Life Lists for Teens

Tips, steps, hints, and how-tos for growing up, getting along, learning, and having fun

Pamela Espeland

free spirit
PUBLiSHiNG®

D1018714

Library of Congress Cataloging-in-Publication Data

Espeland, Pamela
     Life lists for teens : tips, steps, hints, and how-tos for growing up, getting along, learning, and having fun / Pamela Espeland.
        p. cm.
Includes index.
Summary: Hundreds of lists provide guidance in areas of young adult life as diverse as selecting a book or a hair color to selecting a mentor.
     ISBN 1-57542-125-9
     1. Teenagers—United States—Life skills guides. 2. Teenagers—United States—Conduct of life. 3. Time management. [1. Conduct of life—Miscellanea. 2. Life skills—Miscellanea. 3. Lists—Miscellanea.] I. Title.
HQ796.E683 2003
646.7'00835—dc21

                                          2002152116

At the time of this book's publication, all facts and figures are the most current available; all telephone numbers, addresses, and Web site URLs are accurate and active; all publications, organizations, Web sites, and other resources exist as described in this book; and all have been verified. The author and Free Spirit Publishing make no warranty or guarantee concerning the information and materials given out by organizations or content found at Web sites, and we are not responsible for any changes that occur after this book's publication. If you find an error or believe that a resource listed here is not as described, please contact Free Spirit Publishing. Parents, teachers, and other adults: We strongly urge you to monitor children's use of the Internet.

Cover and book design by Marieka Heinlen
Index prepared by Randl Ockey

10 9 8 7 6 5 4 3 2
Printed in Canada

Free Spirit Publishing Inc.
217 Fifth Avenue North, Suite 200
Minneapolis, MN 55401-1299
(612) 338-2068
help4kids@freespirit.com
www.freespirit.com

The following are registered trademarks of Free Spirit Publishing Inc.:
FREE SPIRIT®
FREE SPIRIT PUBLISHING®
SELF-HELP FOR TEENS®
SELF-HELP FOR KIDS®
WORKS FOR KIDS®
THE FREE SPIRITED CLASSROOM®

free spirit
PUBLISHING®

Dedication

To Johnny, who's #1 on my list

Contents

List of Lists

GETTING ALONG 59

STAYING SAFE 90

SCHOOL AND LEARNING 120

GOING ONLINE 156

PLANNING AHEAD 170

SAVING THE WORLD 187

FOCUS ON YOU 209

JUST FOR FUN 229

Introduction

People have made lists since ancient times. The Sumerians of Mesopotamia—who started the first civilization, built the first cities, and invented writing around 3500 B.C.—made lists of their household possessions, animals, kings, and gods, to name just a few. They inscribed their lists on clay tablets and baked them hard in kilns, which is why they're still around today for scholars to decipher and study.

If you're curious, you might visit a museum and see if they have any Sumerian clay tablets in their collection. Or view some online. Go to a search engine like Google and type this word string in the search window: sumerian clay tablet cuneiform. (Cuneiform is the type of writing the Sumerians used.) One site with a lot of examples is hosted by the University of Minnesota: special.lib.umn.edu/rare/cuneiform.

Long before the invention of written language, people probably kept mental and verbal lists—of safe caves to stay in, good plants to eat, ways to hunt animals, and the steps involved in turning a piece of flint into a weapon or tool.

When you scrawl a list on a scrap of paper and stuff it in your pocket, you're part of a human tradition stretching back to prehistory. Which is kind of fun to think about, when you don't have anything better to do.

6 Ways Lists Can Help You

1. **Lists organize your thinking.** Instead of wondering, "How can I do this?" or "Where do I start?" you can try the steps on a list—or make up your own list.

2. **Lists focus your energy.** When you have a step-by-step process for reaching a goal or solving a problem, you're more likely to get it done.

3. **Lists free up time in your day.** When you have a list of things to do or strategies to try, you're less likely to procrastinate.

4. **Lists free up space in your brain.** You don't have to remember what's on a list. You just have to remember where you put it.

5. **Lists are satisfying.** Ask anyone who uses lists: There's nothing like making a big, bold ✓ next to something you've finished doing.

6. **Lists give you confidence.** It's great to know there's no problem so big, no challenge so daunting, that you can't break it down into steps and tackle them one-by-one.

Most "lists books" you'll find in the library or bookstore focus on facts, statistics, or trivia. Some are serious, some are instructive, some are wacky or weird. Depending on what you're interested in, many are very entertaining to read.

It's fun to flip through a collection of "Top 10" lists from the *Late Night with David Letterman* TV show. Or learn about "states that have given birth to more than one president" in *The Book of Political Lists*. (The winner is Virginia, with eight.) Or discover the Earth's lowest points in the *Factastic Book of 1001 Lists*. (The Dead Sea is one.) Or read about the six wives of Henry VIII in *What Are the Seven Wonders of the World? and 100 Other Great Cultural Lists*. (They were Catherine of Aragon, Anne Boleyn, Jane Seymour, Anne of Cleves, Kathryn Howard, and Katherine Parr. Two lost their heads—for real.)

There are lists books about sports, science, animals, plants, bugs, birds, people, places, countries, companies, history, mysteries, math, nature, arts, culture, TV shows, movies, rocks, foods, games, names, stars, cars, UFOs, phrases, proverbs, quotations, abbreviations, and on and on.

Everyone loves lists. And whether we know it or not, we use lists every day. Want to find the meaning of a word? Look in a book of word lists—also known as a dictionary. Need to order a pizza? Scan a phone-numbers list—the telephone book. It's the first day of school and you're wondering what period you eat lunch? Check your when-to-be-where list—your class schedule. Going to a party at a friend's house? Ask for a how-to-get-there list—directions. You bought a shirt that doesn't fit? To return it or exchange it, you'll need the things-you-got-at-the-store list—your receipt.

When you want to know how to use your new digital camera, or put your bike together, or hook up your audio system, or play a video game, you read a how-to-do-it list—also known as a user's guide or instruction manual.

Life Lists for Teens is a user's guide for life—your life. It's not about facts, statistics, or trivia. Instead, it's all about *you*—your feelings, experiences, relationships, body, future, decisions, hopes, problems, and dreams.

This is a book of self-help lists. You can use them to help yourself do, achieve, become, or be something or someone that matters to you. A healthy person. A caring person. Someone who succeeds in school, in relationships, and in life. Someone who knows how to stay safe. Someone who makes a difference in the world. Someone who knows how to lighten up and have fun.

7 Ways to Use This Book

1. You can read it from cover-to-cover, if you want. Then again, there might be lists that don't interest you right now, or don't relate to what's going on in your life, or won't work for you because your circumstances are different.

2. You can scan the Contents to see what's here, then read the lists that have to do with a topic, idea, issue, or problem you care about.

3. You can skim the Index for key words that point you toward specific lists.

4. You can read all the lists on a particular topic you want or need to know more about. For example, the "Going Online" section is a "short course" on using the Internet.

5. You can open this book anywhere and read whatever you find.

6. You can photocopy the lists you want to carry with you, hang on a wall, post in your locker, or tape to a mirror for handy reminders or instant advice. There are seven lists with spaces for you to write in. (You'll find them on pages 93, 179, 190, 195, 228, 229, and 244.) Please make copies for your personal use only.

7. You can use this book as a jumping-off place for creating your own self-help lists.

Self-help books, magazines, articles, and Web sites are almost as popular as lists. Everyone wants to know how to live better, be healthier, get smarter, make wiser decisions, be happier, reach goals, and solve problems. With sound information, support from people who care about you, and a lot of common sense, you really *can* help yourself to be and do your best. This book is full of ideas for you to think about and try to make life easier, more rewarding, more purposeful, and more enjoyable.

I'd love to know which lists in this book work for you. I'd love to hear about your successes. And if you create your own self-help lists, I'd love to read them. You can send your thoughts, insights, comments, and lists to me:

Pamela Espeland
c/o Free Spirit Publishing Inc.
217 Fifth Avenue North, Suite 200
Minneapolis, MN 55401-1299

Or you can send me email at help4kids@freespirit.com.

4 Tips to Keep in Mind

1. **This is a book of lists that are meant to help you.** It is not a book of guarantees. Use your best judgment when deciding which strategies, tips, and ideas to try. Talk with adults you trust when you need more insights and information. Talk with friends you trust to get their perspective and learn what has worked for them.

2. **This is a book of lists that are meant to guide you.** It is not a substitute for professional medical advice if you're sick, or professional counseling if you have a problem you can't handle on your own, or legal advice if you need it.

3. **Almost every list in this book is about a "big topic"**—health, wellness, relationships, feelings, personal safety, learning, self-esteem, goal-setting, problem-solving, Web awareness, service, creativity, and so on. Whole books have been written about each topic. When you want to know more, visit your library or bookstore.

4. **There's a world of help and helpers out there for you to explore.** This book is just the beginning.

I wish you success, satisfaction, and happiness on your life's journey. I hope this book helps you along the way.

Pamela Espeland

Minneapolis, Minnesota

Health an Wellness

Life Lists

12 Serious Reasons to Laugh

1. Laughter boosts your respiration and circulation.

2. Laughter reduces the stress hormones in your body.

3. Laughter stimulates your immune system so you're better able to fight off infections and diseases.

4. Laughter triggers the release of feel-good endorphins, the body's natural painkillers. It gives you an all-over sense of well-being.

5. Laughter is good exercise. Researchers estimate that laughing 100 times is equal to 15 minutes on an exercise bike. Hearty laughter is a workout for your whole body.

6. Laughter gives you a different perspective on your problems. As comedian and actor Bill Cosby has said, "If you can laugh at it, you can survive it."

7. Laughter builds and strengthens relationships. As comedian and pianist Victor Borge liked to say, "Laughter is the shortest distance between two people."

8. Laughter raises your self-esteem. You feel more confident and relaxed in social situations. *Tip:* It's more important to have fun than to be funny.

9. Laughter makes you feel more optimistic about life. You're less likely to feel sad, hopeless, anxious, and depressed.

10. Laughter releases pent-up negative feelings—like anger, frustration, and fear—in a positive, healthy way.

11. Laughter can make you more alert, creative, relaxed, resilient, and productive. It can sharpen your memory and improve your skills in decision-making, negotiating, organizing information, and word association.

12. Laughter is free.

8 Ways to Bring More Laughter into Your Life

It's estimated that toddlers laugh 400 times a day, but adults laugh only 15 times a day. Here's how to recapture some of those "lost laughs."

1. Look for the humor in every situation. Okay...*most* situations. Some things aren't funny, but more things are.

2. Laugh at yourself and your own mistakes. Try not to take yourself so seriously. Don't sweat the small stuff.

3. Surround yourself with things that make you laugh or smile. Clip funny cartoons. Collect funny sayings. Hang funny pictures or posters in your room. Listen to comedy tapes or CDs while you're doing chores. Watch funny movies and videos.

4. Keep a daily humor journal. Write down funny things you see, hear, and think. Jot down jokes, riddles, puns, stories, and sayings. A humor journal is fun to write in, even more fun to read later, when you've built a library of laughter and happy memories.

5. Spend time with a child. Get down on his or her level and get silly.

6. Watch a classic comedy on TV. There must be a reason why even old sitcoms like *I Love Lucy* are still around. Maybe because they're still funny?

7. Do your jokes sometimes fall flat? Do your attempts at humor sometimes make people angry or hurt their feelings? Keep in mind the AT&T Humor Test: Humor must be <u>A</u>ppropriate, <u>T</u>imely, and <u>T</u>asteful.

8. When in doubt, ask yourself, "Am I laughing *with* people or *at* them?" Make sure that your humor goal is always to improve, build up, and support, never to put down, tear down, or embarrass.

"Seven days without laughter makes one weak."
Dr. Joel Goodman

7 Basic Needs All People Share

Needs and wants aren't the same. Wants vary from person to person, but all people share these seven basic needs.

1. **The need for relationships with other people.** From the moment we're born, we need to care about other people. We need them to care about us. We need to feel important and wanted.

2. **The need for touching and holding.** Babies, kids, teenagers, grown-ups, grandparents—everyone needs to be touched and held sometimes. As you get older, you may get mixed messages about touching and holding. This is a problem with our culture. It isn't a problem with you.

3. **The need to belong and feel "one" with others.** This is why we copy the way some people walk and talk and dress. It's also why we join groups, teams, cliques, and clubs.

4. **The need to be different and separate.** Each of us needs to believe that there's no one else like us in the world. This may seem to contradict the need to belong and feel "one" with others. It does! You'll go back-and-forth between these needs throughout your life.

5. **The need to nurture.** It feels good to help other people and show that we care about them.

6. **The need to feel worthwhile, valued, and admired.** At first, we count on other people to help us feel this way. In time, we learn to encourage and praise ourselves.

7. **The need for power in our relationships and our lives.** This is not the same as having power over other people. It's about having choices.

Maria Rodale's 5 Things That Really Matter

Maria Rodale is founding editor of Organic Style *magazine and vice chairman of Rodale Inc., a leading publisher of information on healthy, active lifestyles.*

1. **LOVE.** Everything else pales by comparison.

2. **FAMILY.** Even if they don't deserve it!

3. **FAITH.** It doesn't really matter what you have faith in, as long as it's something.

4. **INTEGRITY.** Doing the right thing will always feel good.

5. **MOMENTS.** Enjoy them while they are happening, but don't try to capture them, or you'll ruin them.

4 Ways to Avoid Burnout

1. **Learn how to say no.** Practice saying it in front of the mirror until you can say it without reservation or hesitation. Use an "I-mean-it!" tone of voice and assertive body language.

   • Be brief, clear, honest, and firm.

   • Remember that you're not rejecting the person. You're rejecting the request.

   • Make "no" the first word you say. *Examples:* "No, I'm not available on Monday." "No, I can't do that."

   • It's okay to give reasons for your refusal, but you don't have to make a speech. *Example:* "No, I have a big paper due on Tuesday morning." "No, I'm already volunteering for the food drive."

   • It's okay to apologize for saying no, if you think that will soften it a bit, but don't go on and on. *Example:* "No, I'm sorry, I don't have time to do that now."

   • Don't be talked into changing your mind.

   • Don't feel guilty. It's your right to say no.

2. **Learn when to say yes.** Say it when you mean it—and when it's right for you.

   • Make sure you have enough information to make a decision. If you feel unsure, anxious, or cornered by the request, chances are you need to know more before agreeing.

   • Say yes if you have the time, energy, and interest.

   • Say yes to something you really want to do, or something you know will be personally rewarding, or something that will benefit another person or group.

   • Say yes if the request will help you reach a goal. *Examples:* meeting new people, learning new skills, broadening your horizons.

   • Say yes if the request honors you as a person.

   • Say yes if the request will help you grow as a person.

   • Say yes if you must. Some requests are nonnegotiable.

3. **Prioritize your activities.** Space them out more efficiently, and build in time for yourself. Try this strategy:

   a. Make a list of all of your activities. Include everything from after-school lessons to assignment due dates, dances to weekend jobs and household chores.

   b. When you're done, mark your *most* important activities #1. Mark the *second-most* important activities #2. And so on. Use a pencil; you're likely to change your mind along the way.

   c. When you've finished, look closely at the results.

   d. If possible, start eliminating the lowest priorities. Work backwards, erasing or crossing out as many items as you realistically can.

   e. Enter the remaining activities on your planning calendar. (What? You don't have a planning calendar? Make that priority #1.)

   f. Look at the schedule you've created for yourself. Does it seem workable? Have you left at least one night a week for yourself, to do whatever you want—or nothing at all?

4. **Get help if you need it.** Ask an accomplished yet reasonably calm friend how he or she does it. Ask a librarian to recommend books. Talk to your school counselor.

8 Ways to Cope with Bad News

CNN, the Internet, TV, radio, newspapers, magazines, email alerts, headlines on your cell phone, pager, or handheld computer.... You want to stay informed, but sometimes it's too much, especially when the news is bad. If you start feeling sad, helpless, depressed, or vulnerable, here's what to do.

1. **Go on a news fast.** Avoid all news for at least a day—or even a week. Notice how you feel, what you miss, and what you do with the extra time you suddenly seem to have. Then, when you're ready to bring news back into your life...

2. **Take it slow.** Limit yourself to an hour or less each day of watching, reading, or surfing.

3. **Choose your news.** Stay away from networks, magazines, or Web sites that focus on the sensational. Avoid so-called "news" programs that are simply excuses for shouting matches. Try watching the news on public television instead.

4. **Place the news in context.** Remember, as you hear about a plane crash, that air travel is still the safest mode of transportation there

is. Remember, as you hear about a murder, that the homicide rate in America has been steadily declining, even though network coverage of murders has been increasing.

5. **Don't read or view disturbing stories.** If you know that certain stories upset you, avoid them.

6. **Take action.** It can be very upsetting to learn about a war or natural disaster that has affected thousands of innocent victims. You may feel a lot better if you make a donation or volunteer to help in some way.

7. **Write a letter.** Some of the most disturbing news stories are about dishonest politicians or greedy business leaders. Don't stew. Send a letter or an email. Give them a piece of your mind.

8. **Avoid pictures.** Seeing the aftermath of a massacre, an earthquake, or a terrorist attack can be much more upsetting than reading about it. Get your news from print media (newspapers or news magazines). You'll keep up with what's happening, but without the blood and guts.

> "Nothing travels faster than light,
> with the possible exception of bad news."
> *Douglas Adams*

7 Ways to Handle Worries

1. **Start a worry book.** Write down everything that worries you. Think of your worry book as a place to store your worries until you're ready to deal with them. Simply writing them down will help you feel as if you're gaining some control over your worries.

2. **Decide whether each worry is a "signal" or just "noise."** A "signal" worry is related to a real problem or concern in your life—something you need to deal with and act on. A "noise" worry is a negative, unproductive thought that keeps repeating itself.

3. **Make plans to deal with your "signal" worries.** Define each one as a problem to be solved. List possible solutions. Pick *one* problem to work on and plan to take positive action. Don't try to tackle every "signal" worry at the same time.

4. **Confront your "noise" worries.** Cross them out in your worry book. Tell yourself, *I don't have to worry about these things anymore.*

Thinking about them isn't helpful to me. When your "noise" worries creep back into your thoughts, do something that takes your mind off of them. Call a friend, watch a video, listen to music, or whatever works for you. Or try a simple meditation. Find a quiet place, get comfortable, and think the same word, phrase, or sound over and over again.

5. **Practice relaxation skills.** Try a simple meditation. Or do some gentle breathing. Slowly inhale; slowly exhale. Focus on your breathing. Follow your breath in and out of your body. If you're extra worried, breathe in, hold for a count of three, then exhale. Be deliberate. Go slow. Stay focused.

6. **Postpone your worries.** Tell yourself, *I'm not going to worry right now. I'll worry later.* Then set a specific time to worry—for example, for 10 minutes starting at 7:00 P.M. With this technique, you take charge of your worries. What should you do when it's "worry time"? Worry! When your 10 minutes are up, do some breathing exercises. Then move on to other activities.

7. **Talk about your worries with someone you trust.** Just getting your worries out in the open can help.

8 Tips for Coping with Tragedy or Disaster

Terrorist attacks. School shootings. Random acts of violence. Most teens will never have personal experience of events like these. But even if you see them on the news, they create strong feelings and fears. Following the 1995 bombing of the Murrah Federal Building in Oklahoma City, the Oklahoma Department of Mental Health and Substance Abuse Services came up with these ideas for helping teens cope.

1. Whether or not you were directly affected by a disaster or violent event, it is normal to feel anxious about your own safety, to picture the event in your own mind, and to wonder how you would react in an emergency.

2. People react in different ways to trauma. Some become irritable or depressed, others lose sleep or have nightmares, others deny their feelings or simply "blank out" the troubling event.

3. While it may feel better to pretend the event did not happen, in the long run it is best to be honest about your feelings and to allow yourself to acknowledge the sense of loss and uncertainty.

4. It is important to realize that, while things may seem off balance for a while, your life will return to normal.

5. It is important to talk with someone about your sorrow, anger, and other emotions, even though it may be difficult to get started.

6. You may feel most comfortable talking about your feelings with a teacher, counselor, or religious leader. The important thing is that you have someone you trust to confide in about your thoughts and feelings.

7. It is common to want to strike back at people who have caused great pain. This desire comes from our outrage for the innocent victims. We must understand, though, that it is futile to respond with more violence. Nothing good is accomplished by hateful language or actions.

8. While you will always remember the event, the painful feelings will decrease over time, and you will come to understand that, in learning to cope with tragedy, you have become stronger, more adaptable, and more self-reliant.

11 Warning Signs That You're Under Too Much Stress

Everyone has some stress, and not all stress is bad. But if some or all of these signs describe you, you may be on stress overload.

1. Having more trouble with teachers.

2. Needing a lot of sleep—or not sleeping well.

3. Wanting to eat all the time—or never eating.

4. Headaches, stomachaches, colds, infections, sore muscles.

5. Escapist behavior—overdoing one thing (TV, music, studying, sleeping, Web surfing) and ignoring other things.

6. Withdrawing from friends and family.

7. Crying for no apparent reason.

8. Feeling like an idiot.

9. Feeling restless and anxious; worrying all the time.

10. Feeling like everything is out of control—like *you're* out of control.

11. Depression, sadness, crabbiness, the blahs.

> "Stress is an ignorant state.
> It believes that everything is an emergency."
> Natalie Goldberg

17 Ways to Manage Stress

Stress isn't "all in your head." It's a physical response to something going on in your life—school pressures, social pressures, or the physical, emotional, and mental changes and challenges of being a teen. Too much stress can lead to health problems, sleep problems, and relationship problems. Try these tips to relieve, reduce, or even prevent stress.

1. **Be active.** Exercise lifts your spirits and helps you feel more relaxed.

2. **Eat right.** A healthy, well-nourished body is a better stress-fighter.

3. **Avoid caffeine.** It can make you feel edgy and tense.

4. **Get enough sleep.** It's hard to deal with stress when you're tired and run-down.

5. **Express your feelings.** Talk about them. Write about them. Stuffing or ignoring your feelings can add to your stress.

6. **Laugh it up.** Laughter reduces stress.

7. **Know how to relax.** Learn and practice relaxation techniques—deep breathing, meditation, tensing and releasing your muscles—and other ways to calm down when stress strikes.

8. **Get organized.** Have a place for everything and keep everything in its place. Then you won't get stressed-out trying to remember where you left your books, your keys, or something else you need *right now*.

9. **Simplify.** Are you cramming too much into your days, nights, and weekends? Prioritize your activities. Start saying no. Make time for yourself—for things you like to do. Including, sometimes, doing nothing at all.

10. **Build strong relationships.** Family members and friends can be your support network when things get too stressful.

11. **Be a planner.** Get a calendar and write down your projects, test dates, and other important stuff. Make a homework and study schedule you can follow. Planning will help you feel more in control of your life.

12. **Talk about your problems.** Find someone you trust and can talk to. Share your problems. Ask for help when you need it.

13. **Don't sweat the small stuff.** Figure out what really matters and let other things go.

14. **Get a new attitude.** Try seeing your problems and pressures from another perspective. Learn to accept the things you can't change.

15. **Forgive your own mistakes.** Are you hard on yourself whenever you mess up? Tell yourself that mistakes are learning experiences. At least you know what *not* to do next time.

16. **Be yourself.** Trying to be something or someone you're not can be stressful.

17. **Be happy with what you have.** Instead of thinking about everything you *want*, think about what you already *have*. Maybe it's enough.

4 Steps to Quitting Caffeine

Caffeine increases your heart rate, speeds up your breathing, can irritate your stomach, depletes your body of vitamin B, may cause heartburn, and can even trigger panic attacks. Former caffeine-a-holics sleep better, have more energy, have less stress, and get fewer headaches. The following tips are for coffee drinkers. If your beverage of choice is caffeinated soda, you can adapt them accordingly.

1. **Do it slowly (so you won't get headaches).** If you drink several cups of coffee every day, cut back by one cup on your first day. A few days later, cut back by another cup. Continue until you give up your last cup.

2. **Switch to decaf.** Start by making a brew that's half caf and half decaf. Over the next week, gradually increase the decaf proportion until you end up with 100 percent decaf.

3. **Substitute other liquids.** For people who drink a lot of coffee, the ritual of having something to drink is as habit-forming as caffeine. Instead of taking a coffee break, take a juice break. Or a sparkling water break. Or a piece-of-fruit break.

4. **Beware of caffeine in hiding.** Many beverages, foods, even over-the-counter drugs contain significant amounts of caffeine. Check out the labels on teas, soft drinks, frozen desserts, yogurts, candies, and pill bottles.

4 Steps to Feeling Peaceful

When you're nervous, excited, or angry, your breathing speeds up and moves up into your chest. When you're calm and relaxed, your breathing is slower, more regular, and farther down in your diaphragm. You can consciously manipulate your breathing to feel more peaceful...even when you're stressed out. Here's how.

1. Find a firm chair and a blank wall to look at. Sit on the chair facing the wall, with your back relaxed but straight. Fold your hands in your lap or lay them flat along the tops of your thighs. Your feet should be flat on the floor.

2. Keeping your head upright, tuck your chin back and in. Keeping your eyes open, look down at about a 45-degree angle. (Don't tilt your head.) You should be staring at the blank surface of the wall in front of you.

3. Keeping your mouth closed, inhale and silently count *one.* Exhale and silently count *two.* Inhale and silently count *three.* Exhale and silently count *four*...and so on up to *ten.*

4. On the next inhalation, start over with *one* and continue counting to yourself. Whenever you reach *ten,* go back to *one* again.

It's that simple. Tips to keep in mind:

- Decide before you start how long you want to spend doing this. In the beginning, 5–8 minutes is enough. Later, you may want to lengthen your sessions to as long as half an hour. Set a timer so you're not distracted by looking at your watch or a clock.

- Don't try to manipulate or control your breathing. Just let it come naturally.

- Don't move your body. Remain absolutely still for the entire time.

- Don't stop before the time is up.

- What if your brain tries to distract you with interesting thoughts, creative thoughts, or bothersome thoughts? As soon as you realize you've been sidetracked, go back to *one* again.

- What if your body tries to distract you with twitches, itches, and "demands" to move? Go back to *one* and start counting again.

- What if the world tries to distract you—if friends stop by, people knock on your door, your brother barges in, the phone rings, or the next-door neighbor starts mowing the lawn? Go back to *one* and start counting again.

7 Steps to Total Relaxation

You can do this exercise anytime you feel stressed or anxious, whenever you feel tension or discomfort in your body, or when you're getting ready to meditate.

1. Sit in a comfortable position or lie down.

2. Close your eyes and relax. (If seated, place your arms on your lap. Fold your hands loosely together. If lying down, place your hands along your sides.)

3. Breathe slowly and deeply from the diaphragm. *How to do this:* Relax your abdominal muscles. Place a hand on your abdomen. Take a deep breath. Pull the air all the way down into your "stomach"—not by sucking it in, but by expanding it, as if you're trying to give yourself a pot belly. Your hand should rise about an inch. If this happens, it means you are breathing from your diaphragm. Exhale, and your stomach will drop.

4. Concentrate on the muscles at the top of your head. Think the word *relax* and consciously relax those muscles. (You may use any gentle or calming word, such as *serene* or *restful*.)

5. Once the top of your head is relaxed, bring your attention to your forehead and the area around your eyes. Continue to say *relax* as you consciously relax these muscles.

6. Now move to the muscles of your temples and ears. Relax them. Then your sinuses and nasal area. Once these areas are relaxed, go on to the back of your neck. Stay with each muscle until it is tension-free.

7. Continue to relax your shoulders, arms, hands, fingers, chest, abdomen...all the way down to the tips of your toes.

Your mind and body will associate the feeling of being relaxed with whatever word you chose for this exercise. The next time you're in a stressful situation, practice deep breathing and silently say the word to yourself. Without moving a muscle, you'll feel calmer.

5 Ways to Deal with Sadness

1. **Try to figure out why you're sad.** Sadness usually results from a loss of some sort. If your parents separate or get divorced, you lose the family life you've always known. If you move to a new neighborhood, you lose people and places you care about. Even a change like the end of the school year—something you probably look forward to—

can cause feelings of sadness as you leave behind favorite teachers, classes, and classmates. Disappointment can lead to sadness, too. Ask yourself: *Who or what have I lost? What changes have taken place in my life, and what I have I lost as a result? Who has disappointed me? Have I disappointed myself?*

2. **Talk to someone you trust.** You don't need someone to try to fix things for you. You can do that yourself, once you've figured out what's going on. But it does help to talk with someone you trust. When you're sad, it's comforting to share your feelings with someone who cares enough to listen.

3. **Write down your feelings.** Writing allows you to express your emotions instead of keeping them trapped inside. It also helps you see your problems from a new perspective, which might lead to solutions. If your sadness is due to the loss of a relationship, write a letter to the person you've lost—the letter is for you to keep and *not to send.* As you write, notice how you feel. Read your writing aloud when you're done. How do you feel afterward?

4. **Check in with your body.** How do you feel physically? Are you hungry, thirsty, or tired? Girls, are you premenstrual? Overactive hormones or a lack of food, water, exercise, fresh air, or sleep can intensify your emotions. If you're feeling sad, pay attention to your physical needs and take care of your body. This will help you feel better physically *and* emotionally.

5. **Try a change of scenery.** Sometimes staring at the same four walls makes you feel stuck in your sadness. Getting outdoors and breathing fresh air helps. Make plans with someone you enjoy spending time with. Seeing new sights or having something to look forward to may raise your spirits.

9 Symptoms of Major Depression

Not all people with depression will have all of these symptoms, or have them to the same degree. But if you have four or more, if nothing can make them go away, and if they last more than two weeks, it's time to get help. See a doctor, counselor, or therapist ASAP.

1. Persistent sad or "empty" mood.

2. Feeling hopeless, helpless, worthless, pessimistic, and/or guilty.

3. Substance abuse.

4. Fatigue or loss of interest in ordinary activities.

5. Disturbances in eating and sleeping patterns.

6. Irritability, increased crying, anxiety, and panic attacks.

7. Difficulty concentrating, remembering, or making decisions.

8. Thoughts of suicide; suicide plans or attempts.*

9. Persistent physical symptoms or pains that do not respond to treatment.

* If you're having suicidal thoughts, *don't wait*. Get help RIGHT NOW. Call one of these 24-hour toll-free national hotlines:

National Hopeline Network
1-800-SUICIDE (1-800-784-2433)

Covenant House Nineline
1-800-999-9999

Girls and Boys Town National Hotline
1-800-448-3000

7 Things to Do When You're Depressed

Depression is more than just feeling sad or blue. It's more than a bad mood that lasts a few days. The mood hangs on, affecting your emotions, body, thoughts, and behavior. If you feel like you've fallen into a deep, dark hole with no way out, you may have depression—a treatable medical illness. That's when you need professional help. You can also help yourself.

1. **Get some exercise.** Exercise affects chemicals in your brain, and brain chemicals have a lot to do with depression. Exercise releases chemicals called *endorphins* that give you a natural high. Endorphins lift your mood, making you feel more energized, and may even help you sleep more soundly. The more often you exercise, the better you'll feel.

2. **Take a break.** Taking time to relax is a way to clear your mind, recharge your batteries, and restore your health. Take a break from your activities and allow yourself to rest for 15–30 minutes every few hours during the day. You might take a nap, soak in the tub, read for pleasure, call a friend, pet your cat or dog, listen to your favorite relaxing music (no sad songs!), daydream, or do a relaxation exercise. Whatever works for you.

3. **Have some fun.** When you laugh, you feel better and happier. It's a good way to temporarily relieve some of the symptoms of depression and to keep your spirits up while you're recovering. Spend time with a friend doing something fun. Or laugh on your own while reading a funny book or watching a funny movie or TV show.

4. **Eat good food.** Nutritious foods give your body and mind the fuel they need to stay healthy and strong. You'll also feel better if you drink lots of water each day. Water quenches your thirst, hydrates your body, and flushes out your system. Start your day with a healthy breakfast. Take a multivitamin to supplement your diet. Avoid caffeine. Choose not to use alcohol or other drugs. Snack on sunflower seeds and pumpkin seeds. They contain a natural antidepressant called *tryptophan*.

5. **Talk about it.** Depression causes painful feelings like sadness, anger, and hopelessness. You may withdraw from people who care about you because you think they won't understand what you're going through. In fact, one of the best ways to deal with painful emotions and start healing is to talk to someone you trust. Talking helps put things into perspective. You'll see that you're not as alone as you may think.

6. **Stick with your treatment plan.** If you're in therapy, on medication, or both, sticking with your treatment plan is the single most important thing you can do to get better and stay well. Make a commitment to follow your treatment plan for a certain length of time—for example, four weeks. During this time, keep in touch with your mental health professional, who can help you adjust the plan as needed. Once you reach the four-week milestone, commit to another four weeks of treatment. Setting and reaching goals will help you feel more in control of your treatment and your life.

7. **Feed your spirit.** When you're depressed, a place inside of you feels empty. This place holds your personal spirit. It needs attention, too. Try writing your thoughts and feelings in a journal, playing a musical instrument, singing, writing a poem, walking on the beach or in a park, volunteering your time, collecting things you love, visiting a museum or art gallery, painting a picture, setting a goal, or saying a prayer. Or come up with other ways to use your creativity and boost your self-esteem.

"You handle depression in much
the same way you handle a tiger."
R.W. Shepherd

11 Types of Helpers and What They Do

If you ever have a problem you can't handle on your own—like depression, trouble sleeping, eating problems, substance abuse, anxiety, a crisis, or behaviors you can't control—there are people who can help you. Some cost money, and some are free. Some are professionals, and some are people who share a similar problem. Here's a brief rundown of the kinds of help out there.

1. **Psychiatrists** are medical doctors who specialize in mental health. They assess people, administer tests, diagnose mental illness, prescribe medications, and provide therapy.

2. **Clinical psychologists** are experts in human behavior. They assess people, administer tests, diagnose mental illness, and provide therapy.

3. **Psychiatric nurse practitioners** are registered nurses trained to deal with mental disorders. They assess people, administer tests, diagnose mental illness, prescribe medications, and provide therapy.

4. **Clinical social workers** have advanced training in social work, with an emphasis on mental health. They can provide you and your family with help and information.

5. **General physicians** may be the first to identify a mental health problem after a physical examination, and may refer you to a specialist for further help.

6. **Psychotherapists** and **counselors** are trained to listen to you and help you make changes in yourself and your life. Your school may have a school counselor available full-time or part-time.

7. **Clergy members** can give you spiritual counsel and comfort.

8. **Crisis centers** offer *immediate* help to individuals or families who need it. If you're suicidal or your family is abusive, for example, a crisis center can provide counseling and care. Crisis counselors are usually mental health professionals trained to listen and find further help for you.

9. **Crisis hotlines** are staffed by mental health professionals or trained volunteers who listen to your problems and recommend other sources of help. Most hotlines are open 24 hours a day, 7 days a week. Look in your Yellow Pages for numbers, or see pages 90–91.

10. **Self-help groups** are support groups of people who share a similar problem. Some groups are run by a mental health professional; others aren't. The group members discuss their feelings, encourage each other, and suggest ways to cope.

11. **Twelve-step groups** (such as Alcoholics Anonymous) are self-help groups that follow a specific program, meet in a variety of locations day and night, don't charge participants a fee, and can be found in nearly every city. These groups have a spiritual emphasis and believe that a higher power can help guide you to recovery.

47 Signs That You Might Be a Perfectionist

You may have heard that perfectionism is a good thing. Don't believe it. Perfectionism is not *about doing your best. It's* not *about striving for high goals or working hard to achieve excellence. In fact, perfectionism can actually* block *your ability to do well. Plus perfection isn't possible. Do you show any, many, or all of these signs?*

16 Things Perfectionists Do...

1. Overcommit themselves.
2. Rarely delegate work to others.
3. Have a hard time making choices.
4. Always have to be in control.
5. Compete fiercely.
6. Arrive late because one more thing had to be done.
7. Always do last-minute cramming.
8. Get carried away with the details.
9. Never seem satisfied with their work.
10. Constantly busy themselves with something or other.
11. Frequently criticize others.
12. Refuse to hear criticism of themselves.
13. Pay more attention to negative than positive comments.
14. Check up on other people's work.
15. Call themselves "stupid" when they do something imperfectly.
16. Procrastinate.

16 Thoughts Perfectionists Have...

1. "If I can't do it perfectly, what's the point?"

2. "I should excel at everything I do."

3. "I always have to stay ahead of others."

4. "I should finish a job before doing anything else."

5. "Every detail of a job should be perfect."

6. "Things should be done right the first time."

7. "There is only one right way to do things."

8. "I'm a wonderful person if I do well; I'm a lousy person if I do poorly."

9. "I'm never good enough."

10. "I'm stupid."

11. "I can't do anything right."

12. "I'm unlikable."

13. "I'd better not make a mistake here, or people will think I'm not very [smart, good, capable]."

14. "If I goof up, something's wrong with me."

15. "People shouldn't criticize me."

16. "Everything should be clearly black or white. Grays are a sign of confused thinking."

15 Ways Perfectionists Feel...

1. Deeply embarrassed about mistakes they make.

2. Disgusted or angry with themselves when they are criticized.

3. Anxious when stating their opinion to others.

4. Extremely worried about details.

5. Angry if their routine is interrupted.

6. Nervous when things around them are messy.

7. Fearful or anxious a lot of the time.

8. Exhausted and unable to relax.

9. Plagued by self-hatred.

10. Afraid of appearing stupid.

11. Afraid of appearing incompetent.

12. Afraid of being rejected.

13. Ashamed of having fears.

14. Discouraged.

15. Guilty about letting others down.

> "Striving for excellence motivates you;
> striving for perfection is demoralizing."
> *Harriet Braiker*

11 Tips for Fighting Perfectionism

1. Be average for a day. Allow yourself to be messy, late, incomplete... imperfect. Then celebrate your success.

2. Get involved in activities that are not graded or judged—activities that focus on process, not product.

3. Take a risk. Sign up for a course with a reputation for being challenging. Start a conversation with someone you don't know. Do an assignment or study for a test without overdoing it. Alter your morning routine. Start a day without a plan.

4. Give yourself permission to make at least three mistakes a day.

5. Stop using the word "should" in your self-talk. Remove "I have to" from your conversation.

6. Share a weakness or limitation with a friend. Recognize that he or she doesn't think any less of you as a result.

7. Acknowledge that your expectations of yourself might be too high, even unrealistic.

8. Savor your past accomplishments. Write about how good they made you feel.

9. Ask your friends to help you "cure" your perfectionism. Maybe they can give you a sign or a word when they notice you are being a perfectionist.

10. Join the human race. It's less lonely when we accept our own and others' imperfections and feel part of life.

11. If you need help, talk with your school counselor or psychologist. Explain your situation and ask for suggestions.

6 Benefits of Failure

If you're a perfectionist, this list is for you. Most people know it's okay to fail occasionally, but perfectionists have a hard time accepting this. Try focusing on what you achieve *when you fail.*

1. **Failure gives you a new perspective on yourself and everything else you do.** It can actually be liberating to fall, pick yourself up, and discover that the world is still turning.

2. **Failure gives you the freedom and motivation to strike out in still more untried directions.** When you realize that failure isn't fatal, you're more willing to take risks and try new things.

3. **Failure gives you a better understanding of others.** Most people fail sometimes, so why shouldn't you know how it feels? Plus, when you fail at something that other people *can* do, you start seeing them differently. You realize there are many ways to succeed, and many types of abilities—some of which you have, some of which you may never have. Your focus becomes less narrow.

4. **Failure gives you permission to do less than your best at something else—and something else after that.** You get more done. You're less likely to procrastinate.

5. **Failure teaches you that there are degrees of accomplishment.** It's not an all-or-nothing proposition. You don't have to be the best to learn something and have fun.

6. **Failure teaches you that not succeeding can be normal.** And necessary. And even desirable. You can learn a lot from failure—but you have to be willing to fail.

5 Reasons Why Misteaks Are Great

Thomas Edison tried 1,500 different filaments for the lightbulb before finding the right one. After the final experiment, an assistant asked, "Mr. Edison, how do you feel about having 1,500 failures to your credit?" Edison replied, "They weren't failures. We now know 1,500 lightbulb filaments that don't work."

1. **Mistakes are universal.** Everybody makes them, from preschoolers to presidents. They give you something in common with the rest of the people on our planet.

2. **Mistakes show that you're learning.** Whether you incorrectly apply a geometry theorem or say something foolish in front of someone

you're trying to impress, a mistake is a point of information that inspires you to do better the next time you're in a similar situation.

3. **Mistakes show that you're trying something new or different.** It's rare that you (or anyone else) will accomplish something perfectly on your first attempt. If you had spent your whole life doing only those things you could master on the first try, you never would have learned to walk, read, or ride a bicycle.

4. **Mistakes allow you to see your own improvements.** If you had videotaped your first attempt at the backstroke, then videotaped yourself after three months of swimming lessons, you'd notice a significant change for the better.

5. **Mistakes allow you to learn from others.** Asking for help isn't the same as admitting you've failed.

> "The greatest mistake you can make in life
> is to be continually fearing you will make one."
> *Elbert Hubbard*

7 Resiliencies All Teens Need

For some teens, life is especially hard. They struggle, they suffer—but they survive. Researchers Sybil and Steven Wolin have identified seven resiliencies that seem to make the difference. How many do you have? To learn more about the Wolins and their work, visit www.projectresilience.com.

1. **INSIGHT** is the habit of asking tough questions—about yourself and about the situations you find yourself in—and giving honest answers. Insight helps you see things as they really are, not as you wish they were.

2. **INDEPENDENCE** means being your own person. Sometimes that means stepping back from the pressures you feel from people and situations. Independence helps keep you focused on what *you* want out of life.

3. **RELATIONSHIPS** are connections with people who matter. Relationships provide a sense of belonging, opportunities to express yourself, and support when you need it.

4. **INITIATIVE** means facing life's challenges head-on. When you take initiative, you begin a positive cycle of solving problems, overcoming fears, and being a winner. Initiative puts you in charge.

5. **CREATIVITY** means using your imagination as a safe haven—a place where you're free to express yourself and rearrange the details of your life as you please. Creativity can help you channel overwhelming feelings and make them manageable.

6. **HUMOR** allows you to find what's funny, even when you're sad or in pain. It's a wonderful way to release tension and to relieve pain or embarrassment.

7. **MORALITY** means doing the right thing, even if it's not the easy or natural thing. It helps connect you to other people through being useful and caring. It helps you feel like you're a good person.

4 Myths About Acne

More than 85 percent of teenagers get acne. What causes acne? It's a mystery. Maybe heredity, stress, and hormones have something to do with it. Here are four things that don't.

Myth #1: Acne is caused by chocolate and French fries. *Fact:* They aren't great for your health, but they don't cause acne or make it worse. Some people eat junk foods when they're stressed out. Coincidentally, stress sometimes triggers acne.

Myth #2: If your hair touches your face, you'll break out. *Fact:* Parents love this myth. They usually give it as the main reason why kids should cut their bangs. But the oil on your hair doesn't cause acne; the oil trapped in clogged pores does. However, keeping your hair clean is still a good idea.

Myth #3: If you have acne, you must be dirty. *Fact:* Blackheads can look "dirty," which is where this myth may have come from. The reality is that acne happens to plenty of clean people.

Myth #4: The more you wash your face, the more you'll get rid of acne. *Fact:* You only need to wash your face twice a day to keep it clean. Don't over-scrub your skin with harsh soaps or exfoliating chemicals. You might dry out your skin to the point where you need to use moisturizers—which may clog your pores and make your acne worse.

IO Tips for Fighting Acne

1. Be gentle to your skin. Wash with mild soaps or cleansers.

2. Use oil-free skin products. Avoid astringents, which can be drying.

3. Try the acne-fighting products available at any drugstore. If one dries out or irritates your skin, switch to another.

4. Don't squeeze or pop pimples. This may cause swelling, skin damage, a bacterial infection, or scarring.

5. Drink lots of water. Much of your skin consists of water, so it functions better when it's hydrated.

6. Avoid being in the kitchen when greasy foods are cooked, if possible. Even though eating greasy foods doesn't cause acne, standing over a pot of hot grease will put an extra layer of oil on your skin.

7. Protect your skin from sunburn. People used to think that sunlight helped to cure acne. But exposure to sunlight can thicken the outer layer of the skin, which may close the pores and cause more problems.

8. Exercise to keep your stress levels down. Stress triggers acne in some people.

9. Eat a healthy diet. Choose foods and beverages that contain vitamins A, B, C, and E—all good for your skin.

10. See a doctor if you have anything other than a mild case of acne.

4 Safe Ways to Learn About Sex

Sex is one of those things you probably shouldn't "learn by doing"—not until you're 100 percent ready. The risks of teen pregnancy and sexually transmitted diseases (STDs) are real. Luckily, there are people you can ask and places you can go for information, advice, and the facts you want and need.

1. **Ask your parents.** They may writhe, they may squirm, they may stammer and blush, they may talk in metaphors (birds and bees?). But chances are, they really want to be the people you go to first with questions about sex, safe sex, STDs, and the rest.

2. **Stay awake in sex ed.** Many schools offer some form of sex education. Often, it's abstinence-based, meaning the main message is "Don't have sex!" Unless you're prepared for the possible consequences of being sexually active, that makes sense. But it's probably not all you want to know.

3. **Read a book.** Check your library or bookstore for a thorough, straightforward, detailed, nonjudgmental, and current book about sexuality, relationships, and health. Two possibilities:

- *Changing Bodies, Changing Lives: A Book for Teens on Sex and Relationships,* 3rd edition, by Ruth Bell and the Teen Book Project (New York: Times Books, 1998).

- *The "Go Ask Alice" Book of Answers: A Guide to Good Physical, Sexual, and Emotional Health* by Columbia University's Health Education Program (New York: Henry Holt and Company, Inc. 1998).

4. **Go online.** Don't just type "sex" into a search engine, or you'll end up with a list of porn sites, a blizzard of porn spam, and parents who cut off your computer privileges. Try these sites. They all have respected sponsors, and they're loaded with information. *Tip:* If you're using a computer with filtering software, you may not be able to access them.

- **www.advocatesforyouth.org** Advocates for Youth works to help young people make informed and responsible decisions about their reproductive and sexual health. The site has a special section for teens.

- **www.goaskalice.columbia.edu** Columbia University's Health Question & Answer Internet Service provides factual, in-depth, straightforward, and nonjudgmental information in a Q&A format.

- **www.itsyoursexlife.com** Reliable and objective information for young adults about sexual health issues. Sponsored by the Kaiser Family Foundation.

- **www.iwannaknow.org** A safe, educational, and fun place for teens to learn about STDs and sexual health. Sponsored by the American Social Health Association (ASHA).

- **www.notmenotnow.org** Information and support for teens who choose abstinence.

- **www.siecus.org** Information from the Sexuality Information and Education Council of the United States (SIECUS). The site has a special section for teens.

- **www.sxetc.org** A site by teens, for teens, operated by the Network for Family Life Education and Rutgers University.

- **www.teenwire.com** Sexuality and relationship information from Planned Parenthood Federation of America.

10 Reasons Not to Get a Tattoo or Body Piercing...

Rock stars have them. Pop stars have them. Athletes have them. So why shouldn't you get a tattoo or a body piercing?

1. It will hurt. Needles will be hammered or drilled into (or through) your skin, and most shops don't use anesthesia.

2. Unless your parents give their permission, they'll probably hit the roof.

3. Your school may have a rule saying that tattoos and piercings aren't allowed or must be covered.

4. Many employers won't hire people who have visible tattoos or piercings.

5. Other places where people stick you with needles—like doctors' offices and hospitals—are required by law to follow sterile operating practices. Most tattoo and piercing parlors aren't. Most states don't regulate tattoo and piercing parlors at all.

6. Anytime you introduce a foreign object into your body, you risk infection. According to one recent study, people with tattoos are nine times more likely to be infected with hepatitis C, a potentially deadly liver disease. According to another recent study, 17 percent of students with piercings had medical complications including bacterial infections, bleeding, and injury or tearing. The same infected blood and needles that spread hepatitis C can also spread HIV, the virus that causes AIDS.

7. Oral piercings can lead to infection, prolonged and uncontrollable bleeding, nerve damage, and swelling. Your tongue could swell up large enough to close off your airway. Mouth jewelry can injure your gums, chip or crack your teeth, and stimulate excessive saliva production, causing problems with chewing, swallowing, and talking. If mouth jewelry comes loose, it's an instant choking hazard.

8. Except for nose piercings and ear piercings high on the ear (through the cartilage), many holes will eventually close up when you remove the jewelry. But a tattoo is permanent. If you decide later in life that you want to get rid of it, your choices are: (a) covering it up with a bigger one, (b) excision (having a doctor cut it out, then stitch you back together), (c) dermabrasion (having a doctor scrape, sand, or chemically peel it off your skin), or (d) laser removal.

9. You can't donate blood for a year from the date you get your tattoo or piercing.

10. Do you like the same clothes you liked last year? The same music? What makes you think you'll like the same tattoo or piercing next week, or next month, or next year?

... and 10 Things to Do
If You Decide to Get One Anyway

You really, really want that tattoo or bellybutton ring. Here's what to do—and don't skip any steps.

1. Ask yourself why you want to do this. Because your friends are doing it? Because you want to rattle your parents? Because you like the way it looks? These aren't the greatest reasons. A tattoo or piercing is serious. It should have real meaning to you.

2. Find out if it's legal. Some states prohibit tattooing or body piercing of minors. Other states require a signed and notarized parental consent form. If you're under 18 and you don't have your parents' permission, be suspicious of any artist who's willing to ink you or pierce you without it.

3. Choose your shop very carefully. Once you find one that looks promising, check with your local health department to see if any complaints have been filed against it. Then check the shop itself. It should be squeaky-clean. If the tattoo or piercing studio looks clean but the bathroom is gross, go somewhere else.

4. Ask to see a valid business license. Ask how long the artist has been in business. You want someone with a lot of experience.

5. Ask to see the autoclave—a device that sterilizes medical equipment. Ask to see the monthly reports of "spore tests," which show that the autoclave is working properly. Ask if the studio follows Universal Precautions, the infection control procedures defined by the Occupational Safety and Health Administration (OSHA). Ask what happens to used needles. They should go into a sharps container—a red plastic container with a biohazard symbol on it. *Needles should never be reused.*

6. If you're getting a tattoo, ask if the shop is APT-certified. The Alliance of Professional Tattooists, Inc. (APT) works to educate the public and tattoo artists about infection control procedures. Visit the Web site: www.safe-tattoos.com. If you're getting a piercing, ask if the artist belongs to the Association of Professional Piercers (APP). Visit the Web site: www.safepiercing.org.

7. Ask to see examples of the artist's finished work. Most artists will have a portfolio. Take the time to examine it closely.

8. If you're getting a tattoo, choose a design you can live with for years...and years...and years. Probably *not* the name of your boyfriend/girlfriend, no matter how much you're in love. Probably *not* a huge spider on the back of your hand, which will be hard to cover up during future job interviews. If you're getting a piercing, start small. Save the barbell-through-the-nose for later.

9. When it comes time to get your tattoo or piercing, these things should happen right in front of you, not in another room or out of your sight: The artist should put on a new pair of disposable latex gloves and a mask. He or she should open a fresh set of needles—one that's been individually packaged, dated, sealed, and autoclaved. If you're getting a tattoo, the package should also include steel (not rubber) tubes, and the artist should pour a new supply of ink into a new disposable container. Everything should be "single-service," used on you and only you. *Tip:* If you're getting a piercing and the artist reaches for a plastic gun, run. Guns can't be sterilized in an autoclave.

10. Ask for printed aftercare instructions so you know what to do and expect when you leave the shop. If you have any complications, call your doctor.

Having second thoughts? Try temporary tattoos or henna tattoos. You can even make your own temporary tattoos, using special paper and an inkjet printer. Try fake tongue balls or magnetic body jewelry.

IO Reasons to Eat Right

1. **Eating right shows you care about your body.** Just like recycling shows you care about the environment, choosing to eat healthy foods makes a positive statement. Eating right proves that you respect your body and want to treat it well.

2. **Eating right enhances your natural good looks.** When you eat lots of fresh fruits and vegetables, plus foods rich in fiber and vitamins, you're taking care of yourself—and it shows. Shiny hair, good skin tone, strong teeth and nails, fresh breath, and a healthy glow are just some of the rewards of a healthy diet.

3. **Eating right can be enjoyable.** Eating is meant to be a pleasant experience. Whether you're in a restaurant, at a picnic, in the school lunchroom, or at home, savor every delicious morsel. Good company, easy conversation, and nutritious food add up to a great time.

4. **Eating right helps keep you healthy.** It's an excellent way to prevent obesity, a heart attack, and some forms of cancer. Getting enough calories and nutrients each day is also important for building strong bones and muscles, developing healthy organs, and strengthening your immune system. You've got a whole lifetime ahead of you. Why not eat right to feel your best?

5. **Eating right helps maintain your weight.** Eating right means paying attention to nutrition as well as to *how much* you eat. If you regularly overeat or eat too little, you'll have a hard time maintaining a weight that's right for your body. It's not healthy to have lots of extra fat or to be underweight. And it's not healthy to be *obsessed* about your weight. The trick is to find the right balance in your diet.

6. **Eating right boosts your brain power.** When you're feeling tired and run-down from a lack of nutrients, it's easy to space out in class or while studying. Fuel your body with the vitamins and minerals needed for good health, and your concentration will improve. Schoolwork, part-time jobs, sports, and extracurricular activities all depend on an alert mind.

7. **Eating right can prevent you from obsessing about food.** Nourishing your body with nutritious meals and snacks makes you less likely to obsess over food or try fad diets that can negatively affect your health. Give yourself a break. Eating is meant to bring pleasure, not pain.

8. **Eating right tastes good.** If you're used to eating canned vegetables or satisfying your fruit requirement with a bowl of sugary fruit-flavored cereal, you don't know what you're missing. Foods packaged in a factory can't compare to all the flavorful foods that nature gives us, from sweet strawberries to fresh corn on the cob.

9. **Eating right gives you energy and makes you feel good.** Fueling your body with healthy foods gives you the get-up-and-go to walk farther, run faster, and dance longer. You'll have more energy to make the most of each day.

10. **Eating right keeps you feeling more positive.** A well-nourished body feels stronger and healthier, which can improve your whole outlook. Taking care of yourself—inside and out—is the key to higher self-esteem and greater self-confidence.

15 Reasons Not to Diet

Americans spend more than $40 billion a year on dieting and diet-related products. More teens than ever are going on diets or dieting all the time. Here are 15 reasons why you shouldn't.

1. **Diets don't work.** When you diet, you lose weight—but from water and muscle, not fat. Your body thinks you're starving it and reacts by slowing down the rate at which you burn calories.

2. **Dieting doesn't make you fit.** Some thin people (not all of them, of course) are actually underweight and may be malnourished. It's also possible to be skinny and totally out of shape because of an inactive lifestyle and lack of muscle tone.

3. **Dieting can make you fat.** Research has shown that most dieters who lose 25 pounds or more on strict diets go back to their old eating habits and regain the weight they lost. Then they diet again and gain even more pounds back. This is called "yo-yo" dieting, and it's a vicious cycle.

4. **Dieting slows down your metabolism.** Your body has a genetically programmed weight called a "set point." Eat too little and it shifts into "survivor mode," slowing down your metabolism to conserve energy and store fat.

5. **Dieting is a futile fight against your genes.** Your ideal weight is based on your particular body type and size, and your body type is predetermined by your genes.

6. **Dieting is unhealthy.** When you're on a low-calorie diet, it's almost impossible to get all the vitamins and minerals your body needs. Diet drinks may contain added nutrients, but your body gets more benefits from the natural vitamins and minerals in wholesome foods.

7. **Dieting makes you sluggish.** When you deprive your body of essential nutrients, it can't function properly. A drastic reduction in calories can make you tired, weak, and less alert.

8. **Dieting can lead to eating disorders.** An obsession with food and weight can lead to anorexia, bulimia, and compulsive overeating.

9. **Dieting can make you cranky.** Have you ever known anyone to be in a peppy, positive mood while she or he is dieting?

10. **Dieting supports poor food choices.** Pre-packaged diet foods and fat-free junk foods don't teach you how to eat healthy, which is the key to long-term weight management. Plus, many prepared foods are loaded with chemicals and sodium.

11. **Dieting doesn't make you more popular or happier.** So you crash diet and lose 10 pounds. Does your life suddenly change? Being thinner won't magically make you more popular, get you a date, or turn you into a better person. Weight loss isn't the key to happiness.

12. **Dieting keeps you from fully enjoying life.** Do you really want to skip your best friend's pool party because you think you're "too fat" for a bathing suit? Do you want to go to dinner with your family and pick at your food?

13. **If you're a girl, dieting can lead to amenorrhea.** Losing too much weight can interfere with or stop your regular menstrual cycle. You may think this is a good thing, but it can cause all kinds of health problems now and when you're older.

14. **Dieting can lower your self-esteem.** Since dieting isn't the way to get healthy and fit, and since dieting doesn't work, it's hard to feel good about yourself.

15. **Dieting can interfere with growth.** Your body needs lots of vitamins, minerals, and calories to mature properly. Not getting enough can mean weaker bones, smaller muscles, and (if you're a girl) amenorrhea.

Bottom line: The only way to lose weight safely and effectively, and keep it off, is through lifestyle changes that include regular exercise and healthy eating habits.

29 Clues to a Diet Scam

According to the Federal Trade Commission (FTC), more than half of all advertisements for weight-loss products contain questionable claims. Forty percent contain at least one claim that's totally false. If an ad for a weight-loss drink, pill, patch, program, or gadget includes any of these words or phrases—or radical before-and-after pictures, or glowing first-person endorsements—don't believe it. Save your money, your health, and your pride. For more on diet scams and supplements, visit www.dietfraud.com.

1. amazing
2. astonishing
3. ancient
4. breakthrough
5. clinically proven
6. easy
7. effortless
8. exclusive
9. exotic
10. guaranteed
11. magical
12. medical miracle

13. miraculous

14. mysterious

15. new discovery

16. revolutionary

17. scientific breakthrough

18. secret

19. eat all you want and still lose weight

20. lose weight naturally

21. lose weight without exercise

22. sweats pounds off

23. absorbs fat

24. blocks fat

25. burns fat

26. melts fat while you sleep

27. fights cellulite

28. natural health product

29. lose up to __ pounds a week! (or a day!)

IO Tips for Sticking to an Exercise Program

1. **Do it with friends.** While some highly disciplined teens prefer solitary exercise, most teens are more likely to stick with an exercise program if they do it with friends.

2. **Pick something you like.** There are so many activities to choose from—running, swimming, power walking, cross-country skiing, aerobics classes. Choose one you enjoy.

3. **Don't let competition ruin the fun.** Exercise should give you a workout, not get you all worked up. Don't choose a competitive sport if you're the type who turns a friendly game into a death match.

4. **Exercise at a set time each day, or at set times on specific days during the week.** It's much easier to get with the program if you schedule it into your life. If you're constantly trying to squeeze exercise in, it's going to get squeezed out.

5. **Start slowly.** You don't have to go out and run 10 miles tomorrow. Aim to exercise three times a week for 20–30 minutes. If all you can manage at first is once a week, that's still better than nothing.

6. **Warm up.** Think of yourself as a car on a cold day. You want to idle a bit before you hit the gas. Always do some warm-up stretches.

7. **Cool down.** When you stop suddenly after strenuous exercise, your heart continues to beat rapidly while the amount of blood reaching it drops suddenly. This can cause faintness, dizziness, nausea, irregular

heartbeats, or even (in the most extreme cases) a heart attack. Never go from 100 mph to zero in no seconds flat. Always keep walking and moving. Do some cooldown stretches.

8. **Think positively.** Instead of telling yourself, "I'm going to stop being a lazy, disgusting slug," say, "I'm going to start taking better care of my body."

9. **Monitor your progress.** You may want to keep a record in your journal or daily planner. Write down whatever you do each day, whether it's a 10-minute walk or a 10-mile bike ride.

10. **Make it a habit.** Promise yourself that you'll stay with your exercise program for three weeks. According to experts, that's how long it takes to form a new habit. The sooner you get started, the faster you'll succeed.

24 Warning Signs of an Eating Disorder

Anorexia (self-starvation) can be fatal. Bulimia (bingeing and purging) can ruin teeth, cause serious heart problems, and permanently damage major organs in the body. Compulsive overeating can lead to obesity. Only a medical professional can actually diagnose an eating disorder. But you can know these warning signs, and if you notice them in a friend, you can tell an adult. If you notice them in yourself, get help ASAP. Tell a parent, tell your doctor, tell a teacher or school counselor or youth leader. For more information, visit www.nationaleatingdisorders.org or call 1-800-931-2237 toll-free.

1. Sudden, abnormal weight loss or weight gain.

2. Eats a lot less than usual, or eats a lot more than usual.

3. Diets all the time, even when thin or at a normal weight.

4. Has a distorted body image—feels "too fat" even when thin.

5. Exercises excessively (too much) or compulsively (can't stop).

6. Is obsessed with weight; is terrified of gaining weight.

7. Always counts calories and food grams; always reads labels on food packages; refuses to eat foods with fat in them; drinks diet sodas all the time.

8. Abuses laxatives, diuretics (for water loss), diet pills, supplements, and "natural" diet aids.

9. Often makes excuses not to eat ("I just ate," "I'm not hungry," "I'm too wired to eat," "My stomach is too upset right now," "I don't like that—I'll eat something later").

10. Leaves the table during meals; spends time in the bathroom right after eating; runs the water to mask any sounds; vomits after eating.

11. Acts weird around food: eats only certain types of foods; chews food, then spits it out before swallowing; skips meals or takes only tiny portions; acts "disgusted" with food; eats only "safe" foods; will only eat from a certain plate or bowl; cuts food into tiny pieces; chews every bite the same number of times; keeps moving food around the plate; cooks for others but won't eat the food.

12. Refuses to eat around other people; avoids restaurants.

13. Eats in secret; gorges on food when alone; hides food; has a lot of empty food packages and wrappers.

14. Is moody, irritable, secretive, sad, cranky, touchy, and/or tired all the time; has dramatic mood swings.

15. Starts wearing very loose-fitting, baggy clothing, or very tight-fitting, revealing clothing.

16. Uses lots of negative self-talk ("I'm a pig," "I'm a loser," "Everyone hates me"); has poor self-esteem.

17. Constantly complains about being "fat," "huge," or "obese"; talks constantly about food and weight; is jealous of people who are thin and vows to be like them.

18. Claims that being thin will change his or her life ("I'll feel better about myself when I'm thin," "People will like me more when I'm thin").

19. Obsesses about his or her body; hates it or parts of it; spends a lot of time in front of the mirror, or refuses to look in a mirror.

20. Withdraws from or avoids friends and family.

21. Lies about eating; feels ashamed or guilty after eating.

22. Cuts himself/herself or hurts self in other ways.

23. Has physical signs of a problem—like dull, stringy hair (or loss of hair), tooth decay, very dry skin, rashes, cold hands, scrapes on the backs of his or her knuckles (from self-induced vomiting), constant sore throat, or fine hair growing on the face or body.

24. Denies that anything is wrong.

14 Do's and Don'ts for Helping a Friend Who Might Have an Eating Disorder

1. **DO** know the warning signs (see pages 36–37).

2. **DO** learn as much as you can about eating disorders. For quick access to information, check out these Web sites. Some also list and describe current books you can find at your library or bookstore.

   - **www.anred.com** (Anorexia Nervosa and Related Eating Disorders, Inc.)

   - **www.edreferral.com** (Eating Disorder Referral and Information Center)

   - **www.anad.org** (National Association of Anorexia Nervosa and Associated Disorders)

   - **www.nationaleatingdisorders.org** (National Eating Disorders Association)

   - **www.somethingfishy.org** (Something Fishy—fishy name, great site)

3. **DO** be compassionate. That way, you're less likely to be judgmental. Nobody *chooses* to have an eating disorder. Nobody *wants* to be sick or obsessed with weight and food.

4. **DO** be honest. Tell your friend that you're concerned, and explain why. Talk in private—don't confront your friend in front of a group. Don't lecture or blame. Use "I-language," not "You-language." *Example:* "I noticed that you haven't been eating lunch lately," not "You're not eating lunch anymore." "I notice that you're losing a lot of weight," not "You're getting too skinny," and NEVER "You look sick," or "You look like you have AIDS or something."

5. **DO** encourage your friend to get help. Suggest that he or she tell a parent, see a doctor, or talk to the school counselor.

6. **DON'T** be surprised if your friend denies having a problem, or tells you to mind your own business, or tries to pick a fight with you.

7. **DON'T** promise not to tell anyone else. Don't threaten to end your friendship if your friend won't change his or her behavior or get help.

8. **DO** tell someone if your friend won't. Tell a teacher, the school counselor, the school nurse, your coach, or another adult you trust. Keep telling until someone promises to help.

9. **DO** be aware of your own attitudes about food, weight, and body image. If you're obsessed about your own weight, if you're always

dieting, if you think that thinness is something to strive for, you won't be much help to your friend—and you won't be very believable.

10. **DON'T** associate food or weight with how your friend looks. Avoid saying things like, "Honestly, you'd look better if you put on a few pounds," or "Now that you've lost the ten pounds you wanted, you really do look better, so maybe you can stop dieting." Your friend will hear, "I look awful!" or "I really WAS fat!"

11. **DON'T** turn into the "food police." Don't monitor what your friend eats or doesn't eat. Don't constantly ask your friend if he or she is eating more (or less), or eating healthy foods, or drinking fewer diet colas. Don't try to convince your friend to eat differently. Don't get into power struggles over your friend's eating.

12. **DO** stick with your friend during the recovery process. Be there and be encouraging, even when your friend has a setback or seems frustrated or wants to give up.

13. **DON'T** give up on your friend or get discouraged. Be patient. Recovering from an eating disorder takes time and a lot of effort.

14. **DO** be realistic. Know your limits. You're not your friend's doctor or therapist. You didn't cause your friend's problem, and you can't solve it on your own. You're not responsible for his or her success or failure. You can't force your friend to change his or her behavior, or even to get help. What you can do is be aware, be there, be supportive, and make sure that at least one trusted adult knows the situation.

15 Ways to Create a Body-Positive World

A negative body image can relate to lower self-esteem, eating disorders, oppressive behaviors towards ourselves and others, and a lack of concern for our own health and well-being. Try these tips to fight back against pressures from friends, family, ourselves, and the media. For more information and resources, visit www.advocatesforyouth.org and go to the section for teens.

1. Encourage positive comments and try to avoid negative comments about your own and other people's bodies.

2. Participate in physical activities that make you feel good about yourself without making anyone else feel bad about their body.

3. Try not to make judgmental comments about food, calories, dieting, and weight. People of all sizes have issues around these and you never know how you will affect people with your comments.

4. Learn the facts and challenge the myths on size and bodies.

5. Compliment people more often on their ideas, personality, and accomplishments than on their appearance and physical being.

6. Try to think of bodies as whole, functional units, rather than breaking them down into parts. Instead of saying, "I'm unhappy with my thighs," say, "I'm pleased that my body is capable of doing this activity well."

7. Don't participate in, encourage, or laugh at jokes that make fun of a person's size or body.

8. Accept all types of bodies as beautiful and challenge limiting societal standards of beauty.

9. Learn about eating disorders and seek help if you suspect that you or a friend has a problem.

10. Wear the clothes that you like and feel comfortable in, rather than avoiding what you think makes you look "too fat" or "too thin."

11. Try to eat when you are hungry, enjoy your food, and take pleasure in the process of eating, without guilt or stress over what you are eating.

12. Object to gender-based assumptions of how bodies should look, such as "women should be thin" or "men should be muscular."

13. Support organizations and activists who work for positive body image and ending sizeism.

14. Teach kids at a young age that they are beautiful just as they are!

15. Understand that size and body oppression relates to other forms of oppression, such as sexism, racism, and homophobia, and then challenge all types of oppression.

16 Safe Ways to Stay Awake

You've got to hand in that paper tomorrow at 8 A.M. sharp. Or you've got to study for that exam, and the textbook...is...soooo...borrrrinnng...zzzzzz. Resist the urge to make a pot of coffee or drink a super-caffeinated soda. Try one or more of these ideas instead.

1. Do sit-ups or jumping jacks, leg lifts or hand squeezes. Run in place. Take a brisk walk. Shake. Exercise gets your heart pumping and moves oxygen-rich blood through your circulatory system.

2. Rub your hands, arms, legs, and face—more ways to stimulate circulation.

3. Eat something crunchy. Try cheese and crackers, an apple, sunflower seeds, or celery sticks with peanut butter. Avoid sugary snacks. They'll give you a brief energy burst, followed by an ugly sugar crash.

4. Drink lots of water or juice.

5. Meditate. Find a comfortable place to sit; keep your spine straight; stare at a spot on the wall, or close your eyes; breathe slowly, deeply, and rhythmically; and think the same syllable, word, or short phrase over and over again. About ten minutes should clear your head.

6. Listen to stimulating music, preferably without lyrics. Working to music may improve your concentration by blocking out other noises.

7. Turn up the lights, or turn on another light. Brighter is better when you're feeling sleepy.

8. Take a 15-minute break. Call a friend and talk. Play a video game. Surf the Web. Whatever.

9. Think wide-awake thoughts. Instead of "I'm so sleepy...I can't stand it...I'm so bored...I have to sleep," try "I *won't* give in. I *will* stay awake. I'm *going* to stay awake. I'm awake!"

10. Read aloud from what you're writing or studying.

11. Chew gum. Blow bubbles.

12. Take a cold shower or a dip in a pool.

13. Open a window, especially if it's cool outside.

14. Put ice cubes down your pants.

15. Drink a liter of carbonated water, then belch the alphabet.

16. If you simply can't keep your eyes open, set your alarm for a half-hour or an hour and take a nap. Even a brief snooze will recharge your brain and body.

"How can you prove whether at this moment
we are sleeping, and all our thoughts are a dream;
or whether we are awake, and talking to one another
in the waking state?"
Plato

The National Sleep Foundation's 7 Sleep-Smart Tips for Teens

Most adolescents and teens today are sleep deprived. If you're one of them, try these tips from the National Sleep Foundation. For more information, call 1-888-NSF-SLEEP or visit www.sleepfoundation.org.

1. Sleep is food for the brain. Get enough of it, and get it when you need it. Even mild sleepiness can hurt your performance—from taking school exams to playing sports or video games. Lack of sleep can make you look tired and feel depressed, irritable, and angry.

2. Keep consistency in mind. Establish a regular bedtime and waketime schedule, and maintain it during weekends and school (or work) vacations. Don't stray from your schedule frequently, and never do so for two or more consecutive nights. If you must go off schedule, avoid delaying your bedtime by more than one hour, awaken the next day within two hours of your regular schedule, and, if you are sleepy during the day, take an early afternoon nap.

3. Learn how much sleep you need to function at your best. You should awaken refreshed, not tired. Most adolescents need between 8.5 and 9.25 hours of sleep each night. Know when you need to get up in the morning, then calculate when you need to go to sleep to get at least 8.5 hours of sleep a night.

4. Get into bright light as soon as possible in the morning, but avoid it in the evening. The light helps to signal to the brain when it should wake up and when it should prepare to sleep.

5. Understand your circadian rhythm. Then, you can try to maximize your schedule throughout the day according to your internal clock. For example, to compensate for your "slump (sleepy) times," participate in stimulating activities or classes that are interactive, and avoid lecture classes or potentially unsafe activities, including driving.

6. After lunch (or after noon), stay away from coffee, colas with caffeine, and nicotine, which are all stimulants. Also avoid alcohol, which disrupts sleep.

7. Relax before going to bed. Avoid heavy reading, studying, and computer games within one hour of going to bed. Don't fall asleep with the television on—flickering light and stimulating content can inhibit restful sleep. If you work during the week, try to avoid working night hours. If you work until 9:30 P.M., for example, you will need to plan time to "chill out" before going to sleep.

8 Ways to Never Start Smoking

If you haven't started smoking, pay attention to everything you hear about not starting. Learn as much as you can. And remember: Smoking is an addiction. The first cigarette is a choice.

1. **Resist curiosity.** It's natural to want to try smoking once—you're probably curious about what it's like. People may tell you that it feels great, it's soothing, it's refreshing, it's a rush, or it's cool. In fact, when you take your first drag, your throat burns, your lungs feel like they're on fire, you cough, you feel sick, your eyes water, your heart rate speeds up, and you become short of breath.

2. **Hang out with nonsmokers.** It's a lot easier to resist cigarettes when the people you hang out with don't have them. If most of your friends smoke, ask them to think about quitting, and offer to help. What if your parents smoke at home? You can still choose not to start.

3. **Find a friend who will support your decision not to smoke.** This makes it easier for both of you to resist smoking. Make a pact with your friend not to smoke. Then stick together.

4. **Avoid situations that involve smoking.** Think twice before going to a party or even where you know people will be smoking. If your plans include hanging out with a group in which almost everyone smokes, change your plans. If someone who smokes asks you out, think about whether you really want to date him or her.

5. **Be ready to say no.** Think up the words you'll use and practice saying them. A simple "No, thanks, I don't smoke" should work just fine.

6. **Don't believe the media hype.** Look at the ads selling cigarettes. Are those smiling, healthy faces with shining white teeth really true to life? A Marlboro Man died of lung cancer. Think of him each time you see a cigarette ad.

7. **Stay busy.** When you're active, you don't have time to think about smoking. Join a sports team or exercise at home, get involved in after-school activities, or find hobbies you enjoy. If you're at a party where a lot of people are smoking, keep your hands and mouth busy. Talk, keep a soft drink in your hand, or chew gum.

8. **Be proud to be a nonsmoker.** Don't feel guilty or insecure about your choice not to smoke. Be confident that you've chosen to avoid a habit that's hard to break and negatively affects your health. Support others who choose not to smoke.

14 Tips for Quitting Smoking

According to the American Lung Association, most adolescents who have smoked at least 100 cigarettes in their lifetime report that they would like to quit, but they are not able to quit. If you're a smoker who wants to quit, try these ideas.

1. **Congratulate yourself.** Just reading this list is a great first step toward becoming tobacco-free.

2. **Get support.** Teens who have friends and family who will help them quit are much more likely to succeed. If you don't want to tell your parents or family that you smoke, make sure your friends know, and consider confiding in a counselor or other adult you trust. And if you're having a hard time finding people to support you (if, say, all your friends smoke and none of them is interested in quitting), you might consider joining a support group, either in person or online.

3. **Set a quit date.** You should pick a day that you'll stop smoking. Tell your friends (and if they know you smoke, your family) that you're going to quit smoking on that day. Try to think of that day as a dividing line between the smoking you and the "new and improved" nonsmoker you've become. Mark it on your calendar.

4. **Throw away your cigarettes**—*all* of your cigarettes—even that emergency pack you have stashed in the secret pocket of your back-pack. Get rid of your ashtrays and lighters, too—that way you'll make it a little bit harder to smoke.

5. **Wash all your clothes.** Get rid of the smell of cigarettes as much as you can by washing all your clothes and having your coats or sweaters dry-cleaned. If you drive and you smoked in your car, clean that out, too.

6. **Think about your triggers.** You've probably smoked a lot of cigarettes since you started smoking, and you're probably aware of certain situations when you particularly tend to smoke—when you're at your best friend's house, drinking coffee after the movies, or just driving around. These situations are your *triggers* for smoking—it feels automatic to have a cigarette when you're in them. Once you've figured out your triggers, you can try a variety of techniques to make it easier to quit:

   - avoid these situations (if you smoke when you drive, get a ride to school, or take the bus for a couple of weeks)

   - change the situation (suggest you sit in the nonsmoking section the next time you go out to eat)

- substitute something else for cigarettes (cinnamon sticks, carrots, gum, straws, toothpicks, and even pacifiers all make good substitutes)

7. **Expect some physical symptoms.** If you smoke regularly, you're probably physically addicted to nicotine, and your body may experience some symptoms of withdrawal when you quit. These symptoms may include:

- headaches or stomachaches

- crabbiness, jumpiness, or depression

- lack of energy

- dry mouth or sore throat

- desire to pig out

The good news is, these withdrawal symptoms will pass—so be patient and don't give in and sneak a smoke, or you'll just have to deal with the symptoms longer.

8. **Keep yourself busy.** Many people find it's best to quit on a Monday, when they have school or work to keep them busy. The more distracted you are, the less likely you are to crave cigarettes. Staying active is also a good way to make sure you keep your weight down and your energy up, even as you experience the symptoms of nicotine withdrawal.

9. **Drink lots of water.** Liquid will help flush the nicotine out of your system and will help you to feel better as the withdrawal symptoms set in. And while you're at it, stay away from caffeine, which can make you even more jumpy.

10. **Quit gradually.** Some people find that switching to cigarettes that have a lower nicotine level and then gradually decreasing the number that they smoke each day is an effective way to quit. (This strategy doesn't work for everyone—you may find you've got to quit cold turkey.)

11. **Use a nicotine replacement.** If you find that none of these strategies is working, you might consider a nicotine replacement. These include gum, patches, inhalers, and nasal sprays. Sprays and inhalers are available by prescription only, and although you can buy the patch and gum without a prescription, you should see your doctor before you do so. That way, you can find out which is best for you, based on your type of addiction. For example, the patch requires the least effort on your part, but it also doesn't provide the almost instantaneous nicotine "kick" you'll get from the gum.

12. **Reward yourself.** Set aside the money you usually spend on cigarettes. When you've stayed tobacco-free for a week, two weeks, or a month, buy yourself a new CD, some clothes, or a book—anything you really like.

13. **What if you slip up?** If you're like many people, you may quit successfully for weeks or even months and then suddenly have a craving that's so strong you feel like you have to give in. Or maybe you accidentally find yourself in one of your trigger situations and give in to temptation. It may be tempting to give up and decide that you've blown it—and to start smoking again. What should you do?

    • Think about your slip as one mistake, not a sign that you've failed. Take notice of when and why it happened and move on.

    • Did you become a heavy smoker after one cigarette? Probably not—it happened more gradually, over time. Keep in mind that one cigarette didn't make you a smoker to start with, so smoking one cigarette (or even two or three) after you've quit doesn't make you a smoker again.

    • Remind yourself why you've quit and how well you've done—or have someone in your support group do this for you.

14. **Remember: It's hard to quit smoking.** If you don't succeed the first time, don't give up. Some people have to quit two or three times before they're successful.

The Benefits of Quitting Smoking: A Timeline from the American Lung Association

Do you smoke? Would you like to quit? This timeline from the American Lung Association may inspire you. If you're not a smoker, give it to someone you care about who is. Learn more at www.lungusa.org.

20 minutes after quitting:

• blood pressure decreases
• pulse rate drops
• body temperature of hands and feet increases

8 hours after quitting:

- carbon monoxide level in blood drops to normal
- oxygen level in blood increases to normal

24 hours after quitting:

- chance of a heart attack decreases

48 hours after quitting:

- nerve endings start regrowing
- ability to smell and taste is enhanced

2 weeks–3 months after quitting:

- circulation improves
- walking becomes easier
- lung function increases

1–9 months after quitting:

- coughing, sinus congestion, fatigue, and shortness of breath decrease

1 year after quitting:

- excess risk of coronary heart disease is decreased to half that of a smoker

Long-term benefits:

- from 5–15 years after quitting, stroke risk is reduced to that of people who have never smoked.
- 10 years after quitting, the risk of lung cancer drops to as little as one-half that of continuing smokers. The risk of cancer of the mouth, throat, esophagus, bladder, kidney, and pancreas decreases. The risk of ulcer decreases.
- 15 years after quitting, the risk of coronary heart disease is similar to that of people who have never smoked. The risk of death returns to nearly the level of people who have never smoked.

7 Reasons Why People—
Even Smart People—Try Drugs

One reason often heard from people using drugs is that they do them to feel good. The problem? Drugs don't care what the reason is. The same effects can occur no matter why you choose to use them. Another reason people give for using drugs is they want to change their situation. The problem? It isn't real. You haven't changed your situation; you've just distorted it for a little while. To learn more, visit www.freevibe.com.

1. **Because they want to fit in.** No one wants to be the only one not participating. No one wants to be left out. So sometimes they make bad decisions, like taking drugs, to cover up their insecurities. They don't think about how drugs can isolate you from your friends and family. They forget to look past that one party to see how things could turn out. Or maybe they just don't see the people around them who aren't using drugs.

2. **Because they want to escape or relax.** You'll hear a lot of people saying things like, "I'm so stressed, I need to get messed up!" or "Drugs help me relax" or whatever. What they're really saying is, "Drinking or doing drugs is just easier than dealing with my problems or reaching out for help." The thing is, the problems are still there when they come down—and not only do they still have to deal with their problems, they have to deal with them when they're not at 100 percent and they're feeling guilty, or even worse, when they're not thinking straight.

3. **Because they're bored.** Lots of people turn to drugs for a little excitement because they say there's nothing else to do but watch the same *Simpsons* rerun for the tenth time or hang out at the Burger King. But people who make these kinds of decisions usually find out that drugs are ultimately really a waste and painful. Drugs don't change the situation, and they just might make it worse.

4. **Because the media says it's cool.** Even though there's an anti-drug ad on every minute and more rock stars and ball players than you can shake a stick at tell you to stay away from drugs, the truth is the entertainment world still manages to make drugs appear very attractive. Kind of like how they encourage people to be really skinny even when they say anorexia is bad. Or when they say you should be super muscular but steroids are bad. But if you're wise, you'll understand that the entertainment world is not the real world, and basing your life on these messages is superficial.

5. **Because they think it makes them seem grown-up.** This is one of the weirdest reasons. Think about it: Why would an adult want to use drugs? Probably for many of the same reasons you would consider. The reality is that the most grown-up people out there aren't users. They're too busy living their lives to bother with stuff, like drugs, that will interfere.

6. **Because they want to rebel.** Sometimes people turn to drugs not so much for themselves, but to make a statement against someone else, such as their families or society in general. Somehow taking drugs makes them outlaws or more individual. The problem is taking drugs, ultimately, robs these people of their ability to be independent, because it makes them dependent—on drugs and their drug connections.

7. **Because they want to experiment.** It's human nature to want to experiment. Trying things out helps you decide if they're right for you. But it's also human nature to avoid things that are obviously bad for you. You wouldn't experiment with jumping off the Brooklyn Bridge. The point is, there are a zillion better things to experiment with—sports, music, dying your hair, seeing bad movies, eating spicy food....

101 Anti-Drugs

Your Anti-Drug is that thing that is more important to you than using drugs. For some people it's their family, for others their goals. Still others get down to specifics with things like soccer, music, and their education. Here are 101 things that other teens have identified as their Anti-Drug. What's yours?

acting	blowing bubbles	computers
after-school activities	boy bands	cooking
animals	boyfriend	culture
art	brain power	dancing
baseball	camping	deejaying
basketball	cheerleading	determination
because not everyone is doing it	chess	drawing
	church camp	dreaming
being happy	comedy	energy
biking	composing songs	everything

exercise	my baby sister	responsibility
faith	my body	school
family	my children	self-confidence
fashion	my freedom	shopping
feeling	my future	singing
friends	my goals	skating
games	my health	sleeping
girlfriend	my impact on others	soccer
God	my style	social life
gymnastics	my team	sports
having fun	nature	student council
helping others	optimism	support
hope	painting	surfing the Internet
imagination	people	survival
jogging	pets	talent
juggling	photography	teachers
karate	poetry	tomorrow
life	prayer	travel
loss of a loved one to drugs	pride	video games
love	racing	volunteering
me	rapping	watching the stars
meditation	raving	weightlifting
modeling	reading	writing
music	respect	youth group

In September 2002, these were the Top 5 Anti-Drugs:

1. music
2. dancing
3. computers
4. family
5. basketball

Visit www.freevibe.com to read what kids and teens say about their Anti-Drug. Write about your own Anti-Drug—tell the world. And get the lowdown on every drug out there—the facts, answers to your questions, and the latest medical and social information.

The Truth About Alcohol: 9 Tips for Teens from NCADI

If you've ever thought "Just one drink won't hurt me" or "Everybody's doing it," check out these facts from the National Clearinghouse for Alcohol and Drug Information (NCADI). To learn more, visit www.health.org or call 1-800-729-6686 toll-free.

1. **Alcohol affects your brain.** Drinking alcohol leads to a loss of coordination, poor judgment, slowed reflexes, distorted vision, memory lapses, and even blackouts.

2. **Alcohol affects your body.** Alcohol can damage every organ in your body. It is absorbed directly into your bloodstream and can increase your risk for a variety of life-threatening diseases, including cancer. It can also make you gain weight and give you bad breath.

3. **Alcohol affects your self-control.** Alcohol depresses your central nervous system, lowers your inhibitions, and impairs your judgment. Drinking can lead to risky behaviors, including having unprotected sex. This may expose you to HIV/AIDS and other sexually transmitted diseases or cause unwanted pregnancy.

4. **Alcohol can kill you.** Drinking large amounts of alcohol can lead to coma or even death. In 1998, 35.8 percent of traffic deaths of 15- to 20-year-olds were alcohol-related. Mixing alcohol with medications or illicit drugs is extremely dangerous and can lead to accidental death.

5. **Alcohol can hurt you—even if you're not the one drinking.** If you're around people who are drinking, you have an increased risk of being seriously injured, involved in car crashes, or affected by violence. At the very least, you may have to deal with people who are sick, out of control, or unable to take care of themselves.

6. **Alcohol can get you in trouble with the law.** It is illegal to buy or possess alcohol if you are under 21.

7. **Just one drink can make you fail a breath test.** In some states, people under the age of 21 who are found to have any amount of alcohol in their systems can lose their driver's license, be subject to a heavy fine, or have their car permanently taken away.

8. **Beer and wine aren't "safer" than hard liquor.** One 12-ounce beer has about as much alcohol as a 1½-ounce shot of liquor, a 5-ounce glass of wine, or a wine cooler.

9. **Everybody isn't doing it.** Most teens *aren't* drinking alcohol. Research shows that 70 percent of people ages 12–20 haven't had a drink in the past month.

NCADI's 7 Warning Signs of a Drinking Problem

You think that a friend might have a drinking problem, but how can you be sure? The National Clearinghouse for Alcohol and Drug Information (NCADI) has made a list of warning signs you can watch for.

1. Getting drunk on a regular basis.

2. Lying about how much alcohol he or she is using.

3. Believing that alcohol is necessary to have fun.

4. Having frequent hangovers.

5. Feeling run-down, depressed, or even suicidal.

6. Having "blackouts"—forgetting what he or she did while drinking.

7. Having problems at school or getting in trouble with the law.

What if you notice one or more of these warning signs? Be a real friend. Encourage your friend to stop drinking or to seek professional help. For information and referrals, visit www.health.org or call 1-800-729-6686 toll-free.

"You get stressed. You drink to chill out.
You think your problems go away. They don't."

Teen boy

Quoted in "Who's Got the Power? You...or Drugs?" brochure
The National Council on Alcoholism and Drug Dependence
www.ncadd.org

How to Help a Friend: FCD's IO Steps for Conducting an Informal Intervention

You're worried about a friend's use of alcohol and/or other drugs. At this point, you don't want to get other people involved. You just want to talk to him or her about it. Follow these 10 steps from Freedom from Chemical Dependency (FCD) Educational Services, Inc., a nonprofit organization that provides alcohol, tobacco, and other drug education and prevention programs for schools throughout the United States and abroad. On the Web, visit www.fcd.org.

1. **Learn all you can about chemical dependency.** It's important to understand that chemical dependency is a health issue rather than one of deficient morals, willpower, or character. It's an illness that can't be cured and can be fatal if left untreated.

2. **Get help for yourself.** Caring about someone with a substance abuse problem is hard. Don't shoulder the entire burden yourself.

   • Talk to a counselor, teacher, coach, doctor, parent, sibling, or someone else you trust. You're not betraying your friend. You needn't mention his or her name, and you can ask the person to keep the information confidential.

   • Join a support group. Al-Anon and Alateen are for people who are concerned about somebody's drinking. Meetings are free. To find a group near you, visit www.al-anon.org or call 1-888-4AL-ANON (888-425-2666) toll-free.

3. **Pick the right time and place.** Talk to your friend when he or she is sober and clear-headed. Talking to a person under the influence is a waste of time. Choose a setting that is calm, private, and free of distractions and interruptions.

4. **Plan what you're going to say.** Give some thought ahead of time to your feelings about your friend. What do you like and respect about her? How has she helped or supported you in the past? What are the specific behaviors or stated attitudes that fuel your concern? What options exist for helping her?

5. **Convey your affection and/or respect.** Let the person know how much she means to you, how important the relationship is to you. Talk about her fine qualities and all the times she has helped and supported you. This minimizes the possibility of anger or defensiveness on her part.

6. **Express your concern.** Be caring and nonjudgmental. *Examples:* "You're my best friend and I'm really worried about you." "I'm afraid you're going to hurt yourself."

7. **Use specific examples.** Provide examples of the worrisome behaviors you have *personally* witnessed. *Examples:* "The last two times we went out, you drank so much I had to get home by myself." "Last season you were the lead scorer, and this year you're warming the bench." Talk about how the person's behavior is affecting you and your relationship. *Examples:* "I miss spending time with you." "I don't like it when you ask me to lie to protect you."

   It's hard to predict your friend's reaction. She might burst into tears and agree with everything you've said. She might get angry, defend or deny her use, blame others, give excuses, or tell you to mind your own business. She might lash out at you as "someone who should talk," considering all of "your problems." This can be very hurtful. Try to see it as the illness talking, not your friend. Don't argue or get angry. Instead...

8. **Offer to help.** From having done research, talked with an adult, and/or attended a support group, you will have learned the various options for helping your friend. Depending on the circumstances, offer to go with her to the school counselor, her parents or doctor, a 12-step meeting, and/or a local resource for evaluating and treating people with substance abuse problems. Instead of asking your friend if she is willing to get help, ask her which of these options she would like to use. Tell her that chemical dependency is not a problem she can solve alone.

   Your friend may make excuses for why she doesn't need to get help. She may promise to "quit" or "cut back" on her own. Know in advance how you will respond to this and any other objections. You may tell her that your concern is so great that you cannot sit back and do nothing. Even if she'll hate you for it. you're going to talk to her parents or somebody at school. Or, if you feel that her use does not pose a serious threat to her or anyone else's safety, you may simply tell her that you wanted to express your concern, and that you are ready to help in any way at any time. If she refuses to get help, you'll need to...

9. **Set limits.** Don't be a coconspirator in the problem. While lying for friends, covering up for them, or cleaning up after them may seem like acts of friendship, they are, in fact, ways to spare your friend from the discomfort and negative consequences that motivate change. Establish limits so you will no longer be in awkward or dangerous situations. *Examples:* "I'm not going to let you copy my homework." "I

only want to spend time with you when you're sober." "I'm not going to lie for you anymore."

10. **Don't expect miracles.** Your intervention may not appear to have "worked." Don't be discouraged. People rarely change long-standing behaviors based on one remark or conversation. But each expression of concern, added to the next, can lead to that point at which your friend is no longer able to ignore the truth.

If You Live with Someone Who Drinks Too Much or Uses Drugs

Are you worried that your mom or dad drinks too much or uses drugs? You're right to be concerned—about their safety and health, about what will happen to you, about their embarrassing you or criticizing you unfairly, about breaking promises, about driving under the influence, and about lots of other things that create unpredictability and confusion. While you can't stop your parent from drinking or using, you can make things better for yourself. If you have a friend in this situation, share this list with him or her. Learn more at the National Association for Children of Alcoholics Web site: www.nacoa.net.

1. One in four kids under age 18 lives in a family where a person abuses alcohol or suffers from alcoholism. Countless others are affected by a family member's use of drugs. So you are *not* alone.

2. Addiction to alcohol or drugs is a disease. When *one* member of the family has this disease, *all* family members are affected.

3. You didn't cause it, and you can't cure it. You need and deserve help for yourself.

4. It's important to find caring adults who can help you. Talking with them really helps. Find an adult—a teacher, school counselor or nurse, friend's parent, doctor, grandparent, aunt or uncle, or neighbor—who will listen and help you deal with problems at home.

5. Join a support group. They're great places to meet other young people who are struggling with the same problems at home that you face. To find a local support group, talk to your school counselor or social worker. Or join Alateen, a group for teens who are affected by someone else's alcohol or drug use. To find a meeting near you, look in the phone book under Alateen, ask your school counselor, clergy person, or another adult you trust, visit the Web site (www.alateen.org), or call 1-888-425-2666 toll-free.

6. Get involved in activities at school and in the community where you can hang out with other young people, use your special talents and strengths, and learn new skills while you are having fun.

7. Even if the person with the disease doesn't get help, you can still get the help you need to feel better and to have a safe and productive life.

Remember the Seven Cs:

I didn't   **C**ause it.

I can't   **C**ure it.

I can't   **C**ontrol it.

I can take better **C**are of myself by

                  Communicating my feelings,

making healthy   **C**hoices, and

                  Celebrating myself.

17 Helpful Toll-Free Numbers

Call toll-free or go online to find help with problems, answers to questions, referrals, resources, information, and more.

Al-Anon/Alateen
1-888-4AL-ANON (1-888-425-2666)
www.al-anon.org or www.alateen.org
Al-Anon is for families and friends of alcoholics—people who live with someone else's problem drinking. Alateen is a recovery program for young people, adapted from Alcoholics Anonymous.

CDC Public Response Service
1-888-246-2675
www.ashastd.org/hotlines/cpr.html
CDC-approved information about biological and chemical terrorism and other emergency public health issues. You can also email questions and requests for information: cdcresponse@ashastd.org.

Cocaine Anonymous World Services
1-800-347-8998
www.ca.org
Information and referrals for people who use cocaine or other mind-altering substances.

Depression and Bipolar Support Alliance
1-800-826-3632
www.ndmda.org
Information about depression and other mood disorders; online directory
of support groups.

Gay and Lesbian National Hotline
1-800-THE-GLNH (1-800-843-4564)
www.glnh.org
Free and anonymous information, referrals, and peer counseling for people
who are gay, lesbian, bisexual, or transgender.

National Center for Victims of Crime
1-800-FYI-CALL (1-800-394-2255)
www.ncvc.org
Refers crime victims and concerned individuals to appropriate local services
including crisis intervention, help with the criminal justice process, counseling, and support groups.

National Clearinghouse for Alcohol and Drug Information (NCADI)
1-800-729-6686
www.health.org
Information and materials about substance abuse. Trained information
specialists can answer your questions 24 hours a day.

National Drug and Treatment Referral
1-800-662-HELP (1-800-662-4357)
findtreatment.samhsa.gov
Substance abuse and treatment referral information. Operated by the U.S.
Department of Health and Human Services.

National Eating Disorders Association
1-800-931-2237
www.nationaleatingdisorders.org
Help, referrals, and answers to your questions about eating disorders.

National Health Information Center
1-800-336-4797
www.health.gov/nhic
Help finding health information; referrals to health professionals and
resources; publications about health.

National Information Center for Children and Youth with Disabilities
1-800-695-0285
www.nichcy.org
Information about disabilities in children and youth to age 22.

National Institute of Mental Health (NIMH)
1-800-421-4211 (Depression information)
1-88-88-ANXIETY (1-888-826-9438)
www.nimh.nih.gov
Call the toll-free numbers to request brochures about depression or anxiety, or visit the Web site to view them online.

National Mental Health Association Resource Center
1-800-969-NMHA (1-800-969-6642)
www.nmha.org/infoctr/index.cfm
Information on mental illnesses and treatments, and referrals for local treatment services.

National Sexual Violence Resource Center
1-877-739-3895
www.nsvrc.org
Information, help, and support for victims of sexual violence. A project of the Pennsylvania Coalition Against Rape. Visit their site for teens: www.teenpcar.com.

National Organization for Children of Alcoholics
1-888-55-4COAS (1-888-554-2627)
www.nacoa.net
Resources for children and families affected by alcohol and other drug dependencies.

Planned Parenthood Federation of America
1-800-230-PLAN (1-800-230-7526)
www.plannedparenthood.org
Information about birth control, emergency contraception, parenting, pregnancy, abortion, STDs, and sexual health. Call to get connected with a clinic near you. Visit a site created for teens by Planned Parenthood: www.teenwire.com.

Suicide Awareness/Voices of Education
1-888-511-SAVE (1-888-511-7283)
www.save.org
Educational information about depression and suicide prevention.

Life Lists

Getting Along

12 Tips for Making and Keeping Friends

1. **Reach out.** Don't always wait for someone else to make the first move. A simple hi and a smile go a long way.

2. **Get involved.** Join clubs that interest you. Take special classes inside or outside of school. Check out neighborhood and community organizations.

3. **Let people know that you're interested in them.** Don't just talk about yourself. Ask questions about them and their interests. This is a basic social skill that many people lack. It will make you seem like a brilliant conversationalist.

4. **Be a good listener.** Look at people while they're talking to you. Pay attention to what they say.

5. **Risk telling people about yourself.** When it feels right, let them in on your interests, your talents, and what's important to you. BUT...

6. **Don't be a show-off.** Not everyone you meet will have your interests and abilities. (On the other hand, you shouldn't have to hide them— which you won't, once you find people who like and appreciate you.)

7. **Be honest.** Tell the truth about yourself, what you believe in, and what you stand for. When someone asks your opinion, be sincere. Friends appreciate honesty in each other. BUT...

8. **Be kind.** There are times when being tactful is more important than being totally honest. The truth doesn't have to hurt.

9. **Don't just use your friends as sounding boards for your problems.** Include them in the good times, too.

10. **Do your share of the work.** Any relationship takes effort. Don't depend on your friends to stay in touch with you, make all the plans, and make all the decisions.

11. **Be accepting.** Not all of your friends have to think and act like you do. (Wouldn't it be boring if they did?)

12. **Learn to recognize the so-called friends you can do without.** Some people get so lonely that they put up with anyone, including friends who aren't really friends at all.

Rate Your Friends: 15 Qualities to Look For

Think about someone you consider a friend. How many of these qualities does he or she have? Do this for all of your closest friends. Because nobody's perfect, few people will have all of these qualities all of the time. But the more a friend has, the better that friendship is for you.

My Friend...

1. is someone I trust.

2. encourages me to succeed and achieve—and celebrates my successes (instead of being jealous or negative).

3. is a person of good character (meaning: honest, sincere, loyal, respectful, responsible).

4. resolves conflicts peacefully.

5. has strong, positive relationships with his or her parents and/or other adults.

6. is serious about school.

7. knows how to make plans and set goals.

8. has a positive view of the future.

9. gets along with many different kinds of people; isn't biased or prejudiced.

10. is kind and compassionate.

11. respects himself or herself.

12. avoids dangerous situations.

13. takes positive risks.

14. gives back to the community and serves others.

15. is a positive influence on me and others.

"A friend is someone you can be alone with and have nothing to do and not be able to think of anything to say and be comfortable in the silence."

Sheryl Condie

16 Things to Say
When Someone Teases You

1. _____. *(Nothing. Just ignore it. If that doesn't work, turn and walk away.)*

2. I don't like it when you tease me, and I want you to stop.

3. I know you're just trying to upset me. Give it up. It's not going to work. Let's talk about something else, okay?

4. What's your point?

5. Whatever.

6. So?

7. Tell me when you get to the funny part.

8. Who cares about that?

9. You know, I really don't care what you think.

10. Do you have a problem with that? I don't have a problem with that.

11. I thought you were above all that.

12. Thank you for noticing.

13. Thanks! That's my best part/quality/feature.

14. Give me a break!

15. Big deal.

16. *(Yawn.)*

4 Steps for Handling Betrayal

Sometimes friends make mistakes. They accidentally say or do things that hurt each other. Good friends admit the error and apologize, forgive each other and move on. But what if friends say or do something on purpose *to hurt each other? That's called* betrayal, *and it's a major break in trust. If a friend betrays you—or you betray a friend—you need to talk.*

1. **Share your side of the story.** If your friend hurt you in some way, communicate this. Let him or her know how you feel and why. If you did something hurtful to your friend, explain why you did it.

2. **Listen to your friend's side of the story.** If your friend betrayed you, find out why. After you've listened, ask yourself if you feel confident that you've heard the *real* reasons behind your friend's actions. If you don't feel that the truth has been revealed, you may have trouble trusting your friend, even if he or she promises never to betray you again. If the betrayal was yours, listen to what your friend has to say. Don't get defensive.

3. **Apologize and forgive.** This is an essential step for putting the betrayal behind you. Make a promise to each other that this will *never* happen again. Then keep your promise.

4. **Decide whether you're still friends.** If a friend who has betrayed you can't guarantee that it will never happen again, the relationship may be damaged beyond repair. You no longer have an important ingredient for friendship: trust. If you betrayed someone, find out whether you're truly forgiven. Whatever you and your friend decide, be honest about what you're doing and why.

8 Steps to Conflict Resolution

Conflict between people is normal and inevitable, and not all conflict is bad. Constructive conflict helps us learn, grow, and build stronger relationships with other people. Follow these steps to work out your differences.

1. **Cool down.** Don't try to resolve a conflict when either of you is angry. Take a time-out or agree to meet again in 24 hours.

2. **Describe the conflict.** Each person should tell about it in his or her own words. No put-downs allowed! *Important:* Although each person may have a different view of the conflict and use different words to describe it, neither account is "right" or "wrong."

3. **Describe what caused the conflict.** What specific events led up to the conflict? What happened first? Next? Did the conflict start out as a minor disagreement or difference of opinion? What happened to turn it into a conflict? *Important:* Don't label the conflict as anyone's "fault."

4. **Describe the feelings raised by the conflict.** Again, each person should use his or her own words. Honesty is important. No blaming allowed!

5. **Listen carefully and respectfully while the other person is talking.** Try to understand his or her point of view. Don't interrupt. It might help to "reflect" the other person's perceptions and feelings by repeating them back. *Examples:* "Your feelings are hurt." "You thought you should have first choice about what game to play."

6. **Brainstorm solutions to the conflict.** Follow the three basic rules of brainstorming:

   • Everyone tries to come up with as many ideas as they can.

   • All ideas are okay.

   • Nobody makes fun of anyone else's ideas.

   Be creative. Affirm each other's ideas. Be open to new ideas. Make a list of brainstormed ideas so you're sure to remember them all. Then choose one solution to try. Be willing to negotiate and compromise.

7. **Try your solution.** See how it works. Give it your best efforts. Be patient.

8. **If one solution doesn't get results, try another.** Keep trying. Brainstorm more solutions if you need to.

If you can't resolve the conflict no matter how hard you try, agree to disagree. Sometimes that's the best you can do. Meanwhile, realize that the conflict doesn't have to end your relationship. People can get along even when they disagree.

11 Rules for Fighting Fair

1. **Try not to start an argument at a bad time.** When you're overly angry, rushed, tired, hungry, distracted, or otherwise feeling badly, it's not the time to fight. Instead, agree to discuss the sore spot at an agreed time when you're both likely to be in a good frame of mind, alone, and have the time for a meaningful discussion.

2. **Have a discussion, not a yelling match.** Speak in a normal tone of voice. Rather than make angry, accusatory messages, express your feelings by using "I-messages." *Example:* "I really felt worried when you didn't call."

3. **State factually what's bothering you.** Speak in the first person. Saying, "I'm upset that you didn't call about being late," is more effective than saying, "You never call when you're going to be late." Absolute statements like "You never..." or "You always..." are never quite true and always cloud the issue at hand.

4. **Stick to the subject being discussed.** Don't bring up past, old hurts or unrelated issues. That's another argument for another day.

5. **Don't hit "below the belt."** Unkind, hurtful statements about the person's character, appearance, or personality only bring anger and retaliation.

6. **Maintain eye contact.** Don't walk away or turn your back.

7. **Accept responsibility for your own behavior,** but no one else's.

8. **Recognize that feelings are neither right or wrong.** They just are. Recognize that while feelings can't be judged, behavior can and should be.

9. **Stay as calm and in control as possible.** If feelings and emotions become too overwhelming, ask to take a break and then come back to the discussion at an agreed time. If the other person needs such a break, graciously provide one.

10. **Clarify decisions made.** When a problem has been negotiated or settled, clearly restate what has been agreed to and what actions will be taken, who will take them, and when. *Example:* "When I'll be late for dinner, I'll call by 5 P.M. to let you know."

11. **No physical attacks allowed! Ever!**

16 Steps for Mediation from the Resolving Conflict Creatively Program

Peer mediation is a proven way to help others resolve conflicts. Through their Resolving Conflict Creatively Program (RCCP), an organization called Educators for Social Responsibility (ESR) has helped thousands of teachers and students learn how to respond nonviolently to conflict. For more information, call 1-800-370-2515 or visit www.esrnational.org.

I. INTRODUCTION

1. Introduce yourself as a mediator.

2. Ask those in the conflict if they want your help in solving the problem.

3. Find a quiet area to hold the mediation.

4. Ask for agreement to the following:

—try to solve the problem

—no name-calling

—let the other person finish talking

—confidentiality

II. LISTENING

5. Ask the first person "What happened?" Paraphrase.

6. Ask the first person how she or he feels. Reflect the feelings.

7. Ask the second person "What happened?" Paraphrase.

8. Ask the second person how he or she feels. Reflect the feelings.

III. LOOKING FOR SOLUTIONS

9. Ask the first person what she or he could have done differently. Paraphrase.

10. Ask the second person what she or he could have done differently. Paraphrase.

11. Ask the first person what she or he can do here and now to help solve the problem. Paraphrase.

12. Ask the second person what she or he can do here and now to help solve the problem. Paraphrase.

13. Use creative questioning to bring disputants closer to a solution.

IV. FINDING SOLUTIONS

14. Help both disputants find a solution they feel good about.

15. Repeat the solution and all of its parts to both disputants and ask if each agrees.

16. Congratulate both people on a successful mediation.

8 Ways to Be a Better Talker

1. *Stop* and *think* **before you talk.** As the old saying goes, "Make sure brain is engaged before putting mouth in gear."

2. **Say what you mean and mean what you say.** Most people appreciate directness and honesty. On the other hand, be tactful and respectful. Honesty doesn't have to hurt or offend.

3. **Watch your language.** Among some of your friends, it might be all right to use colorful words. But don't assume the whole world wants to hear #$%, $%^&*, and @#$%^&* on a regular basis.

4. **Use "I-messages" to communicate your wants, needs, and feelings.** Here's the basic formula for an "I-message":

   I feel _____
   (emotion)

   when _____
   (this happens)

   because _____.
   (it causes this problem for me)

   I want/need _____.
   (this to happen—an idea for a solution)

5. **If you feel that you're not getting through, talk more softly.** Do this instead of raising your voice. The other person will have to lean in and listen harder to what you're saying.

6. **Check your tone of voice.** Are you whining? Yelling? Sneering? Mocking? Being ironic? As another old saying goes, "It's not what you say, it's how you say it."

7. **Try seeing the situation from the other person's point of view.** Instead of thinking, "How can I get what I want?" think, "How can we both get what we need?" This will influence your choice of words, your tone of voice, and the outcome of your conversation.

8. **Build a feelings vocabulary.** It's hard to tell another person how you're feeling if you don't have the right words. Are you sad—or are you miserable, devastated, worried, or heartbroken? Are you mad—or are you irritated, resentful, furious, or enraged? Are you scared—or are you shy, anxious, petrified, or in a panic? The more clearly you can explain your feelings, the more likely it is that other people will really understand you.

To build your feelings vocabulary, listen to other people talk about their feelings. Ask adults to help you explain your feelings when you're stuck. Look up feelings words in a thesaurus and find synonyms. Read books about feelings.

5 Ways to Be a Great Listener

Some experts claim that people misinterpret what they hear in over 70 percent of all communications. That's because they listen passively. It's easy to be an active listener. Practice these active listening skills. Before long, other people will start seeing you as one of the most brilliant and fascinating people they know.

1. Make and keep eye contact. Don't stare the person down. Just look into his or her eyes.

2. Show that you're paying attention with an occasional nod, grunt, or brief comment. *Examples:* "I see what you mean." "I hear you." "No kidding!" "Tell me more." "Really?" "Go on." "Hmmmm." "Uh-huh."

3. Ask for clarification if the other person says something you don't understand. This is not the same as challenging or interrogating him or her. *Examples:* Instead of saying "What are you talking about?" say "I'm sorry, I don't quite understand what you're saying." Instead of, "Start over. You're not making any sense!" try "Run that by me again. I'm not sure I got it."

4. Every so often, mirror what the other person is saying. Summarize what you've heard. This shows that you're paying attention. *Examples:* "Wow. So James told Mrs. Smith that you were copying his answers?" "You think that Keesha was rude to you at lunch today." "Your parents have been giving you a hard time."

5. Every so often, offer a brief comment on the other person's feelings. *Examples:* "You must have been surprised." "I can tell you were upset." "I'll bet you were terrified." "You must feel really sad about that."

"Nature gave us one tongue and two ears
so we could hear twice as much as we speak."

Epictetus

7 Ways to Be a Terrible Listener

1. Interrupt often with your own ideas, opinions, and point of view.

2. Give advice (unless the other person asks for it, in which case *wait* until he or she stops talking).

3. Act bored. *Examples:* tap your feet, roll your eyes, check your watch, look around the room, yawn.

4. Argue with or challenge the other person.

5. Blame or criticize the other person.

6. Pay attention to someone or something else. *Examples:* watch TV, play a video game, surf the Web, listen to music, talk on the phone to someone else.

7. Think about what you'll say as soon as the other person stops talking. (That's not listening. That's rehearsing.)

8 Things to Try If You're Shy

Almost everyone feels shy at times. Surveys show that more than 90 percent of Americans say they've been shy at some point during their lives. Nearly half say they're still shy. If you want, you can try to be less shy. Here's how.

1. Talk with adults you know and trust. Explain that you sometimes feel shy. Ask for help and ideas. Ask them to share stories about times when they felt shy.

2. Start each day with a single goal. *Examples:* "Today I'll say hi to at least one person in the hall." "Today, if James teases me, I'll tell him to stop."

3. Make a mental list of three topics you feel comfortable talking about. Pick one and try starting a conversation with someone you'd like to know better.

4. Make yourself do something you normally wouldn't do. Join a club. Invite someone over to your house. Offer to read aloud to younger kids at your school.

5. Instead of saying no to invitations, say yes. The more time you spend with other people, the easier it gets.

6. Make a new friend. The more friends you have, the less shy you'll feel.

7. Build your positive self-esteem. Spend time with people who care about you. Do things that make you feel proud of yourself. Use positive self-talk. Help others.

8. Most of all, always respect yourself—even when you're feeling shy.

8 Tips for Appearing Assertive

When you appear *assertive, you're more likely to* feel *assertive. When you* feel *assertive, you're more likely to ask for what you want and need. And you're less likely to be bullied, teased, or ignored. You might practice these tips in front of a mirror, or with a friend or parent.*

1. Stand up or sit up straight. If you stand, place your feet slightly apart so you feel balanced and stable.

2. Hold your head up.

3. Keep your back and shoulders straight. Don't hunch or slouch.

4. Look the other person in the eye. Don't look at the ground, over the other person's head, or to the side. Maintain eye contact, but don't stare.

5. Speak clearly, audibly, and firmly. Don't mumble, whisper, whine, or sound apologetic. Don't sound like you're asking a question unless you are. (*Examples:* "I need you to listen to me? I have something important to tell you?") Hold your voice as straight as your posture.

6. Say what you mean, and mean what you say.

7. Use gestures and facial expressions to emphasize your most important points.

8. Don't back off or lean back when you're talking, or when the other person is talking to you. If anything, move closer—but not *too* close. Keep a comfortable distance between you.

"The bravest thing you can do when you are not brave is to profess courage and act accordingly."
Corra May White Harris

4 Myths About Friendship and Dating

Myth #1: Girls and boys can't be friends. *Reality check:* In fact, the most successful couples are usually close friends. This myth may come from the idea that girls are looking for a long-term relationship while boys are only interested in sex. True, some couples are attracted to each other purely for physical reasons. But wanting to form a meaningful connection isn't just a girl thing. Having a girlfriend or boyfriend you care about, respect, and enjoy being around is one of the best relationships you'll ever have.

Myth #2: If you aren't dating yet, something must be wrong with you. *Reality check:* Nothing is wrong with you. Some teens just aren't interested in dating yet. Some don't date because of family or religious values. Others concentrate on school, extracurricular activities, and community service projects. They're focused on the future—college or career—and they don't want dating to get in their way. Still others don't feel the need to rush. They're having plenty of fun hanging out and aren't ready for the commitment or responsibility of a relationship. They like having girls who are friends and boys who are friends.

Myth #3: When a boy hangs out with girls, he's cool. When a girl hangs out with boys, she's easy. *Reality check:* Being a girl with friends who are boys, and being a boy with friends who are girls, can be great. But sometimes the talk around school rewards boys for forming these friendships and restricts or punishes girls. Boys who spend time with lots of girls are cool; girls who spend time with lots of boys are sluts. Even parents sometimes have this view. They're proud if their son has several "girlfriends" but worry that their daughter will get a "bad reputation." This is a double standard. Don't buy into it.

Myth #4: Boys put out all the money. Girls have to pay them back somehow, right? *Reality check:* Wrong—especially if "somehow" means sexual favors, which many people think it does. No one should be pressured, intimidated, or guilted into getting physically close with someone else. This goes for boys *and* girls. And guess what? Boys don't have to pay for everything. Girls have their own money. If you want to date someone but don't have the cash, find free or inexpensive things to do—like a walk in the park, a bike ride, a movie matinee, or a video. If you don't want to be seen as "owing" anyone, pay your way. And if you really like each other, share the expenses or take turns paying.

8 Tips for Asking Someone Out

1. **Get to know each other as friends first.** It's a lot easier to date someone you already have something in common with—like shared interests and values.

2. **Have some ideas for what you might like to do.** Is there a new movie you'd like to see when it opens on Friday? A school play? A concert? A restaurant you want to check out? You don't have to make firm plans—you want to be open to your date's ideas, too. But having something in mind avoids this type of non-conversation: "So, you want to do something?" "Like what?" "Oh, you know—something." "Something like what?" "I dunno. Just something."

3. **Ask early if the event you'd like to attend happens on a specific day.** Three or four days in advance is usually enough. For a big school dance, you might want to plan further ahead—a few weeks. Don't ask *too* early or you'll seem too eager. Inviting someone to the senior prom when you're both freshmen is premature.

4. **Ask in person or over the phone.** Start by talking about ordinary things—your day, your friends, school, whatever. Then relax and take a deep breath. Smile even if you're on the phone; you'll sound more confident. Then pop the question. Use your own words, as long as the phrase "Will you go out with me?" is somewhere in there. Don't ask in an email. You want this to be a real conversation.

5. **Describe what you'd like to do together.** *Example:* "There's a new comedy starting on Friday. It'll be at the MegaTheater. We could go to the 7:30 show and get a bite to eat after. How does that sound to you?"

6. **Wait for an answer.** Listen. Don't interrupt.

7. **If the answer is "yes," great.** You've got a date. Now nail down the details. Will you meet there? Who will pay for the movie and food? Since you're asking, you might want to pay, if you can afford it. Or, since you're already friends (see #1 above), you might say, "Great! I'll buy the tickets, and maybe you can cover the food?"

8. **If the answer is "no," don't hang up.** Don't argue, and don't try to change the person's mind. After all, you're friends (see #1 above). Respect your friend's decision. You might say, "Okay, I'm disappointed, but if you don't want to, that's how it is. So, where do we go from here? Still friends?" Even if you're crushed, tell yourself that there *is* someone out there for you—just not this particular person, or not this particular person right now. Don't let the "no" influence how you feel about yourself.

3 Things to Say
When Someone Asks You Out

1. YES—if all of these things are true:

- Your parents allow you to date.

- You like the person who's asking you out, and you already know each other as friends.

- The person has a plan for the date, and you like the plan. Or you have another suggestion—a comedy instead of an action movie, for example—and the person is willing to do that instead.

- You really mean "Yes."

Don't say it if you don't mean it, or you sort of mean it, or you need to think about it, or you need to talk it over with your parents or friends first, or you might back out later, or you definitely will back out if something better comes along.

2. MAYBE—if some or all of these things are true:

- You need to check with your parents first.

- You want to talk with your friends first and get their opinion. (Although this is your date, and your opinion matters most.)

- You're waiting for someone else to ask you out.

- You're not sure if you want to go out with the person. You need time to think about it.

- You want to know the person better before you go out.

In any case, don't leave the person hanging. Give him or her a specific time or date when you'll decide. You might say, "I have to ask my parents if it's okay. I'll get back to you tomorrow." Or, "Thanks for asking. This is a surprise to me. Can I think about it for a day or two?" Don't make up a fake excuse.

3. NO—if any of these things is true:

- You're not allowed to date yet.

- You're hoping someone else will ask you out.

- You already have plans for that day.

- You don't want to go out with the person.

Be honest when you can, and tactful when honesty would be hurtful. For example, if you're not allowed to date, that's easy: "I'm sorry, but my parents won't let me start dating until next year." If you're hoping someone else will ask you out, that's harder. You might just say something vague, like: "I'm sorry, but I already have plans for Friday night. Thanks for asking." If you do, in fact, have plans but you'd like to date the person, say so: "I'm really sorry! I wish I could go, but Aimee is having an overnight on Friday. Could we do it some other time?" If you don't want to go out with the person, period, be gentle: "Thank you for asking, but I'd really rather just stay friends." Or, "Thank you for asking, but there's someone else I'm interested in." Or, "Thanks, but no thanks. I just don't see us going out together. I'm sorry, but that's how I feel."

9 Rules for Breaking Up with Someone

You've been going together for a month (or a week, or a year), and for whatever reason, it's not working out. Maybe you've met someone else you like more. Maybe you don't want to date anyone. Or maybe this relationship just isn't right for you. You want to break up, but you don't want to be cruel about it. Here's one way to handle a tough situation.

1. **Think about what kind of relationship you want to have after the breakup, if any.** Would you like to stay friends? This won't be your decision alone; maybe the other person won't want a friendship with you. Or would it be better not to see each other anymore, period? This might be hard if you go to the same school, hang out with the same friends, live in the same neighborhood, or worship at the same place.

2. **Don't start dating another person until you've broken up with the first person.** This isn't fair to anyone, including you. You can't bring your best to a new relationship when you're being dishonest about an old one.

3. **Do it soon.** There's no point in letting the relationship drag on if you know you want to end it. Don't wait for someone else to come along, or stay together for a wrong reason: because you don't want to be alone, because it's convenient, because the world sees you as a couple, because the other person wants you to stay together.

4. **Do it in person.** Not over the phone, not in a letter, not by email or an instant message. In person. Face-to-face. Privately, not in a crowd. And don't send someone else to bear the bad news. The *only* exception to this rule is if you feel unsafe around the other person.

5. **Be honest, but try to be kind.** And try to relax. If this is how you really feel, you're doing the right thing. You might say something like, "I'm sorry, but you and I just aren't right for each other. I think it's best for both of us if we break up." Or, "I'm sorry, but this wasn't meant to be." Or, "I'm sorry, but I don't feel the way I used to about you." Of course, you'll come up with much better words. No one else can tell you how to say this.

6. **Don't blame the other person.** Saying, "This is your fault," or, "If you were different, this might have worked out," or, "You're not the right person for me," is unnecessarily hurtful. Plus it invites the other person to say, "Wait! I can change!"

7. **Don't pick a fight.** This might be a fast way to break up—plus a fight is "proof" that you don't belong together—but it's mean, and it doesn't give either of you a chance to talk openly and honestly.

8. **If the other person wants to talk, listen.** Even if the person tries to get you to wait, or rethink your decision, or give him or her another chance. Hear the person out, then say something like, "I'm sorry, but I've made up my mind."

9. **If the other person just wants to get away from you, let him or her go.** Maybe he or she is too upset or hurt to talk right now. You can talk another time.

9 Ways to Tell When Someone Is Lying to You

None of these signs is absolute proof *that someone is lying. But they can alert you to keep your ears and eyes open.*

1. **The eyes.** Some people avoid eye contact when they are lying. They get "shifty eyed."

2. **The smile.** People smile less when they are lying. Or they try to cover up their lie by forcing themselves to smile. How can you tell the difference between a real smile and a forced smile? A real smile makes wrinkles around the eyes; a forced smile doesn't. A forced smile lasts longer than a real one.

3. **The hands.** Liars touch their faces more often than truth-tellers to relieve some of the anxiety they feel when lying. Practiced liars keep their hands hidden.

4. **The voice.** Liars may sigh. Their voices may rise, as if their sentences end with question marks. Their voices may sound inappropriate for the surroundings or the occasion—too eager or too restrained, too casual or too urgent.

5. **Mismatches.** Does he say, "I love you," in a sing-song voice? Does she claim, "I am so happy for you," in a flat, lifeless voice? Are gentle words paired with angry gestures, or sad eyes with a happy voice?

6. **Motive.** What, if anything, does the person have to gain from lying to you? Is there money involved? Does the person think you want something from him or her?

7. **Reasonableness.** Does what the person is saying make sense to you? Or do you have to stretch your imagination to believe your ears?

8. **Rightness.** You've had enough experience with friends, family, teachers, and others to have a good idea of how people typically act and sound in given situations. Use what you know to stay close to the truth.

9. **Your gut feelings.** Trust them. Sometimes they are the only "evidence" you have to go on.

> "One may sometimes tell a lie,
> but the grimace that accompanies it tells the truth."
> *Friedrich Nietzsche*

10 Tips for Talking to Parents

Maybe you've got a problem at home. Whatever it is, don't just stuff it or whine to your friends. Talk to your parents! If you and they already talk a lot, this shouldn't be too hard. If you talk to each other sometimes, hardly ever, or never, it will be harder. But it's still worth a try.

1. **Choose your time wisely.** Don't try to start a serious conversation when your parents are obviously 1) cranky, 2) stressed out, 3) busy doing something else, or 4) sleeping.

2. **Be respectful.** Your parents will be much more willing to hear you out if they don't feel like they're being attacked or ridiculed.

3. **Speak precisely and concisely.** Say what you mean and don't take forever to say it.

4. **When you approach your parents with a problem, come prepared with suggestions for solving it.** Why should they do all the work? (Make sure that you present these as suggestions, not demands.)

5. **Make a genuine effort to see their point of view.** Put yourself in their shoes. Try to empathize with them. You're not the only person with an opinion, a brain, or feelings.

6. **Watch your body language.** Glaring, turning your back, slouching, shaking a fist, pointing a finger, sneering, gagging, and rolling your eyes are not recommended.

7. **Keep your voice down, please.** Nobody likes to be yelled at.

8. **Avoid "you statements."** "You don't understand me" or "You never let me do what I want" don't help to get your point across. Instead, use "I statements"—like "I guess I haven't done a very good job of explaining myself to you" or "I feel like you don't trust me to make decisions about what's most important to do in school."

9. **Pay attention.** You'll be more effective if you look at your parents (not at the wall or out the window) while they're speaking.

10. **Be willing to compromise.** Give a little and you might get a lot.

7 Good Times—and 7 Bad Times— to Ask Your Parents for Something You Want

Good Times:

1. When it's your parents' payday.

2. When your parents are relaxed, cheerful, and unpressured.

3. When you are relaxed, cheerful, and unpressured.

4. When your parents are in an affectionate, supportive, and accepting mood.

5. When your parents are alone and are not going to be influenced by what their peers will think.

6. When you've been responsible, well-behaved, and worthy in your parents' eyes of having your request fulfilled.

7. What about time of day? Only you know when the best times can be found in your household. Perhaps before dinner, when your parents are unwinding...or after dinner, when things have settled down...or in the middle of a lazy, refreshing weekend.

Bad Times:

1. When your parents are rushed or distracted.

2. When your parents are burdened with problems of their own.

3. When they feel unloved and abused by their children.

4. When there's an audience (neighbors, business associates, grand-parents) whose presence may adversely affect your parents' decision.

5. When there's already an ill wind blowing in your direction. You know what this feels like. It's when you want to *avoid* your parents, not cozy up to them and ask for a favor.

6. When calamity has struck or is about to strike. *Examples:* relatives coming to visit; illness; financial problems.

7. When it's a few days before your parents' payday.

12 Ways to Show Your Parents What a Fine, Upstanding, Totally Responsible Person You Really Are

1. **Get things clear.** Be sure that you and your parents agree on existing limits, rules, and expectations—what they are and what they mean.

2. **Make lists of agreed-upon responsibilities.** Post them where every-one can see them. There'll be no question whether Tuesday is your night to do dishes or take out the trash, or whether mowing the lawn is something you do for money or as part of your chores.

3. **Make contracts.** Write out the precise understandings, obligations, and conditions underlying agreements and commitments between you and your parents.

4. **Come up with a schedule.** This is an especially good idea if you're the forgetful type.

5. **When in doubt, check it out.** Why risk trouble just because of con-fusion or misunderstanding? Ask for clarification if you don't under-stand a rule or expectation.

6. **Observe your own behavior.** Often, there are patterns to a person's irresponsible behaviors. Analyze yourself. Do you tend to goof up only in certain areas? If so, why? If you can discover patterns, you can find solutions.

7. **Write yourself a note.** Leave it in a place so obvious that it screams to be noticed.

8. **Do it NOW.** The longer you put something off, the greater the chance you'll forget it, or something else will come along to entice you away. Get it over with—whether it's a chore, a phone call, a practice session, or an appointment.

9. **Take the bull by the horns.** Be active. Don't let problems occur through passivity or inattention. Responsibility exists; look for it, talk about it, and ask your parents to be specific when they accuse you of being irresponsible.

10. **Give advance notice.** Anticipate problems so you can work out solutions ahead of time. *Example:* If you agree to baby-sit your little brother next Friday night and you've just been invited to a party at the same time, don't wait until Friday afternoon to say you can't baby-sit. Bring it up as early as you can. You'll avoid looking irresponsible and inconsiderate, and you'll increase the chances that plans can be changed.

11. **Get in trouble for a good reason.** If you're going to be labeled irresponsible, try to be irresponsible on a high plane of behavior—one where you take an action based on careful consideration, high principle, and integrity. Make sure your parents realize that the course you charted was a conscious choice and not mindless stupidity.

12. **Make that call.** When you don't turn up on schedule, it's parent nature to assume the worst: you've been kidnapped, murdered, mugged, or drugged. By the time you get home, your parents will be so worried that they'll want to kill you. All of this can be avoided with one phone call. This doesn't mean you're a baby checking in. It means you're smart enough to know what's in your own best interests, which in this case happens to coincide with your parents' best interests. If you simply lost track of time, call anyway.

5 Steps for Getting More Freedom

If you and your parents argue a lot, it's probably related to the Freedom Gap. You want more, which makes them anxious and fearful; they want you to wait until you're older, which makes you crazy. You push, they pull. You rebel, they crack down. But if you're a responsible, trustworthy person, you should be in a position to negotiate for more freedom. Here's how.

1. **Set up a meeting with your parents.** Pick a time that works for everyone. Plan to show up a few minutes early.

2. **Choose a comfortable, quiet place to meet.** If home is usually busy and noisy, consider meeting in a park, taking a walk together, or finding a table at a favorite restaurant.

3. **Prepare an agenda for your meeting in advance.** Write down the points you plan to raise so you don't forget what you want to say or get distracted. An agenda will keep you on track.

4. **Do your part to keep the meeting positive, upbeat, and civil.** This shouldn't be a gripe session. Be clear about what you want; hear what your parents have to say. Try to reach a consensus—an agreement about what you want and what your parents are willing to give.

5. **If at first you don't succeed, don't be discouraged.** Especially if this is your first attempt at negotiating with your parents, you may get a few wires crossed. If the meeting goes nowhere, suggest that you adjourn and reconvene in a week or so. Then be on your best behavior until you meet again.

6 Ways to Stay Close to Your Family

Family closeness is good for you. Teens who have close relationships with their parents are more likely than other teens to be emotionally healthy. Plus it just feels good to be in a warm, loving, supportive family. See if your family is willing to try some of these ideas.

1. **Try to eat at least one meal together every day.** It doesn't have to be dinner, but dinner is a good time to share the events of the day.

2. **Have a family night.** You can do this once a week, once a month, or whenever you want (and schedules allow). Choose a night and mark it on the calendar so everyone remembers. That can be your evening to cook a meal together, order take-out food, see a movie or play, attend

a sporting event, visit a museum, go to a concert, work on a family project, play a board game, or do anything else your family enjoys.

3. **Volunteer together.** Volunteering your time and energy will help you feel good about yourselves *and* the people (or animals) you're helping. You might serve food at a food kitchen, clean up litter in your community, or walk dogs at a local animal shelter. Explore volunteering options that are available within your community or through your place of worship. Participate in National Family Volunteer Day, held on a Saturday in November. To learn more about National Family Volunteer Day, visit www.pointsoflight.org or call 1-800-VOLUNTEER (1-800-865-8683) toll-free.

4. **Plan a family vacation.** A vacation doesn't have to be far away or expensive to be fun. How about camping? Or taking a long weekend to explore sights in your community or state? Or what about a vacation in your own home?

5. **Create new family traditions.** How does your family celebrate Thanksgiving? Valentine's Day? The New Year? What about Christmas, Hanukkah, Kwanzaa, or Ramadan? Each family observes holidays in its own way, and these events can be a special time of celebration and family closeness. Think about your family's traditions. Do you honor them each year? Find new ways to personalize the holidays while maintaining your old traditions.

6. **Stay in touch with relatives.** Is there one person in your family who sends all of the birthday cards or letters to relatives? Why not give that person a hand? You can also keep in touch with relatives on your own by sending notes, email, videos, or audiocassettes with greetings and messages.

"Call it a clan, call it a network, call it a tribe, call it a family: Whatever you call it, whoever you are, you need one."

Jane Howard

12 Steps to Successful Family Meetings

Family meetings are a great way to make plans, coordinate schedules, discuss family goals, celebrate successes, and identify and solve family problems. See if your family is willing to have regular family meetings. Here's how to make them work.

1. **Name the time and place.** Decide *how often* you'll meet (once a month, once a week, whenever a big issue comes up), *what time* (after dinner, after homework), for *how long* (a time limit keeps meetings from dragging on), and *where* (the kitchen, the living room).

2. **Post an agenda in a conspicuous place.** Encourage family members to write down items they'd like to discuss. While late-breaking issues can always be brought up, the agenda lets people do some thinking ahead of time. Make sure there's at least one fun item on every agenda.

3. **Set some ground rules.** Important rules include listening respectfully, not interrupting each other, and being sure not to tease, whine, or raise voices.

4. **Decide what to do about no-shows.** If someone can't come because of an unavoidable conflict, try to reschedule. If one or more family members just decide not to show up, don't reschedule. It's their loss, and they have to abide by decisions made without their input.

5. **Decide on a way to begin each meeting.** Start each meeting on a positive note, even if you've gathered to discuss a conflict. Some families begin by letting each person talk about his or her day. What was the best thing that happened? Were there any surprises?

6. **Appoint a "chair" for each meeting.** This is the person who brings the agenda and runs the meeting. The position should be rotated among all family members so no one person dominates.

7. **Take turns talking.** Some families pass around a "talking stick" for the person who's speaking to hold. You can use anything for a talking stick. If you'd like, you can make one for your family. Start with a wooden spoon and add paint or decoration. Whoever is holding the talking stick gets to speak without being interrupted.

8. **Take notes.** Appoint a scribe for each meeting. The scribe's job is to write down ideas, decisions, plans, etc. He or she can also remind people between meetings of actions they need to take.

9. **If you have a family problem, work together to solve it.** Virtually any conflict can be resolved if you:

- define the problem in terms that don't accuse people of wrongdoing (*example:* "I can't study with music on," NOT "Your music is driving me crazy!"), then
- brainstorm solutions together, then
- discuss the options available to you, then
- pick the best one and make a plan of action, then
- monitor and adjust the solution as needed.

More problem-solving tips:

- Think constructively. Focus on solving the problem rather than finding blame.
- Don't label people's ideas as lame, clueless, or silly.
- Don't accuse. Say how you feel.

10. **Keep the mood positive.** While family meetings are the place to bring problems and complaints, they shouldn't degenerate into gripe sessions.

11. **Try to honor your time limit.** When meetings go on too long, people get restless. When people get restless, tempers flare and thinking gets sloppy. Better to schedule another meeting than to run overtime.

12. **Come up with a way to end the meetings.** Go for something upbeat. *Example:* Create a fun slogan to end every meeting. Other ideas include having each person say one positive thing about another family member or express one thing they're grateful for. Try not to end a meeting when people are angry or upset.

A Bill of Rights for Children of Divorce

If your parents are divorced (or divorcing) and you're having a hard time because of their actions and attitudes, think about sharing this list with them.

As a child of divorce, I hold these truths to be self-evident:

1. I have the right to be free of your conflicts and hostilities. When you badmouth each other in front of me, it tears me apart inside. Don't put me in the middle or play me against my other parent. And don't burden me with your relationship problems. They're yours, not mine.

2. I have the right to develop a relationship with both of my parents. I love you both. I know you'll sometimes be jealous about that, but you need to deal with it because you're the adult and I'm the child.

3. I have a right to information about things that will affect my life. If you're planning to divorce, I have a right to know, just as soon as is reasonable. Likewise, if you're planning to move, get remarried, or any other major life change, I have a right to know about it.

4. Just as I have a right to basic information about my life, I also have a right to be protected from bad information. This means you shouldn't tell me about sexual exploits or other misbehavior by my other parent. And don't apologize to me—for my other parent—because this implies a negative judgment of my other parent. If you apologize to me, apologize for yourself.

5. I have a right to my own personal space in both of my homes. This doesn't mean I can't share a room with my brother or sister, but it does mean that I need you to give me some space and time of my own. I also need some special personal items in my own space. And this might include a picture of my other parent. Don't freak out about it.

6. I have a right to physical safety and supervision. I know you may be very upset about your divorce, but that doesn't mean you should neglect my needs. I don't want to be home alone all the time, while you're out dating some new person.

7. I have a right to spend time with both parents, without interference. My right to spend time with each of you shouldn't depend on how much money one of you has paid the other. That makes me feel cheap, like something you might buy in a store.

8. I have a right to financial and emotional support from both of my parents, regardless of how much time I spend with either one of you. This doesn't mean I expect twice as much as other kids get. It just means you should stop worrying about what I got from my other parent and focus on what you're providing me.

9. I have a right to firm limits and boundaries and reasonable expectations. Just because I'm a child of divorce doesn't mean I can't handle chores, homework, or other normal responsibilities. On the other hand, keep in mind that even though I may have a little sister or brother (or stepsister or stepbrother), I'm not the designated baby-sitter.

10. I have a right to your patience. I didn't choose to go through a divorce. I didn't choose to have my biological parents live in two different homes, move away, date different people, and in general turn my world upside-down. More than most children, my life has been beyond my control. This means I'll need your help and support to work through my control issues.

11. Finally, I have a right to be a child. I shouldn't have to be your spy,
your special confidant, or your mother. Just because you hate to talk
to each other, I shouldn't have to be your personal message courier. I
exist because you created me. Therefore, I have a right to be more
than a child of divorce. I have the right to be a child whose parents
love me more than they've come to hate each other.

Code of Etiquette for Children of Divorce

1. Don't play one parent off against the other.

2. Treat your parents' new romantic interests with the same courtesy
you extend toward all guests.

3. Don't assume that your parents' dates wish to steal your mom's or dad's
affections from you. It's a different kind of affection they're after.

4. Don't ask your parents for details of what they do on or with dates.

5. Never brag about one parent's "new friend" to the other parent.

6. Put yourself in your parents' shoes. They, too, may feel angry, confused, scared, lonely, and betrayed. Try to help each other rather
than hurt each other.

7. Give stepparents a break. It's as hard for them as it is for you.

8. Don't get caught in the middle of your parents' arguments. As you
leave the room, say, "I love you both, but I'm not going to take sides."

Alex J. Packer's 10 Great Reasons to Have Good Manners

*Nobody's polite anymore. Why should you be? Because, in an age when people
are ruder than ever, having good manners sets you apart and works to your
benefit. Alex J. Packer, Ph.D., author of* How Rude! The Teenager's Guide to
Good Manners, Proper Behavior, and Not Grossing People Out, *explains how.*

1. Good manners put people at ease. People at ease are more likely to
agree to your requests.

2. Good manners impress people. People who are impressed by your
behavior are more likely to treat you with respect.

3. **Good manners build self-esteem.** Teenagers with self-esteem are more likely to get what they want out of life.

4. **Good manners are attractive.** Kids who know what to say and do in social situations are more likely to have the friends and relationships they want.

5. **Good manners allow people to live and work together without unnecessary friction.** This makes your everyday world more pleasant.

6. **Good manners can save your life.** Teenagers who know what to do if they accidentally disrespect or insult the wrong person are less likely to be shot.

7. **Good manners are rare.** Young people who have them sparkle like diamonds and immediately get elevated status in the eyes of adults.

8. **Good manners make you feel good.** You can hold your head high, knowing that you're doing your part to stop humanity's slide into the cesspool of incivility.

9. **Good manners make others feel good.** You can help to create a world in which people treat one another with care, respect, and compassion.

10. **Good manners don't cost anything.** You can have the BEST for free.

10 Ways to Swear Off Swearing from the Cuss Control Academy

You can only go so far in life if you look good but sound bad. Swearing makes a bad impression, reduces the respect people have for you, shows you don't have control, offends more people than you think, and can lead to violence. You can choose to have character and class, or to be considered rude, crude, and crass. Try these tips for taming your tongue. For more information, visit www.cusscontrol.com.

1. **Recognize that swearing does damage.** You don't win an argument by swearing. You don't prove that you are smart or articulate. You don't earn respect or admiration. Swearing doesn't get you what you want.

2. **Start by stopping casual swearing.** Pretend that your sweet little grandmother or your young sister or brother is always next to you. Use inflections for emphasis instead of offensive adjectives. Instead of using the "s" word or the "f" word to describe things, be more descriptive.

3. **Think positively.** A positive mental attitude not only eliminates lots of swearing, it also brings you contentment and brightens your personality.

4. **Practice being patient.** When you are stuck in line or in traffic, ask yourself if a few more minutes matters.

5. **Cope, don't cuss.** Consider even the smallest annoyance a challenge, and feel proud of yourself for dealing with it cheerfully and efficiently.

6. **Stop complaining.** Before you start griping or whining about something, remind yourself of a very important reality: No one wants to hear it! Why would they?

7. **Use alternative words.** English is a colorful language, but chronic cursers repeatedly use the same unimaginative words that have been around for centuries. Take the time to develop your own list of alternatives to the nasty words you now use.

8. **Make your point politely.** Think of the response to what you are about to say, and decide if you need to reword your statement to be more effective. Take the time to make your point in a mature and convincing manner.

9. **Think of what you should have said.** It's easy to blurt out a swear word at an inappropriate time. Think of what you could have said, then say the tamer word. If you make a statement that you later realize was negative, confrontational, or rude, think of how you could have phrased it. Over time, these exercises will train you to think and act differently.

10. **Work at it.** Breaking the swearing habit takes practice, support from others, and a true desire to be a better person—not only by controlling your language, but the emotions that prompt you to swear. Here are a few exercises to condition yourself:

    • Think in clean language. Switch negative thoughts into positive solutions.

    • When you are on your way to a situation you know will test your temper and your tongue, plan ahead what you will say and how you will say it.

    • Tell your family or friends what you are doing, and you will be more cautious around them.

    • Determine when and why you swear the most, and develop your own tricks for changing your behavior.

12 Ways to Be a Great Guest

You're invited to a party, an overnight, or whatever. Here's how to be a guest with the best.

1. **Show up.** Or, if it turns out that you're not able to attend, let your host know ASAP.

2. **Be on time.** If the invitation is for an open house from 4:00–7:00 or a party that starts around eightish, you're free to arrive anytime before 7:00 or after eightish. If the invitation is for a dinner at 6:30 or a graduation at 3:00, don't be late.

3. **Don't arrive early.** Most hosts are running around like crazy and getting things ready until the very last minute.

4. **Never bring people who weren't invited.** Especially not to events where numbers matter—a sit-down dinner, a wedding reception, a weekend at a cabin, a concert or show requiring tickets. If you think that numbers might not matter, you can ask for permission to bring another guest.

5. **Dress appropriately.** This shows respect for your host and the occasion. If you're not sure what to wear, it's usually better to overdress than underdress.

6. **Introduce yourself to people you don't know.** Especially if those people include your host's parents.

7. **Don't hog the food.** It's there for everyone, not just you. If the invitation doesn't include dinner, eat something before you arrive so you're not starved.

8. **Don't bring anything illegal.** Underage drinking and illegal drugs put hosts in legal and financial jeopardy.

9. **Don't snoop.** No peeking into closets, drawers, or medicine cabinets.

10. **Do your best to be cheerful.** Even if you've had a bad day. Even if you've just been dumped by your boyfriend/girlfriend. Don't let your woes ruin the mood.

11. **Don't overstay your welcome.** Watch for clues that the party or event is winding down. When your host yawns, turns off the music, turns up the lights, and starts cleaning up, it's time to go.

12. **Thank your host.** For informal parties, it's usually enough to say thanks when you leave. If your host's parents were involved, thank them, too. For smaller, more formal, or fancier events, send a thank-you note.

8 Tips for Writing a Thank-You Note

Before learning how to write a thank-you note, you may wonder, "Why bother?" First, because it's the right thing to do when someone gives you a gift, extends hospitality, or does something especially kind or thoughtful for you. Second, because people (especially adults) are incredibly impressed by kids and teens who write thank-you notes. And third, because a thank-you note makes you seem deserving of more gifts and kindnesses in the future.

1. **If you're not sure whether to write a thank-you note, write one.** It's better to overthank than underthank. You should write a note for any gift received by mail, UPS, or Fed Ex for a birthday, graduation, Christmas, Hanukkah, etc. Generally, it's not necessary to write notes for presents given in person if you said thank-you at the time. Other times you might write: when a friend's mom has driven you to soccer practice all season; when a teacher or mentor has been especially helpful to you; when a friend's parents let you stay at their house for a week while your parents are away.

2. **Write immediately.** The longer you wait, the harder it gets, and the more like a chore it seems.

3. **Write by hand.** Use personal note stationery or a nice card that's blank inside. Don't write on a computer unless your handwriting is unreadable. Don't use email.

4. **Never begin with "Thank you for...."** Start with some news, a recollection of the event or visit, a reaffirmation of your friendship, or other charming chitchat.

5. **Always mention the gift by name.** Saying "Thank you for your generous gift" sounds like a form letter.

6. **If the gift was one of hospitality, mention special moments.** Don't just write, "Thanks for letting me stay with you." Let your hosts know the things that made your visit special.

7. **If the gift was one of money, tell how you're going to spend it.** If you have no idea, make something up.

8. **If you don't like the gift, don't say so.** This isn't being dishonest. It's being polite. Telling Grandma that you hated the sweater she sent for your birthday won't inspire her to send money next time. It may inspire her to send nothing next time.

9 Ways to Be a Host with the Most

1. **Start with a clear invitation.** Is it a slumber party? A birthday party? A swim party? What? When does it start and end? Is it at your house? If not, where? Should your guest(s) bring or wear anything special?

2. **Answer the door and greet your guest(s).** Don't send your little sister to do this. It's your party. Say, "Hi, [name]. I'm glad you could come."

3. **Take coats. Guests often arrive with coats, bags, and (you hope) gifts.** Offer to take them or, if you're busy greeting many guests at once, tell them where to put them ("The coat closet is over there," "You can toss your coat in my bedroom down the hall to the right.")

4. **Say "Thank you" if someone hands you a gift.** But don't dump your guest to open it. Put it on a table and plan to open it later. If *everyone* brings a gift (for your birthday, for example) and *everyone* wants to watch you open your gifts, then it's okay to do that later in the party. If just a few people bring gifts, or you suspect that the gifts are very "uneven" (some people brought fabulous gifts, others just brought cards), have the grand opening after everyone leaves.

5. **Offer nourishment.** Take beverage orders or, if it's self-serve, point your guests toward the food and drink.

6. **Make introductions.** If some people don't know each other, introduce them. Give a clue or two about why they were invited. *Examples:* "Jessie has been my best friend since kindergarten." "Amal helps me with my biology homework."

7. **Explain the house rules.** Especially if your guests include people who haven't been to your house before, give them a brief run-down of what is and isn't okay. *Examples:* "My sister's room is off-limits." "We can watch the wide-screen TV in the family room, but let me handle the DVD player or my father will kill me."

8. **Circulate.** Spend time with all of your guests, not just your best friends or that really cute new guy or girl. Do your best to make sure that everyone has a good time. That's what parties are for.

9. **Thank your guests for coming.** When the party's over, tell your guests how much you enjoyed having them. Walk them to the door.

II Toll-Free Crisis Hotlines

No matter what you're going through, no matter how alone or hopeless or desperate you feel, no matter what your problem or crisis might be, you can talk to someone who cares and is trained to help. Or use this list to help a friend. All hotlines are staffed 24/7.

National Hopeline Network
1-800-SUICIDE (1-800-784-2433)
www.hopeline.com
For people who are depressed, suicidal, or concerned about someone they love. Connects callers to a certified crisis center and trained counselors.

National Runaway Switchboard
1-800-621-4000
www.nrscrisisline.org
Confidential, anonymous crisis intervention, information, help, and referrals to shelters. Can relay messages to or set up conference calls with parents, at the request of the child. For kids, teens, and families.

Covenant House Nineline
1-800-999-9999
www.covenanthouse.org
Immediate crisis information, support, and referrals for runaways, abandoned youth, and those who are suicidal or in crisis. You can also email Nineline and a trained counselor will respond to your concerns online ASAP.

Girls and Boys Town National Hotline
1-800-448-3000
www.girlsandboystown.org/hotline
A crisis, resource, and referral line. Call for advice on any issue—abuse, depression, suicide, identity struggles, family troubles, and other problems. You can also email your questions to a counselor, who will respond ASAP, or visit the online chat room.

The Trevor Helpline
1-800-850-8078
www.thetrevorproject.org/helpline.html
A suicide prevention hotline for gay or questioning youth. For people in crisis and those who want to help someone in crisis.

National Sexual Assault Hotline
1-800-656-HOPE (1-800-656-4673)
www.rainn.org
Free, confidential counseling and support for victims of sexual assault. Calls are immediately routed to the nearest rape crisis center. Operated by the Rape, Abuse, and Incest National Network (RAINN).

Childhelp USA National Child Abuse Hotline
1-800-4-A-CHILD (1-800-422-4453)
www.childhelpusa.org
Crisis intervention and professional counseling on child abuse and domestic violence issues. For abused children, troubled parents, individuals concerned that abuse is occurring, and anyone who wants information about child abuse.

National Domestic Violence Hotline
1-800-799-SAFE (1-800-799-7233)
www.ndvh.org
Crisis intervention, information about domestic violence, referrals for victims and people calling on their behalf, and guidance on how to talk to someone in an abusive relationship and offer help.

National Center for Missing and Exploited Children
1-800-THE-LOST (1-800-843-5678)
www.missingkids.com
Report a missing child or sightings of missing children, child sexual exploitation, or child pornography (www.cybertipline.com).

CDC National STD and AIDS Hotlines
1-800-227-8922
1-800-342-AIDS (1-800-342-2437)
www.ashastd.org
Anonymous, confidential information on HIV/AIDS and other sexually transmitted diseases (STDs). Answers your questions about prevention, risk, and treatment; makes referrals. Visit the Web site created for teens: www.iwannaknow.org.

National Clearinghouse for Alcohol and Drug Information
1-800-729-6686
www.health.org
Answers to your questions about substance abuse.

16 Adults You Can Talk To

Sometimes you just want to talk, and sometimes you really need to talk because of an event, concern, or crisis in your life. Especially if you feel that your life is spinning out of control, you may not know who to visit or call. You may not be able to think straight. And it may seem like you're all alone with your problem. You're not alone! There are many people who will talk with you. Here's a list of possibilities. If one doesn't work, try another.

1. A parent, stepparent, or foster parent.

2. A grandparent.

3. An aunt, uncle, or adult cousin.

4. A friend's parent.

5. A neighbor you know well.

6. A teacher.

7. A counselor at school.

8. A coach.

9. The school principal.

10. A mentor.

11. A doctor.

12. A professional counselor, psychologist, or therapist.

13. A leader at your place of worship.

14. A social worker.

15. A scout, club, or youth group leader.

16. An adult friend, like a Big Sister or Big Brother (visit bbbsa.org).

If you're in crisis, you need to talk with someone RIGHT NOW, and you can't get hold of an adult you know and trust, call one of these 24-hour toll-free national hotlines:

1-800-SUICIDE (1-800-784-2433) (National Hopeline Network)

1-800-621-4000 (National Runaway Switchboard)

1-800-999-9999 (Covenant House Nineline)

1-800-448-3000 (Girls and Boys Town National Hotline)

Adults I Can Talk To

List the names and contact information for at least three adults you can talk to. These should be people you trust. People you can count on to listen when you need to talk, offer good advice (if you want advice), and be there for you. Copy this list, keep it with you, and keep it current. TIP: If you can't think of at least three adults, see the list on page 92.

NAME: _____

Daytime phone: _____

Nighttime phone: _____

Cell phone: _____

Pager: _____

Email: _____

NAME: _____

Daytime phone: _____

Nighttime phone: _____

Cell phone: _____

Pager: _____

Email: _____

NAME: _____

Daytime phone: _____

Nighttime phone: _____

Cell phone: _____

Pager: _____

Email: _____

NAME: _____

Daytime phone: _____

Nighttime phone: _____

Cell phone: _____

Pager: _____

Email: _____

10 Myths About Bullies and Bullying

Myth #1: Bullying is just teasing. *Fact:* Bullying is much more than teasing. While many bullies tease, others use violence, intimidation, and other tactics. Sometimes teasing can be fun; bullying always hurts.

Myth #2: Some people deserve to be bullied. *Fact:* No one deserves to be bullied. No one "asks for it." Most bullies tease people who are "different" from them in some way. Being different is not a reason to be bullied.

Myth #3: Only boys are bullies. *Fact:* It seems that most bullies are boys, but girls can be bullies, too.

Myth #4: People who complain about bullies are babies. *Fact:* People who complain about bullies are standing up for their right not to be bullied. They're more grown-up than the bullies are.

Myth #5: Bullying is a normal part of growing up. *Fact:* Getting teased, picked on, pushed around, threatened, harassed, insulted, hurt, and abused is not normal. Plus, if you *think* it's normal, you're less likely to say or do anything about it, which gives bullies the green light to keep bullying.

Myth #6: Bullies will go away if you ignore them. *Fact:* Some bullies might go away. But others will get angry and keep bullying until they get a reaction. That's what they want.

Myth #7: All bullies have low self-esteem. That's why they pick on other people. *Fact:* Some bullies have *high* self-esteem. They feel good about themselves, and picking on other people makes them feel even better. Most of the time, bullying isn't about high or low self-esteem. It's about having power over other people.

Myth #8: It's tattling to tell an adult when you're being bullied. *Fact*: It's smart to tell an adult who can help you do something about the bullying. It's also smart to tell an adult if you see someone else being bullied.

Myth #9: The best way to deal with a bully is by fighting or trying to get even. *Fact:* If you fight with a bully, you might get hurt (and hurt someone else). Plus you might get into trouble for fighting. If you try to get even, you're acting the same as the bully. And the bully might come after you again to get even with *you*.

Myth #10: People who are bullied might hurt for a while, but they'll get over it. *Fact:* Bullying hurts for a long, long time. Some kids have dropped out of school because of bullying. Some became so sad, afraid, desperate, and hopeless that they committed suicide. Many adults can remember times when they were bullied as children. People don't "get over" being bullied.

10 Things to Do
When Someone Bullies You

What should you do when someone bullies you? There isn't just one right answer. It depends on the situation. But there are some things you can do that are generally wiser and more effective than other things.

1. **Stand up straight, look the bully in the eye, and say in a firm, confident voice, "Leave me alone!"** Bullies don't expect people to stand up to them. They usually pick on people who don't seem likely to defend themselves. So they're surprised when someone acts confident and strong instead of scared and weak. This might be enough to make them stop.

2. **Stand up straight, look the bully in the eye, and say in a firm, confident voice, "Stop it! I don't like that."** See #1 above.

3. **Shout, "Cut it out!" as loudly as you can.** This may surprise the bully and give you a chance to get away. Plus, if other people hear you, they might turn and look, giving the bully an audience he or she doesn't want.

4. **Tell a friend.** Make sure it's a friend who will listen, support you, and stand up for you. And don't just tell a friend. Tell an adult, too.

5. **Tell a teacher.** Especially if the bullying happens at school. Most bullying happens where adults aren't likely to see or hear it. Your teacher can't help you unless you tell (or someone else tells).

6. **Tell your parents.** Give them the details—who, what, when, and where—and ask for their help.

7. **Stay calm and walk away.** Especially if you can walk toward a crowded place or a group of your friends. Bullies generally don't pick on people in groups.

The next three strategies sometimes work. Assess the situation and follow your instincts before you try them.

8. **Tell a joke or say something silly.** Sometimes humor can defuse a tense situation.

9. **Laugh and act like you just don't care.** Some bullies will give up if people don't react to their bullying.

10. **Run away.** If you feel you're in real danger—for example, if you're facing a gang of bullies—then run as fast as you can to a safe place.

12 Things NOT to Do When Someone Bullies You

1. **Cry.** Bullies love having power over others. They enjoy making people cry. When you cry, you give bullies what they want. On the other hand, you might be so upset that you can't help crying. If this happens, get away as quickly as you can. Find a friend or an adult who will listen and support you.

2. **Hunch over, hang your head, and try to look so small the bully will stop noticing you.** This gives bullies what they want—someone who appears even more scared and weak.

3. **Try to get even with the bully.** The bully might get angry and come after you again. Plus getting even makes *you* a bully, too.

4. **Hit, push, or kick the bully.** Since bullies tend to be bigger and stronger than the people they pick on, chances are you'll get hurt. Plus you might get in trouble for fighting.

5. **Threaten the bully.** The bully might get angry and come after you even harder.

6. **Call the bully a bad name.** This will only make the bully angry.

7. **Ignore the bully.** Bullies want a reaction from the people they're bullying. Ignoring them might lead to more and worse bullying.

8. **Tell the bully's parents.** Some kids become bullies because their parents bully them. The bully's parents are more likely to believe their child, not you. They might even get defensive and blame you for doing something to "deserve" the bullying.

9. **Stay home from school.** Unless you feel you're in real danger, you should never stay home from school to avoid a bully. Remember that bullies love power. Imagine how powerful they feel when they can scare someone away from school! Plus staying home from school gets in the way of your learning and hurts you even more.

The next three strategies sometimes backfire. Assess the situation and follow your instincts before you try them.

10. **Tell a joke or say something silly.** Never tell a joke about the bully or make fun of him or her.

11. **Laugh and act like you just don't care.** Some bullies will bully harder to get the reaction they want.

12. **Run away.** Sometimes it's better to stand your ground and stick up for yourself.

Are You a Bully? 12 Ways to Tell

1. Do you pick on people who are smaller than you, or on animals?

2. Do you like to tease and taunt other people?

3. If you tease people, do you like to see them get upset?

4. Do you think it's funny when other people make mistakes?

5. Do you like to take or destroy other people's belongings?

6. Do you want other students to think you're the toughest kid in school?

7. Do you get angry a lot and stay angry for a long time?

8. Do you blame other people for things that go wrong in your life?

9. Do you like to get revenge on people who hurt you?

10. When you play a game or sport, do you always have to be the winner?

11. If you lose at something, do you worry about what other people will think of you?

12. Do you get angry or jealous when someone else succeeds?

If you answered "yes" to one or two of these questions, you may be on your way to becoming a bully. If you answered "yes" to three or more, you probably are a bully, and you need help finding ways to change your behavior. Parents, teachers, school counselors, and other adults can help you. Just ask!

13 Ways to Make Your School Safe

Although schools are still among the safest places to be, no school is immune to violence. The responsibility for keeping your school safe rests with educators, parents, and your community, but there are things you can do to help. Talk with your teachers, parents, and counselor to find out how you can get involved. Try these ideas that students in other schools have tried.

1. Listen to your friends if they share troubling feelings or thoughts. Encourage them to get help from a trusted adult—such as a school psychologist, counselor, social worker, leader from the faith community, or other professional. If you are very concerned, seek help for them. Share your concerns with your parents.

2. Create, join, or support student organizations that combat violence, such as "Students Against Destructive Decisions" (www.saddonline.com) and "Young Heroes Program" (active in several cities).

3. Work with local businesses and community groups to organize youth-oriented activities that help young people think of ways to prevent school and community violence. Share your ideas for how these community groups and businesses can support your efforts.

4. Organize an assembly and invite your school psychologist, school social worker, and school counselor—in addition to student panelists—to share ideas about how to deal with violence, intimidation, and bullying.

5. Get involved in planning, implementing, and evaluating your school's violence prevention and response plan.

6. Participate in violence prevention programs such as peer mediation and conflict resolution. Employ your new skills in other settings, such as the home, neighborhood, and community.

7. Work with your teachers and administrators to create a safe process for reporting threats, intimidation, weapon possession, drug selling, gang activity, graffiti, and vandalism. Use the process.

8. Ask for permission to invite a law enforcement officer to your school to conduct a safety audit and share safety tips, such as traveling in groups and avoiding areas known to be unsafe. Share your ideas with the officer.

9. Help to develop and participate in activities that promote student understanding of differences and that respect the rights of all.

10. Volunteer to be a mentor for younger students and/or provide tutoring to your peers.

11. Know your school's code of conduct and model responsible behavior. Avoid being part of a crowd when fights break out. Refrain from teasing, bullying, and intimidating peers.

12. Be a role model—take personal responsibility by reacting to anger without physically or verbally harming others.

13. Seek help from your parents or a trusted adult—such as a school psychologist, social worker, counselor, or teacher—if you are experiencing intense feelings of anger, fear, anxiety, or depression.

9 Things You Can Do to Stop School Violence

1. Refuse to bring a weapon to school, refuse to carry a weapon for another, and refuse to keep silent about those who carry weapons.

2. Welcome new students and help them feel at home in your school. Introduce them to other students. Get to know at least one student unfamiliar to you each week.

3. Lobby your school board, city council, or state legislature to set up a toll-free school violence hotline so that students can report threats confidentially.*

4. Tell a teacher, parent, or even the police if you overhear someone talking about their plans to bring a gun to school. Or report it anonymously. You may save someone's life.

5. Contact Congress and tell them you want something to be done about gun violence. For names, phone numbers, and email address of elected officials, visit www.congress.org or www.visi.com/juan/congress/.

6. Report any crime immediately to school authorities or police.

7. Become a peer counselor, working with classmates who need support and help with problems. Ask your guidance counselor how you can become a peer counselor.

8. Ask each student activity or club to adopt an anti-violence theme. The school newspaper could run how-to stories on violence prevention; the art club could illustrate costs of violence. Career clubs could investigate how violence affects their occupational goals. Sports teams could address ways to reduce violence that's not part of the game plan.

9. Start (or sign up for) a "peace pledge" campaign, in which students promise to settle disagreements without violence, to reject weapons, and to work toward a safe campus for all. Try for 100 percent participation. Visit www.pledge.org for a pledge you can download and print.

* Or find out if one already exists and make sure that everyone knows about it. Check to see if these hotlines are available in your area: 1-866-SPEAK-UP (1-866-773-2587) or 1-87-REPORT-IT (1-877-376-7848).

6 Big Differences Between Flirting and Sexual Harassment

Some people confuse flirting with sexual harassment. They say or do something to another person, that person doesn't like it, and they think, "What's the big deal?" or "She/he is overreacting." In fact, flirting and sexual harassment are very different.

1. Flirting makes the other person feel good, happy, flattered, attractive, and in control. Sexual harassment makes the other person feel bad, angry, sad, demeaned, ugly, and powerless.

2. Flirting boosts the other person's self-esteem. Sexual harassment hurts the other person's self-esteem.

3. Flirting is reciprocal and complimentary. Sexual harassment is one-sided and degrading.

4. Flirting is wanted and done among people who consider themselves equals. Sexual harassment is unwanted and done as a way for one person to have power over another.

5. Flirting is legal. Sexual harassment is illegal. In schools, it's illegal according to Civil Rights Act Title IX of the Federal Education Amendments. In the workplace, it's illegal according to Civil Rights Title VII.

6. Flirting is okay. Sexual harassment is not okay.

7 Ways to Tell If You're Flirting or Harassing

Sexual harassment can be hard to pin down, which is part of the problem. Some people think a comment like "Hey, babe!" is harmless and flirtatious. Others think it's insulting or even scary. Harassment is in the "eye of the beholder"—or the ear. How can you tell if you've crossed the line? You can ask yourself these questions.

1. Did the other person respond favorably to what you said and did? Or did the person ignore you or seem embarrassed or upset?

2. How would you feel if someone said or did the same thing to a member of your family?

3. Were you more interested in how the other person felt, or in scoring points with your friends?

4. If you were being featured on the evening news, would you want this to be part of the story?

5. Would you have acted this way if your girlfriend or boyfriend had been around? Your parents? Your sister or brother?

6. How would you feel if the roles were switched? Would you like the way you've been treated?

7. Is there a difference in power between you and the other person? Are you bigger? Older? Stronger? More popular? Alone or in a group of your friends?

9 Things You Can Do to Stop Sexual Harassment in School

One student in five fears being hurt or bothered in school. Four students in five personally experience sexual harassment. In some cases, the harassment starts before third grade. Here's what you can do. To learn more, visit the American Association of University Women Web site (www.aauw.org) and do a search for "sexual harassment."

1. If someone harasses you, tell that person to stop. Say you do not like what they are doing to you. If you are too uncomfortable confronting the people directly, do it in writing.

2. If you are harassed, tell a grown-up—a parent, a teacher you trust, or someone in your school who has been designated to handle issues of sexual harassment. Be persistent. If the first school official doesn't respond, go to someone else until you are taken seriously. Whether a fellow student or an adult is harassing you, the school is required by law to listen to your claim and take action.

3. Remind yourself that sexual harassment is wrong, is illegal, and should stop. Don't tell yourself (or believe it if anyone else tells you) it's your fault. Don't ignore what is happening to you and just hope it will stop.

4. Remember that someone you date, someone you used to date, or someone who wants to get involved with you can harass you. If you feel scared, uncomfortable, or threatened by the way someone is "flirting" with or treating you, tell a trusted friend or adult and get help.

5. Keep a journal of your experiences with sexual harassment. This will help you if you ever need to remember particular details. Getting your feelings on paper also might make you feel better. If the person harassing you or that person's friends send you any notes or emails, keep them. Your records might later help substantiate the harassment.

6. Step in and interrupt any harassment you observe and tell an adult you trust. Don't be a bystander.

7. Ask to see your school's sexual harassment policy. Read it and see what it tells you to do if you experience or witness sexual harassment. The policy might also help you understand what behaviors are considered harassment.

8. Identify the sexual harassment or Title IX officer for your school or district and ask that person questions you may have about your legal rights. (Title IX is the law that prohibits sex discrimination in education.) If you have tried talking to the appropriate people and nothing has been done, you might consider seeking help from someone outside the school such as the U.S. Department of Education's Office for Civil Rights. As a last resort, pursue other avenues such as filing a lawsuit against the school in either state or federal court.

9. Meet or get involved with a leadership or other student group that works on sexual harassment issues. The more you know about preventing harassment, the better off you'll be if it ever happens to you. If no such student group exists, organize your peers to address this issue. Many resources can help you begin a club or student group focusing on harassment and other related issues such as body image and dating violence. Ask a teacher, school counselor, or media specialist to help you find appropriate resources and Web sites.

25 Ways to Resist Negative Peer Pressure

When 1,000 students ages 13–17 were asked to name the worst influence facing today's youth, peer pressure was #2—right after drugs. You don't have to give in. Here are 25 ways not to.

1. Walk away.

2. Ignore the person.

3. Pretend that the person must be joking. ("What a riot! You are so funny.")

4. Say no—calmly but firmly.

5. Say no and give a reason. ("No. Cigarette smoke makes me sick.")

6. Say no and state a value or belief that's important to you. ("No. I've decided not to have sex until I get married.")

7. Say no and warn about the possible consequences. ("No way! We could all get expelled.")

8. Say no and change the subject. ("No, I'm not interested. Say, what did you think of that stunt Clarisse pulled in math class today?")

9. Say no and offer a positive alternative. ("No thanks, I'll pass. I'm going for a bike ride. Want to come?")

10. Say no and ask a question. ("No! Why would I want to do that?")

11. Say no and use humor. ("Forget it. I'd rather go play on the freeway; it's safer.")

12. Say no and apply some pressure of your own. ("No. Say, I always thought you were smarter than that.")

13. Share your feelings. ("I don't like being around people who are drinking.")

14. Use your parents as an excuse. ("My dad would kill me if I ever did that.")

15. Stick up for yourself. ("I'm not going to do that. It wouldn't be good for me.")

16. Confront the person. ("I can't believe you'd ask me to do that. I thought you were my friend.")

17. Call another friend to help you.

18. Always have an out—a Plan B. ("Sorry, I can't come to the party. I promised my sister I'd take her to a movie.")

19. Lie. ("Gotta run. I told my mom I'd clean out the garage.")

20. Laugh.

21. Hang out with people who don't pressure you to do risky things.

22. Ask a peer mediator to help.

23. Tell an adult.

24. Trust your instincts. If something doesn't feel right, it probably isn't right.

25. Avoid the person from then on.

"Keep out of the suction
caused by those who drift backwards."
E.K. Piper

10 Tips for Staying Safe in Relationships

Sexual pressures don't happen only in dating situations. Parties, concerts, post-game gatherings, and other social scenes can also turn risky. And girls aren't the only ones who are victims of unwanted sexual advances, sexual abuse, violence, and rape. Boys can be, too.

1. Make sure you get together in a public place.

2. Don't go to parties alone. Always make sure you have people you trust along with you. This will help you stay safe if there's a clique present, or teens you hardly know, or if the ratio of boys to girls is uneven, or if alcohol or other drugs are used at the party.

3. Set personal boundaries *before* things get physical.

4. Remember that just because someone pays for a movie or buys a gift doesn't mean he or she is entitled to sex. Just because someone acts or looks "sexy" doesn't mean she or he wants to have sex. Just because someone gets angry doesn't mean that you "made" the person act that way, or that you "deserve" to be hurt or intimidated.

5. Don't drink or use other drugs. They will affect your ability to take care of yourself and make good decisions.

6. Don't worry about hurting someone's feelings. If you're uncomfortable with what another person is doing, clearly and firmly say "No!" or "Stop!" When someone says no to a sexual advance from you or tells you to stop, stop. Remember that just because someone doesn't want sex doesn't mean he or she is rejecting you as a person.

7. Be prepared in case something goes wrong. Have money or a cell phone so you can get another way home if necessary.

8. If the person you're with doesn't seem to respect you, respect yourself and look for a healthier relationship.

9. If something doesn't look, sound, or feel right, it probably isn't right. Weigh the risks. Stay in control of your actions.

10. If someone is physically or sexually abusing you, stop seeing the person and get help. Talk to your parents, a counselor, or another adult you trust. If you don't know who to talk to, call one of these 24-hour toll-free national hotlines:

National Domestic Violence Hotline
1-800-799-SAFE (1-800-799-7233)

National Sexual Assault Hotline
1-800-656-HOPE (1-800-656-4673)

20 Ways to Tell
If a Relationship Is Unhealthy

Are you in a relationship where things don't feel right? Where the give-and-take isn't there? This list can help you decide.

A relationship is unhealthy if a friend, boyfriend, or girlfriend...

1. doesn't like you to spend time with anyone else; gets jealous or angry if you do.
2. criticizes you or makes fun of you in front of other people.
3. gets angry when you disagree with him or her.
4. has a terrible temper.
5. makes you feel afraid to be with him or her.
6. ever—that's EVER—hits you, kicks you, shoves you, or throws things at you.
7. ever—that's EVER—forces you to have sex.
8. wrongly accuses you of flirting with other people or seeing other people behind his or her back.
9. makes you feel trapped.
10. expects you to justify everything you do, every place you go, and every person you see.
11. wants to make all the decisions in your relationship.
12. gives you orders.
13. tries to control you.
14. tells you what you should or shouldn't wear.

15. drives your other friends away.

16. criticizes your beliefs.

17. makes you feel that nothing you do is ever good enough.

18. makes you feel that it's your fault if he or she treats you badly.

19. spies on you when you're apart.

20. threatens to hurt himself or herself if you break off the relationship.

If any of these things are happening to you, you need to get out of the relationship. Talk with an adult you trust—someone who can help you and maybe get help for the other person involved.

Dating Bill of Rights

These rights apply to boys, girls, men, women, and anyone who asks someone out or gets asked out. No exceptions!

I have the right to:

1. trust myself above all others.

2. decent treatment by anyone I date.

3. refuse to date anyone.

4. be safe on a date.

5. pay my own way on a date.

6. be assertive on a date.

7. refuse to have sex.

8. disagree with my date.

9. say NO.

10. get angry.

11. fulfill myself with or without a partner in my life.

12. know who I am.

13. know who I am dating.

14. determine who I will date.

15. use my own transportation on a date.

16. leave any dating situation my instincts tell me to.

17. prosecute for battery and sexual assault.

18. emotional support and understanding.

19. a healthy dating relationship.

20. control my own destiny.

21. be loved.

22. be cared about.

23. intimacy.

24. high self-esteem.

25. *trust myself above all others.*

10 Things Teens Want Other Teens to Know About Preventing Teen Pregnancy

When it comes to teen pregnancy—why it happens and how to prevent it— teens get loads of advice from adults, but they aren't often asked to offer their own. Along with Teen People *magazine, the National Campaign to Prevent Teen Pregnancy set out to change this by asking teens directly what they would say to other teens about preventing pregnancy. For information about teen pregnancy, abstinence, contraception, and more, visit www.teenpregnancy.org.*

1. Thinking "it won't happen to me" is stupid. If you don't protect yourself, it probably will. Sex is serious. Make a plan.

2. Just because you think "everyone is doing it" doesn't mean they are. Some are, some aren't—and some are lying.

3. There are a lot of good reasons to say "no, not yet." Protecting your feelings is one of them.

4. You're in charge of your own life. Don't let anyone pressure you into having sex.

5. You can always say "no"—even if you've said "yes" before.

6. Carrying a condom is just being smart—it doesn't mean you're pushy or easy.

7. If you think birth control "ruins the mood," consider what a pregnancy test will do to it.

8. If you're drunk or high, you can't make good decisions about sex. Don't do something you might not remember or might really regret.

9. Sex won't make him yours, and a baby won't make him stay.

10. Not ready to be someone's father? It's simple: Use protection every time or don't have sex.

3 Rules for Life from the National Center for Missing and Exploited Children

Teenagers 12–17, especially girls, are the most victimized segment of the U.S. population. These three rules—clear, simple, and easy to remember—can help keep you safe. For more information, visit www.missingkids.com.

1. **Don't Go Out Alone.** There is safety in numbers, and this rule isn't just for little kids, it applies to everyone. We are always safer if we take a friend, sister, or brother.

2. **Always Tell An Adult Where You're Going.** Letting someone know where you'll be at all times is smart. If you're faced with a risky situation or get into trouble, your family and friends will know where to find you.

3. **Say No If You Feel Threatened.** If someone—anyone—touches you in a way that makes you feel uncomfortable, you have the right to say no. Whether it is peer pressure about sex, drugs, or doing something that you know is wrong, be strong and stand your ground. Don't be afraid to make your feelings known.

10 Questions to Ask Yourself Before You Run Away

You may believe that your problems at home can't be solved. You may be fed up, frustrated, desperate, angry, and sure that running away is your only choice. First, take a few minutes to ask yourself these questions.

1. What else can I do to improve my home situation before I leave?

2. What would make me stay at home?

3. How will I survive?

4. Is running away safe?

5. Who can I count on to help me?

6. Am I being realistic?

7. Have I given this enough thought?

8. What are my other options?

9. If I end up in trouble, who will I call?

10. When I return home, what will happen?

If you still think you have to run away, contact the National Runaway Switchboard:

1-800-621-4000

Trained, caring people there can put you in touch with support groups, hotlines, and counseling centers. They can help you find a shelter. They can get a message to your parents when you're on the run—or set up a conference call with your parents when you're ready to talk. Their services are confidential, and they want to help. For more information, visit www.nrscrisisline.org.

12 Suicide Warning Signs from the National Association of School Psychologists

Suicide is one of the leading causes of death for kids in middle school and high school. Although kids thinking about suicide are not likely to seek help, they do show warning signs.

1. **Suicide notes.** These are a very real sign of danger and should be taken seriously.

2. **Threats.** Threats may be direct statements ("I want to die." "I am going to kill myself") or indirect comments ("The world would be better without me." "Nobody will miss me anyway").

3. **Previous attempts.** If someone has attempted suicide in the past, there is a greater likelihood that he or she will try again. Be very observant of any friends who have tried suicide before.

4. **Depression (helplessness/hopelessness).** Watch out for behaviors or comments that indicate that your friend is feeling overwhelmed by sadness or pessimistic views of his future.

5. **"Masked" depression.** Sometimes risk-taking behaviors can include acts of aggression, gunplay, and alcohol/substance abuse. While your friend does not act "depressed," her behavior suggests that she is not concerned about her own safety.

6. **Final arrangements.** This behavior may take many forms. In adolescents, it might be giving away prized possessions such as jewelry, clothing, journals, or pictures.

7. **Efforts to hurt oneself.** Common self-destructive behaviors include running into traffic, jumping from heights, and scratching, cutting, or marking the body.

8. **Inability to concentrate or think clearly.** If your friend starts skipping classes, getting poor grades, acting up in class, forgetting or poorly performing chores around the house, or talking in a way that suggests he is having trouble concentrating, these might be signs of stress and risk for suicide.

9. **Changes in physical habits and appearance.** Changes include being unable to sleep or sleeping all the time, sudden weight gain or loss, and/or lack of interest in one's own appearance or hygiene.

10. **Sudden changes in personality, friends, behaviors.** Changes can include withdrawing from friends and family, skipping school or classes, loss of involvement in activities that were once important, and avoiding friends.

11. **Death and suicidal themes.** These might appear in classroom drawings, work samples, journals, or homework.

12. **Plan/method/access.** Someone who is suicidal may show an increased interest in guns and other weapons, may seem to have increased access to guns, pills, etc., and/or may talk about or hint at a suicide plan. The greater the planning, the greater the potential for suicide.

Never ignore these signs. You can help!
See the following list for ideas about what you can do.

5 Ways to Help a Friend Who Might Be Suicidal from the National Association of School Psychologists

Suicide can be prevented if adults and friends are aware of the warning signs and know what to do.

1. **Know the warning signs!** Read over the list on pages 109–110. Make a copy and keep it in a safe place.

2. **Do not be afraid to talk to your friends.** Listen to their feelings. Make sure they know how important they are to you, but don't believe you can keep them from hurting themselves on your own. Preventing suicide will require adult help.

3. **Make no deals.** Never keep secret a friend's suicidal plans or thoughts. You cannot promise that you will not tell—you have to tell to save your friend!

4. **Tell an adult.** Talk to your parent, your friend's parent, your school's psychologist or counselor—a trusted adult. And don't wait! Don't be afraid that the adults will not believe you or take you seriously— keep talking until they listen! Even if you are not sure your friend is suicidal, talk to someone. It's okay if you "jump the gun"—this is definitely the time to be safe and not sorry!

5. **Ask if your school has a crisis team.** Many schools (elementary, middle, and high schools) have organized crisis teams, which include teachers, counselors, social workers, psychologists and principals. These teams help train all staff to recognize warning signs of suicide as well as how to help in a crisis situation. These teams can also help students understand warning signs of violence and suicide. If your school does not have a crisis team, ask your Student Council or faculty advisor to look into starting a team.

> "Suicide is a permanent solution to a temporary problem."
> Phil Donahue

Do's and Don'ts
When a Friend Is a Crime Victim

Teens are twice as likely as any other age group to be victims of violent crimes. Girls are more likely to be victims of sexual assault; boys are more likely to be victims of assault and robbery. If a friend tells you that he or she is a crime victim, remember:

1. **DO** believe your friend. Being a victim is nothing to joke about. Take your friend seriously and believe what he or she tells you.

2. **DON'T** be judgmental. Let your friend know that you are there for him or her.

3. **DO** listen to your friend. You may be the only person your friend trusts enough to tell.

4. **DON'T** interrupt. Let your friend tell his or her entire story.

5. **DO** tell your friend it is not his or her fault. Victims often blame themselves for crimes committed against them.

6. **DON'T** blame your friend. It is important that friends remain on your side during these times.

7. **DO** encourage your friend to tell a trusted adult. Whether a parent, teacher, or coach, adults often have more resources to help out.

8. **DON'T** keep it a secret. If your friend does not tell an adult, tell one yourself. Really. You could save your friend's life.

9. **DO** get help. Call the National Center for Victims of Crime at 1-800-FYI-CALL (1-800-394-2255) or email gethelp@ncvc.org.

10 Ways to Keep
from Being Ripped Off

Caveat emptor. *"Let the buyer beware."* That Roman saying is still good advice, even if it is thousands of years old. Advertisers aren't going to watch out for you. Here's how to watch out for yourself.

1. **Read everything—especially the fine print.** You'll find out some fascinating facts.

2. **Don't sign anything that has blank spaces.** This includes contracts, checks, and agreements.

3. **Get everything in writing—and keep copies for yourself.** An oral agreement is only worth the paper it's written on.

4. **Beware of "bait-and-switch" ads.** It's illegal to advertise something at an incredibly low price just to attract customers, then "switch" them to another item when they come into the store. If this happens to you, report it to local authorities such as the Better Business Bureau.

5. **Know your rights.** You don't have to pay for anything that comes in the mail if you didn't order it, as long as you don't use it. Return it at the sender's expense. Read the guarantees that come with the products you buy.

6. **Be suspicious of "too-good-to-be-true" offers.** Your own greed can be your own worst enemy. If something sounds too good to be true, it probably isn't true.

7. **Never give out personal information on the phone.** You may be conditioned to politely answer questions, but this habit is worth breaking when it comes to telling strangers about yourself. You don't know that callers are who they say they are. You don't know how they will use the information you give them. Simply say, "Sorry, I'm not interested," and hang up.

8. **Never pay any money for something you have "won" or something that's supposed to be "free."** Free means free. If you have to spend any of your money or time for something you have "won," then you haven't "won" anything.

9. **Take your time.** Don't be pressured into buying something because it's your "last chance," "a limited offer," "one of a kind," or "a golden opportunity." Remember that there's *no* material item you literally "can't live without."

10. **Never forget that you can't get something for nothing.** This is the bottom line. Put it first on your personal list of buying do's and don'ts.

"The smart consumer is the one who says 'Whoa! Just a minute.'"

Consumer Protection Association of America

www.consumerpro.com

11 Tips for Staying Safe at an ATM Machine

Providing 24-hour access to cash, ATM machines are a great convenience. They're also frequent crime scenes. Here's how to make sure you leave with your money.

1. **Choose your ATM carefully.** Look for one that's in front of the bank, well-lit, and visible to passersby, not hidden by trees or shrubbery.

2. **If you use an enclosed ATM center, make sure it has a large window so passersby can see in.** If there's someone inside when you arrive, wait outside for him or her to leave. Never hold the door open so another person can enter.

3. **Avoid using ATMs at night.** If you're in desperate need of cash, use one inside a supermarket, convenience store, or gas station. Or take another person with you. If the lights at the ATM aren't working, don't use it.

4. **Spend as little time as possible at the ATM.** Have your card already out and in your hand before you approach it. Don't stand there digging through your purse or wallet to find it.

5. **Don't let anyone see you enter your PIN number.** Use your body to shield the keyboard.

6. **Stay alert and aware of your surroundings.** If someone is crowding you or seems interested in your transaction, leave. If someone offers to help you, say no. If someone follows you into an ATM center and you feel uncomfortable, leave. Find another ATM.

7. **Once you're through with your transaction, put everything away and leave quickly.** Count your money later. Never walk away from an ATM holding your cash.

8. **Take your receipt with you.** Don't let a potential criminal know how much money you've just withdrawn, or how much you have in your account.

9. **Keep your PIN number private.** Memorize it. Don't write it on your card (duh) or keep a copy in the same wallet as your card.

10. **If your card is lost or stolen,** notify your bank immediately.

11. **Never give any information about your ATM card or PIN number over the phone.** If someone calls you to "verify your PIN," even if that person claims to be a police officer or a banker, don't give it. Notify the police instead.

The Chicago Police Department's
12 Tips for Staying Safe
on Public Transportation

If you live in or near a city, chances are you ride the bus, train, or subway. Here are some safety tips you should know.

1. Plan your trip. Call the bus, train, or subway company or your local transportation authority and request schedules. Or go online to find them.

2. Tell a family member or friend about your travel route and time. Call them when you arrive safely.

3. Have your exact fare ready in advance. That way, you won't have to fumble for your money at the fare box, or display extra cash.

4. Use the busiest, best-lit stop possible both to get on and get off a bus or subway. If you must wait, stay near the attendant's stand or in the best-lit area available.

5. Find a seat on the aisle if possible. This allows you to observe everything around you, and to avoid getting "boxed in" against the window.

6. Sit near the driver or operator, if possible, but avoid sitting right next to the door. Thieves may try to snatch jewelry or personal belongings from people near the door and then exit quickly.

7. Don't let yourself doze off on a bus or subway, or become too engrossed in reading, listening to music, or playing a hand-held game. It can make you an easy target.

8. Keep your backpack, purse, shopping bag, packages, or other belongings in your lap, on your arm, or between your feet. Do not leave them on an empty seat.

9. Avoid displaying expensive-looking watches, rings, necklaces, or other jewelry. Don't invite trouble.

10. Be wary of noisy passengers arguing or causing a commotion. This could be staged to distract you while others are trying to steal your valuables.

11. Observe the behavior of those around you. If you feel uneasy or threatened, change your seat or alert the conductor or driver.

12. Minimize the chances of losing your property by avoiding crowded buses and train cars.

12 Things to Do
If Someone Is Stalking You

Most states define stalking as "the willful, malicious, and repeated following and harassing of another person that threatens his or her safety." It is also described as "psychological terrorism" and "emotional rape." Stalking is persistent, repetitive, obsessive attention that gives you the creeps and makes you feel afraid. A stalker might be a former boyfriend (or girlfriend—boys and men are stalked, too), someone you know only casually, or a stranger. Stalking is serious, and it's a crime; all 50 states have anti-stalking laws.

1. **Listen to your intuition.** If it feels wrong, it is wrong.

2. **Know that the stalking is not your fault.** You didn't ask for it. You didn't invite it. You don't want it. What you wear, how you act, what you say, where you go—none of these is a "reason" for someone to stalk you.

3. **Understand that stalking is not a compliment.** Don't be flattered by this kind of attention. It doesn't mean that your stalker "loves" you. Stalking isn't about love; it's about intimidation and control.

4. **Be firm.** Tell the person in no uncertain terms that you don't want any kind of relationship with him or her. Don't be nice or polite about it. Don't worry about hurting the stalker's feelings. Don't try to reason or bargain with the person.

5. **Tell everyone you know.** Tell your parents, friends, teachers, coaches, school counselors, neighbors, and other adults you trust that you are being stalked. Give them a physical description of the stalker—or copies of a photo, if you have one. Tell them what kind of car your stalker drives.

6. **Talk with a victim specialist, who can help you develop a safety plan.** Check the front of your local phone book under "Emergency Assistance" or "Community Service." You'll find victim specialists at your local domestic violence or rape crisis program.

7. **Call the police.** Tell them that you are being stalked, and give them all the details they ask for. If the stalker commits other crimes—physically assaulting you, breaking into your home or locker, vandalizing or destroying property that belongs to you or your family—report them immediately. This may be enough to arrest and convict your stalker. At the very least, your complaints will be documented.

8. **Keep a detailed written record of your stalker's behavior.** Write down any incidents of being followed, spied on, watched, or threatened. Take pictures if you can. Log every phone call. Keep letters. Print out and save emails. This is all evidence of the stalking, and it will help to build your case if you decide you want to get a restraining or protective order.

   Should you or shouldn't you get a restraining order or a protective order? Some experts say yes; some say no, because it might give you a false sense of security and/or enrage the stalker. A piece of paper can't protect you. Only you can do that, with help from your family, friends, and other members of your support system.

9. **If you have a cell phone and your stalker has the number, change it.** Only give your new number to your family and closest friends.

10. **Try not to go anywhere alone.** Bring a parent or friend. You're not being a baby—you're protecting yourself. You're not giving up your freedom—the stalker has taken your freedom away for now.

11. **Be prepared in case of emergency.** Make a list of phone numbers you might need—police, friends, trusted adults—and keep it with you.

12. **Get help for yourself.** Stalking is scary. Some stalking victims have symptoms of anxiety, depression, and post-traumatic stress disorder. Talk with a counselor.

How to Know If You're Being Abused—and What to Do

Abuse happens everywhere to all kinds of people. Age, gender, ethnic group, religious beliefs, whether you're rich or poor, popular or not so popular—none of this matters. Anyone can be a victim. And anyone can be an abuser— a parent, stepparent, other relative, neighbor, caregiver, teacher, youth leader, religious leader, coach, employer, camp counselor, family friend.

1. **You are being abused if someone who's responsible for your well-being—someone who's supposed to take care of you—has:**

   • touched you in a sexual way, or forced you to touch them, or forced you to watch sexual acts, or showed you sexually explicit videos or Web sites. This is *sexual abuse.*

   • injured or physically hurt you on purpose. This is *physical abuse.*

   • made you feel worthless. This is *emotional abuse.*

- left you alone to care for yourself for an extended period of time, or failed to provide for your basic physical needs (food, shelter, appropriate clothing, health care). This is *neglect*.

The U.S. government defines child abuse and neglect as "the physical and mental injury, sexual abuse, negligent treatment, or maltreatment of a child under the age of 18 by a person who is responsible for the child's welfare under circumstances which indicate that the child's health or welfare is harmed or threatened."

2. **If you are being abused:**

- *Know that it is not your fault.* Abuse is NEVER the victim's fault. It is ALWAYS the abuser's fault. No exceptions!

- *Get help.* Tell an adult you trust. Keep telling until someone really listens and promises to help you.

3. **If you need immediate help:**

- Look in your phone book or Yellow Pages for an Abuse Hotline. Or:

- Call the Childhelp USA National Child Abuse Hotline at 1-800-4-A-CHILD (1-800-422-4453). Call anytime—24 hours a day, 7 days a week. Or:

- Dial 911.

8 Do's and Don'ts for Calling 911

1. **DO call 911 to report a *real* emergency.** *Examples:* a fire, a serious traffic accident or injury, a medical crisis (chest pain, trouble breathing, bleeding, unconsciousness, seizure), an intruder, a prowler, a crime in progress, violence or a threat of violence, shots fired, someone with a weapon—any potentially life-threatening situation.

2. **DON'T call 911 to report a *non*-emergency.** *Examples:* a minor accident with no injuries, vandalism, a theft or break-in that has already happened.

3. **DON'T just start talking a mile a minute.** Let the dispatcher ask you questions. He or she has been trained to ask questions that will help to prioritize the emergency and make sure the right help is sent.

4. **DO stay calm.** Speak slowly and clearly. Answer the dispatcher's questions. You'll probably be asked your name, your phone number, your address, the exact location where help is needed (be sure to say if this is *different* from your address), what happened, what type of

emergency it is, and who needs help. This is one time when it's okay to give your personal information to a stranger.

5. **DON'T hang up until the dispatcher says it's okay.** Stay on the phone in case he or she needs more information.

6. **DON'T call 911 on a dare or as a joke.** This can delay a response to someone who really needs help. Most 911 calls are traced. Using 911 for anything but reporting an emergency is a crime.

7. **DON'T program 911 into your phone's speed dial.** You won't forget it, and you might hit the button by accident.

8. **If you dial 911 by mistake, DON'T hang up the phone.** Stay on and tell the dispatcher that there's no emergency. If you just hang up, emergency personnel will be sent to your location.

Tip: You don't need money to dial 911 on a pay phone.

School and Learning

7 Keys to School Success

As authors and educators, Judy Galbraith and Jim Delisle have surveyed and interviewed countless students across the country and around the world. They've found that successful students—those who do well in school and enjoy it—share certain characteristics. Which ones do you have?

1. You believe that you are responsible for your own performance. You don't blame others when you do poorly (*example:* "I've got a lousy teacher for biology this year"), and you don't credit others for your achievements (*example:* "I got a good grade in history because my teacher likes me").

2. You think that school is important, but not *all*-important. You give yourself time and space to enjoy other, more social aspects of growing up—friends, activities, fun.

3. You understand that school isn't always 100 percent fulfilling. You accept that it can also be boring, maddening, and frustrating at times.

4. You perceive yourself as a competent, capable person.

5. If you achieve less than perfection, you don't label yourself a failure.

6. You don't place too much emphasis on success.

7. You know that mistakes are part of learning and growing up. You don't dwell on your mistakes or let them slow you down.

> "I don't know the key to success,
> but the key to failure is trying to please everybody."
> **Bill Cosby**

5 Steps to School Success: The Checkpoint System

Before takeoff, an airplane pilot goes through a series of checkpoints to make sure that everything is ready for a safe journey. Having your own checkpoints will help you succeed at school.

1. **At Home:** Before you leave the house, check to make sure you have everything you need for the day (backpack or bookbag, supplies, books, lunch or lunch money, homework, signed notes, special projects, planning calendar or assignment notebook, good mood...).

2. **At Your Locker:** Before going to class, stop at your locker and check to see that you have everything you need.

3. **In Class:** Before leaving class, record your assignments. If you need to ask questions or clarify directions, do it *before* you walk out of the classroom. Make sure that you know the due date of every assignment.

4. **At Home:** Check your daily schedule, then stick to it. Keep your commitment to study and do your homework at the same time each day, if at all possible.

5. **At Home:** Before going to bed for the night, put your backpack or bookbag, supplies, books, homework, signed notes, special projects, and anything else you'll need for the next day in one place, preferably the same place every night. This will make it easier to leave for school in the morning.

10 Ways to Be Smart

Schools usually deal with two types of intelligence: language smarts and math smarts. These are what you're taught and tested on. Harvard professor Howard Gardner believes that there are at least nine intelligences, maybe ten or even more. (His theory of multiple intelligences keeps evolving.) Which of these intelligences do you have?

1. **Linguistic Intelligence.** You enjoy writing, reading, listening, and speaking, and you do them with ease. You enjoy memorizing information and building your vocabulary, and you may be an excellent storyteller.

2. **Musical Intelligence.** You can detect rhythms, patterns, and tempos in things that seem to have none at all—like chirping birds, crickets, and even some of the music your parents listen to. You can "hear" tone and pitch, and you may be talented at playing one or more musical instruments, either by ear or with instruction. You may appreciate many kinds of music.

3. **Logical-Mathematical Intelligence.** You instinctively put things in order and comprehend quantities—often in your head. Numbers and math concepts come easily to you, and you love brainteasers, logic puzzles, games, and computers.

4. **Visual-Spatial Intelligence.** You readily notice when a building (or painting, or person) is not quite symmetrical. If you're an athlete, you can judge almost perfectly the angle needed to score a goal in hockey or a basket in basketball. You can mentally rotate complex forms, and you can draw whatever you see. You're good at taking things apart and putting them back together, and you love games.

5. **Bodily-Kinesthetic Intelligence.** You are good at handling and manipulating objects, and you move your body with grace and ease. You enjoy training your body to do its physical best, and you may be a great mimic. You may be talented at one or more crafts—carving, sewing, weaving, making pots.

6. **Interpersonal Intelligence.** You easily understand other people, perceiving their moods and feelings. You're a natural leader and a skilled mediator; you can break up a fight between two of your friends and still remain on each person's good side.

7. **Intrapersonal Intelligence.** You understand yourself very well; you're profoundly aware of your feelings, dreams, and ideas, and you're true to your goals. People may say that you "march to the beat of a different drummer." You enjoy journaling. (Are you keeping a journal while reading this book?)

8. **Naturalist Intelligence.** You feel a deep connection to the natural world and its inhabitants—plants and animals. You enjoy experiencing and observing the out-of-doors, and you may be a talented gardener and/or cook.

9. **Existential Intelligence.** You enjoy and have a talent for grappling with Big Questions—like the meaning of life and death, who we are, why we're here, and why the world exists.

10. **(not yet official) Spiritual Intelligence.** You are sensitive to and have an interest in spiritual and religious matters. You experience wonder and awe; you're aware of an "otherness"; you have faith.

Randall McCutcheon's 5 Reasons to Sit in the Front Row at School

In the words of award-winning teacher Randall McCutcheon, "There is no reason to cheat off the student sitting next to you when you can tap his or her talents through the legitimate use of logistics. In other words, put up a good front by sitting up front."

1. You will often meet brighter, even more ambitious students than yourself by sitting in the front row. It is true that the academically gifted are likely to plop down anywhere, but a higher percentage, row-wise, will be near the teacher. (In college, graduate students inevitably gravitate in that direction.) Make friends with these people, play up to them, pat their heads, give them your full attention.

2. Front-row students are more likely to take good notes that you can borrow if you absolutely must miss class. If you don't understand some of the lecture material and the teacher is usually busy after class, these students are the next best thing. Plus, they will be able to provide superior insight when trying to second-guess potential test questions.

3. You are less likely to fall asleep when sitting in the front row. Snoring is visible, noisy, and embarrassing. So is drooling on your desk.

4. By sitting up front, you give the teacher a chance to get to know you. If the teacher is at all approachable, you have, as they say, headed off the other students at the pass (and passing, after all, is the name of the game). Clearly, if the teacher is prone to fits of gabbiness, then it is a simple matter to introduce yourself, and at the same time, remove yourself from the stigma of being just another face in the crowd.

5. When you sit in the front row, your confidence level will increase. Besides the obvious merit of no guilt trip for skipping out or falling asleep, it is likely you will feel more positive when studying for exams if you have attended and listened. A positive attitude can be critical in passing the threshold of trying, and thus, in passing the class.

Bonus tip: It is a good idea to choose your position in the front row next to a student that you are certain the teacher likes. Remember the childhood advice not to sit too close to the fire (i.e., naughty students) or you would get burned? Well, a corollary is true: Sit by likable, bright students and you will get en-light-ened.

8 Do's and 5 Don'ts
for Class Discussions

When it comes to class discussions, some students don't know what to say. Others are afraid of saying the wrong thing. Some students fear that if they speak up, they'll be branded show-offs or know-it-alls or teacher's pets. Should you just sit there silently? Probably not. Your grade in some classes may depend, at least partly, on whether and how you participate in class discussions.

Do...

1. Ask legitimate questions based on reading you've done ahead of time.
2. Ask legitimate questions about what others say in class.
3. Listen carefully to what others have to say.
4. Add any information you may have to a point someone else makes.
5. Share personal experiences related to the topic when this will enhance the discussion.
6. Make statements or ask questions showing that you came to class prepared.
7. Give yourself 3–5 seconds of thinking time before answering a question. Your answers will be more accurate and interesting.
8. Be kind when you disagree with what somebody else says.

Don't...

1. Make comments that take up too much class time.
2. Make comments just to hear yourself talk.
3. Make a habit of going off the subject.
4. Interrupt others.
5. Get into arguments.

5 Reasons to Take Notes in Class

Some people can remember everything they hear. The rest of us need to take notes! Here are five reasons why.

1. Most of the information presented in class is given *orally* by the teacher. Often, this includes information that isn't covered in the textbook. If you don't write it down, you won't have it when you need it.

2. Class notes are your best record of what happens during class, and your best source of material for test reviews.

3. Writing things down reinforces what you hear and helps you to remember.

4. Taking notes makes you a more active listener. You're less likely to doze off.

5. Note-taking skills are critical for success in high school and college. You may think you don't need them now, but you'll definitely need them later. Now is the time to learn them.

19 Note-Taking Tips

Before Class:

1. Review your assignment so you're ready to listen.
2. Review your notes from the last class.

During Class:

3. Write down the date and title of each lecture.
4. Don't worry about punctuation or grammar.
5. Use abbreviations for speed and efficiency.
6. Don't write down every word the teacher says.
7. Don't write down everything the teacher writes on the board.
8. Underline, circle, or star anything the teacher repeats or emphasizes.
9. Don't write more than one idea per line.
10. Listen for digressions—times when the teacher gets off the subject. It's okay to take a mental break during these, but don't fall asleep.

11. Write down any questions the teacher asks, since these are likely to appear on future tests.

12. Don't cram your writing into a small space. Leave room to add more notes later.

13. Put question marks by any points you don't understand. Check them later with the teacher.

After Class:

14. Read your notes as soon as possible after class—ideally, within 24 hours.

15. Reorganize your notes, type them, or enter them into a computer, if this will help you understand and remember them.

16. Spell out any abbreviations you may not remember later.

17. Highlight important points in your notes. Use a yellow highlighter for handwritten, typed, or printed-out notes; use boldface or color for notes on a computer screen. This will help you to find facts fast when you review for tests.

18. Jot down any additional questions you may need to ask the teacher.

19. If you're absent from class, get the notes from a friend.

16 Benefits of Doing Your Homework

Most teachers don't give homework just to make your life miserable. Homework can actually be good for you. Here are 16 reasons why.

1. Homework reinforces what you learn in school. It lets you review facts, ideas, and skills you might forget.

2. Homework gives you practice in skills you haven't yet mastered or fully learned.

3. Homework gives you chances to explore subjects in depth and detail.

4. Homework enriches your store of general knowledge. It adds to what you already know and helps you to learn new things.

5. Homework encourages self-discipline and responsibility.

6. Homework helps you learn time-management skills.

7. Homework gives you time to be creative.

8. Homework allows for tasks that are too time-consuming to finish during regular school hours.

9. Homework helps you get ready for the next day's classes.

10. Some homework introduces material that will be covered in future lessons. It gives you a head start on learning the new material.

11. Some homework asks you to apply skills you already have to new situations. It helps you see that what you're learning has broader applications.

12. Some types of homework—like book reports, science projects, and creative writing—require you to apply many different skills to a single task. This is good practice for all kinds of situations.

13. Homework gives you practice in using resources such as libraries, reference materials, encyclopedias, and the Internet.

14. Homework can bring people closer together. If you get stuck on an assignment, try asking your parents for help. This gives them the chance to learn more about what you're doing in school.

15. Homework can help you develop good habits and positive attitudes.

16. Homework encourages a love of learning.

BUT... homework shouldn't take up every minute of your time away from school. It shouldn't leave you feeling stressed out, exhausted, frustrated, and pressured. It shouldn't keep you from spending time with your family and friends, and time doing other things that matter to you. It shouldn't just be boring "make work." It should never be given as punishment. Homework really should be good for you! If you think you have too much homework, or the wrong kind of homework, talk with your parents. Talk with your teachers.

10 Web Sites for Homework Help

Abuzz
www.abuzz.com
"An interactive knowledge sharing community" hosted by *The New York Times*. Abuzz sends your questions to volunteer experts, and you get an email alert when someone replies.

Altavista Babelfish Translation
world.altavista.com
Translate almost anything from another language to English, or from English to another language.

Bartleby.com
www.bartleby.com
You have to read *Hamlet* by tomorrow and the library closed early? No problem. Bartleby.com has the complete texts of works by many authors, plus reference books online.

B.J. Pinchbeck's Homework Helper
school.discovery.com/homeworkhelp/bjpinchbeck
Hundreds of links to homework help. This site was started by B.J. ("Beege") and his father in 1996, when Beege was 9 years old. More than 10,000 people visit each day.

Encarta Homework
encarta.msn.com/homework
Tons of links plus specific suggestions for test preparation, writing reports, being a better writer, and other helpful homework tips.

Fact Monster
www.factmonster.com
An online almanac, atlas, dictionary, encyclopedia, and much more.

Infoplease Homework Center
www.infoplease.com/homework
Find answers to your homework questions in the Infoplease almanac, dictionary, encyclopedia, and biography databases. A Family Education Network Web site.

RefDesk
www.refdesk.com
General Colin Powell's favorite Web site. Huge numbers of reference links, plus a homework help section (refdesk.com/homework.html).

StarTribune Homework Help
www.startribune.com/homework_help
Volunteers ages 18 and up (some are teachers, some aren't) post answers to your question, usually within 24 hours. Answers are not emailed.

Yahooligans! School Bell
www.yahooligans.com/School_Bell
Links to thousands of homework-helping sites.

10 Tips for Talking to Teachers

Are you having a problem with a class or an assignment? Can you see room for improvement in how a subject is taught? Do you have a better idea for a special project or term paper? Don't just tell your friends. Talk to the teacher! Here's how.

1. **Make an appointment to meet and talk.** This shows the teacher that you're serious and you have some understanding of his or her busy schedule. Tell the teacher how much time you'll need, be flexible, and don't be late.

2. **If you know other students who feel the way you do, consider approaching the teacher together.** There's strength in numbers. If a teacher hears the same thing from four or five people, he or she is more likely to do something about it.

3. **Think through what you want to say before you go into your meeting with the teacher.** Write down your questions or concerns. Make a list of the items you want to cover. You may even want to copy your list for the teacher so both of you can consult it during your meeting. (Or consider giving it to the teacher ahead of time.)

4. **Choose your words carefully.** *Example:* Instead of saying, "I hate doing reports; they're boring and a waste of time," try, "Is there some other way I could satisfy this requirement? Could I do a video instead?" Strike the word "boring" from your vocabulary. It's a buzz word for teachers.

5. **Don't expect the teacher to do all of the work or propose all of the answers.** Be prepared to make suggestions, offer solutions, even recommend resources. The teacher will appreciate that you took the initiative.

6. **Be diplomatic, tactful, and respectful.** Teachers have feelings, too. And they're more likely to be responsive if you remember that the purpose of your meeting is conversation, not confrontation.

7. **Focus on what you need, not on what you think the teacher is doing wrong.** The more the teacher learns about you, the more he or she will be able to help. The more defensive the teacher feels, the less he or she will want to help.

8. **Don't forget to listen.** Strange but true, many students need practice in this essential skill. The purpose of your meeting isn't just to hear yourself talk.

9. **Bring your sense of humor.** Not necessarily the joke-telling sense of humor, but the one that lets you laugh at yourself and your own misunderstandings and mistakes.

10. **If your meeting isn't successful, get help from another adult.** "Successful" doesn't necessarily mean that you emerged victorious. Even if the teacher denies your request, your meeting can still be judged successful. If you had a real conversation—if you communicated openly, listened carefully, and respected each other's point of view— then congratulate yourself on a great meeting. If the air crackled with tension, the meeting fell apart, and you felt disrespected (or acted disrespectful), then it's time to bring in another adult. *Suggestions:* a guidance counselor, the gifted program coordinator, or another teacher you know and trust who seems likely to support you and advocate for you. Once you've found help, approach your teacher and try again.

The Student Bill of Rights

Author and educator Roger C. Schank believes that students should have some say in their education. His Student Bill of Rights might inspire you to lobby for an education that's more exciting, meaningful, and fun. If you want to know more about Dr. Schank's thinking or read his hyper-book on educational reform, visit www.engines4ed.org.

1. **Testing:** No student should have to take a multiple-choice or fill-in-the-blank test.

2. **Real-Life Skills:** No student should have to learn something that fails to relate to a skill that is likely to be required in life after school.

3. **Memorization:** No student should be required to memorize any information that is likely to be forgotten in six months.

4. **Clarity of Goals:** No student should be required to take a course, the results of which are not directly related to a goal held by the student, nor to engage in an activity without knowing what he or she can expect to gain from that activity.

5. **Passivity:** No student should be required to spend time passively watching or listening to anything unless there is a longer period of time devoted to allowing the student to participate in a corresponding active activity.

6. **Arbitrary Standards:** No student should be required to prepare his or her work in ways that are arbitrary or to jump through arbitrary hoops defined only by a particular teacher and not by the society at large.

7. **Mastery:** No student should be required to continue to study something he or she has already mastered.

8. **Discovery:** No student should be asked to learn anything unless there is the possibility of his or her being able to experiment in school with what he or she has learned.

9. **Defined Curriculum:** No student should be barred from engaging in activities that interest him or her within the framework of school because of breadth requirements imposed by the curriculum.

10. **Freedom of Thought:** No student should be placed in a position of having to air his or her views on a subject if the opposing point of view is not presented and equally represented.

8 Steps to Stress-Free Studying

1. **Take some downtime between school and home.** Relax and de-stress from school before tackling your homework.

2. **If you have chores to do, just do them.** Get them out of the way. Then you'll be able to study without interruption. If chores seriously cut into your homework time, talk with your parents. Maybe you can save some of them for the weekend, or share them with a sibling, or trade them for other chores that aren't as time-consuming.

3. **Study in the same place every day.** The same *quiet* place, if at all possible. Don't study on your bed. If you do, you'll fall asleep. Sit at a desk or table.

4. **Have everything ready before you start studying.** Books, pencils, pens, calculator, reference materials, paper, etc. Jumping up to get things will break your train of thought.

5. **Clear your desk or table of distractions.** No games, puzzles, magazines, or toys. If you have a computer, close your Web browser, unless you need it for research. Then you won't be tempted to surf.

6. **Do your easiest, most fun assignment first.** This probably contradicts a so-called rule you've heard before—to do your hardest, least fun assignment first. But if the easy-and-fun-one won't take much time, doing it first will put you in a studying mood. Plus you'll have already accomplished something by the time you face the more difficult task.

7. **Take short breaks when you're feeling stuck or tired.** Stretch, walk around, or have a snack.

8. **Reward yourself after each assignment you finish.** Call a friend, shoot some hoops, or listen to a favorite song. Do something you enjoy. You've earned it.

6 Ways to Remember What You Study

1. **Recite.** Read aloud. Recite what you're learning to yourself, a study partner, or a parent. Hearing and speaking can help information stick in your mind.

2. **Write.** Write what you want to learn and remember. This reinforces your reading.

3. **Use mnemonics.** Make up words, names, or sentences to help you remember facts and ideas. *Examples:*

   • To remember a sequence, use a sentence or key words. For the colors of the spectrum, memorize ROY G. BIV—for Red, Orange, Yellow, Green, Blue, Indigo, and Violet. For the Great Lakes, try HOMES—for Huron, Ontario, Michigan, Erie, and Superior.

   • To remember a date, try a rhyme. *Example:* "In fourteen-hundred-and-ninety-two, Columbus sailed the ocean blue...."

   • To remember the meaning of a word, associate it with something you know. *Example:* Mentally link "obnoxious" with a song or commercial that drives you crazy.

4. **Overlearn.** Keep studying something even after you know it. Overlearning is especially useful if you get very nervous during tests.

5. **Visualize.** Picture what the information looks like on the page you're studying. Make mental pictures of facts and ideas. Draw real pictures, if that helps you to learn.

6. **Apply what you learn in your everyday life.** If you use it, you won't lose it.

"Never forget what you need to remember."
Garrett Bartley

10 Test Preparation Tips

The night before:

1. Gather everything you think you'll need for the test and are allowed to bring. Paper? Your favorite pen or pencil? Reference materials? Calculator? Notes? What else?

2. Do a quick review of your notes and materials. Then spend time doing something you enjoy. Watch a movie, hang out with friends or family, exercise.

3. Set your alarm and get a good night's sleep.

The morning of:

4. Eat a healthy breakfast. Avoid processed foods, sugary foods, artificial sweeteners, and caffeine. Have some fresh fruit or vegetables.

5. Prepare a small snack to bring to the test, if eating is allowed. More fresh fruit or vegetables, a muffin, a sandwich—no candy.

6. If you have time, exercise. It will get your blood flowing and sharpen your mind.

7. Plan to do something fun that afternoon or evening, as a reward for taking the test.

The hour before:

8. If possible, do something you enjoy that relaxes you. Last-minute cramming is usually more stressful than helpful.

9. Plan to arrive at the test site early. Leave yourself plenty of time to get there.

10. If you're feeling anxious, use positive self-talk. *Examples:* "I'm ready. I can do this. I'm rested and prepared. I'm at my best."

"Proper preparation prevents poor performance."
Charlie Batch

I2 Ways to Keep Cool During Tests

A little test anxiety can be good for you. It keeps you alert and motivated. Too much can make you physically ill or block your ability to perform. Try these tips for managing test anxiety.

1. Arrive early. Being late or almost late will heighten your anxiety. Plus the sooner you arrive, the better choice of seats you'll have. Sit away from windows, doors, and other distractions.

2. Bring a newspaper or magazine to read while you're waiting for the test to start. Don't talk to friends about the test, or what you think might be on it, or how worried you are, or how worried they are. This will only feed your anxiety.

3. When the test is being handed out, calm yourself with a few deep breaths.

4. Read the instructions carefully—twice.

5. Unless you're not allowed to look ahead, review the whole test. Start by answering the questions you know for sure. Then work on the next-easiest questions. This will build your confidence.

6. In a timed test, pace yourself to answer as many questions as possible. Pay special attention to the ones worth the most points. Even if you can't answer them right away, jot down any thoughts or ideas you have on scratch paper.

7. Are you drawing a total blank on a question? Skip it for now and come back to it later.

8. If you start feeling too anxious (heart pounding, palms sweating), calm yourself with a few deep breaths. Stretch and relax your arms and legs. Tense and relax your muscles. Close your eyes and think good thoughts. Or try some positive self-talk. *Examples:* "I can do this. I know this material."

9. If the test is a lot harder than you thought it would be, don't panic. Just do your best. There will be other tests.

10. What if other students start handing in their papers and you're still working? Unless you're running out of time, ignore them. There's no bonus for finishing early.

11. Think about something fun you'll do after the test, as a way to reward yourself.

12. If you finish early, use the time to check your answers. Change any you know are wrong. Let the others stand.

12 Test-Taking Tips

When it comes to tests, it's not how much you know that counts, but how well you use what you know. When you want to be "in the know" at test-taking time, try these tips from award-winning teacher Randall McCutcheon.

1. **Memorize.** Few tests require you to do much thinking. Therefore, refine your cramming techniques. Be selective about what you try to remember. Force yourself to choose only the most important elements that were covered in class. Drill on those items. Recite aloud the important elements over and over again. Make use of mnemonics.

2. **Use your time wisely.** Most teachers talk at a rate of about 100 words per minute. You are able to think about four times that fast. Use that "extra" time to make sense of what is being said. You will significantly reduce the need for long hours of studying later.

3. **Be note-worthy.** Take notes only on the right-hand half of your notebook pages. Save the other half for your own comments and the teacher's. Teachers are constantly giving clues to potential test questions by repeating a fact several times, by writing it on the board, or by subtly saying that it will be on an upcoming exam.

4. **Break away.** When you are reviewing for a test, be sure to take many breaks. After an hour or two of studying, people reach a point of diminishing returns. Study the most difficult material first, while you are most alert. Do not form a "study group" unless you plan to study. You may end up with a social group that gets together to avoid the loneliness of *not* learning.

5. **Know thy teacher.** Students whose work is most similar to that of their instructors get the best grades. Your teachers are not likely to change, so you must adapt your learning style to their teaching style.

6. **Watch your test.** Before you begin any test, examine it. Allocate your time wisely. Assign a certain number of minutes per section; answer easy questions first to gain momentum; save some time at the end for review. You always need to review in order to catch silly mistakes and obviously wrong answers.

7. **Haste makes waste.** The classic error in test-taking is *not reading the directions* (or any question) carefully. Next time, pretend that you are attempting to disarm an atomic bomb.

8. **Play games.** Make test-taking into a game. Be positive. Practice possible questions and answers before the exam. Drill yourself. Try to outguess the teacher. During the test, restate difficult questions in terms that you can understand. And when all else fails... think.

9. **Know the M.O.** A test-maker, like any other criminal, has a *modus operandi*—a method of operating. Obtain old tests given by your teacher. Most teachers are ambitious enough to continually create new questions, but there will always be patterns that you can decipher. For example, in true-false questions, the teacher will probably favor one over the other. In multiple choice questions, sentence structure or answer length are often repeated even if the exact questions are not.

10. **Write to learn.** Write neatly, be brief, and be clear. Grading short answer and essay questions can be largely a subjective exercise—don't give a "burned out" teacher a reason to take out frustrations on you. Practice writing answers to essay questions you yourself make up. Use mnemonics or other memory devices to retain factual information. Finally, when answering essay test questions, you will have greater success if you follow a specific structural approach. In short, be organized.

11. **Reach out.** In times of quiet desperation, when you suddenly realize that you are facing a major exam and you have no idea how to prepare, pay a visit to the teacher. You will be surprised at how much valuable information can be acquired if you are both direct and tactful. You won't know what help your teacher can give you if you don't ask.

12. **Correct old tests.** When most students are handed back their tests, they glance at the grades and discard the remains. Wrong. You should analyze each incorrect answer for future reference. You may never be tested over the same material again, but you *will* be tested again. Anyone can make a mistake. Successful students try to avoid repeating the same kinds of errors.

4 Things to Do
When Someone Tries to Cheat Off You

1. **Change your seat.** This may not be possible in classes with assigned seating, or classes where cliques sit together.

2. **Cover your paper.** This sends a strong message to the cheater that you're not willing to let him or her copy from you. It also sends a message to the observant teacher.

3. **Speak to the cheater after the test.** Some students cheat because they're lazy or not interested in doing their schoolwork. Others cheat because they're under great pressure to achieve. These students often feel confused, anxious, guilty, and ashamed. If you notice someone

copying your answers, cover your paper. Then pick a time to talk with the person. Don't actually *accuse* him or her of cheating. This could lead to denial and maybe a punch in your nose. Instead, you might say something like this: "During the math test, it seemed like you might have been glancing over at my paper from time to time. You probably weren't, and I'm probably just being paranoid, but I needed to say something anyway." Letting the cheater know that you noticed may prevent future cheating.

4. **Speak to the teacher after the test.** Most schools have a strong student code against ratting and tattling, so you probably don't want to say, "So-and-so cheated off me during the test." Plus, you'd have to prove it, and if your school has no-exceptions rules about cheating, this could involve you in a very unpleasant process. Instead, you might say something like this: "I wonder if we could move the desks farther apart during tests. I know I'd be more comfortable if people couldn't accidentally see each other's papers." Most teachers will get the hint and increase their vigilance.

10 Ways to Learn New Words

A large vocabulary can help you express your thoughts and feelings more clearly. It can make what you say sound more interesting. It can improve your performance on tests and make you a better reader. Follow these tips to build a bigger vocabulary.

1. Develop word radar. Become aware of new words as you read and hear them.

2. Make an effort to remember new words. Keep a list in your notebook, or start a word box with index cards. Write a new word on the front of each card and the definition on the back. Store your cards alphabetically in a file box.

3. If you come across a new word in a textbook you can't write in, jot down the word on a sticky note and put it in the book.

4. Try to figure out the meanings of new words from their context—the familiar words and phrases that surround them. If you find a word you can't understand, look it up in the dictionary.

5. Use a "word-a-day" calendar in your home study center. Learn each day's new word. Or subscribe to an online "word-a-day" service. Merriam-Webster has one; go to www.m-w.com. Or sign up for Wordsmith's Word-a-Day email at wordsmith.org. Want to know the

very latest and greatest words? Join the Word Spy mailing list at
www.wordspy.com.

6. Use a thesaurus. The root meaning of the word "thesaurus" is "treasury." Think of your thesaurus as a treasury of new words, waiting to
be discovered by you. For an online version of the *Merriam-Webster
Collegiate Thesaurus,* go to www.m-w.com. Search *Roget's II: The New
Thesaurus* at www.bartleby.com.

7. Use your head. When someone around you says a word that's new to
you, ask what it means.

8. Be a word detective. Let your curiosity inspire you to learn more
about a word than its meaning. Check its pronunciation. Find out
where it came from. Examine its roots and track down related words.

9. Put on your Sherlock Holmes hat and head for the *Oxford English
Dictionary,* called the "OED" for short. Most libraries carry this important reference work. It traces words back through time to their earli-
est uses, showing how spellings and meanings have changed.

10. Become an *etymologist*—a student of words.

"The limits of my language are the limits of my mind.
All I know is what I have words for."
Ludwig Wittgenstein

100 Words All High School Graduates (and Their Parents) Should Know from the Editors of the American Heritage® College Dictionary

*The quality of your vocabulary affects your success in college and the work-
place. According to the editors of* The American Heritage College Dictionary,
*these are the 100 words that each high-school graduate should know. Of
course, they're not the only 100 words you should know. But if you're able to
use them correctly, you're likely to have a superior command of the language.
Get a jump on high school and learn them now. Use a dictionary to look up
the ones you don't already know.*

1. abjure
2. abrogate
3. abstemious
4. acumen
5. antebellum
6. auspicious
7. belie
8. bellicose
9. bowdlerize
10. chicanery
11. chromosome
12. churlish
13. circumlocution
14. circumnavigate
15. deciduous
16. deleterious
17. diffident
18. enervate
19. enfranchise
20. epiphany
21. equinox
22. euro
23. evanescent
24. expurgate
25. facetious
26. fatuous
27. feckless
28. fiduciary
29. filibuster
30. gamete
31. gauche
32. gerrymander
33. hegemony
34. hemoglobin
35. homogeneous
36. hubris
37. hypotenuse
38. impeach
39. incognito
40. incontrovertible
41. inculcate
42. infrastructure
43. interpolate
44. irony
45. jejune
46. kinetic
47. kowtow
48. laissez faire
49. lexicon
50. loquacious
51. lugubrious
52. metamorphosis
53. mitosis
54. moiety
55. nanotechnology
56. nihilism
57. nomenclature
58. nonsectarian
59. notarize
60. obsequious
61. oligarchy
62. omnipotent

63. orthography
64. oxidize
65. parabola
66. paradigm
67. parameter
68. pecuniary
69. photosynthesis
70. plagiarize
71. plasma
72. polymer
73. precipitous
74. quasar
75. quotidian
76. recapitulate
77. reciprocal
78. reparation
79. respiration
80. sanguine
81. soliloquy
82. subjugate
83. suffragist
84. supercilious
85. tautology
86. taxonomy
87. tectonic
88. tempestuous
89. thermodynamics
90. totalitarian
91. unctuous
92. usurp
93. vacuous
94. vehement
95. vortex
96. winnow
97. wrought
98. xenophobe
99. yeoman
100. ziggurat

5 Ways to Be a Better Speller

1. Pay attention to how words are spelled. Do this when you read *and* when you write.

2. Keep a personal list of new and difficult words.

3. Play word games. Try Scrabble, Boggle, UpWords, Scattergories, and Hangman. You can also play word games on your computer and online.

4. Teachers and other reading specialists have made lists of Spelling Demons—words that seem to give students the most trouble. Ask your teachers if they have lists they can give you. Look in the library for books of lists.

5. Set up a schedule for studying spelling words. *Example:*

   ### On the day spelling words are assigned:

   - Test yourself on the words for that week. Find out which ones you'll need to study.

   ### For the rest of the week:

   - Schedule regular study sessions for every day or every other day. Keep them short—no more than 15–20 minutes. Several short sessions are more effective than a night-before-the-test cram-a-thon.

   - Squeeze brief practices into spare moments—in the car, while you're waiting to be picked up from soccer practice, on the bus, during breakfast.

   ### On the night before the test:

   - Review *all* the words—the hard ones and the easy ones.

   - Get help studying. Have a friend or family member dictate your spelling words to you. Write them down, leaving a blank space underneath each one. Afterward, check your work. For any misspelled word, write the correct spelling under the incorrect spelling.

   - Write *all* of your spelling words once. Then write them all again... and again... until you've mastered them.

   ### When you get the test back:

   - Study the words you misspelled until you know them.

   - Add the words you spelled correctly to your personal list of new words.

10 Ways to Smash Writer's Block

Your writing assignment is due tomorrow, but you... can't... write... one... single... word. Now what?

1. Don't panic! Spend a few minutes reading a cartoon book, the comics section of the newspaper, or a funny story. This may unblock your brain and put you in the mood for writing.

2. Freewrite. Put pen to paper (or fingers to keyboard) and write anything. Even if it's "Help! I have writer's block! Help! Oh, help!" Keep writing for 5–10 minutes.

3. Forget about grammar, spelling, punctuation, and all the other rules. You can fix your writing later.

4. Copy a few paragraphs or pages from your favorite book. Or imitate your favorite writer's style.

5. Talk your paper to the mirror, the family cat or dog, your baby brother or sister, a parent or friend. Talk it into a tape recorder. Then jot down the main ideas you just said out loud, or transcribe the tape you made.

6. Draw a picture of your writer's block. Use your imagination. It doesn't matter *what* you draw, just *that* you draw. The act of drawing gets your "whole brain" working and stimulates creative thinking.

7. Write the ending first. Or the middle. You don't have to start at the beginning. But once you do start, it's easier to keep going.

8. Make a list of key words and ideas. Write related words and ideas in clusters around them.

9. Move around. Stretch. Take a walk. Do jumping jacks. Shake your arms and shoulders. Dance.

10. Relax! Daydream for a few moments. Do a simple meditation. Take a break. The more you worry about writer's block, the bigger it gets, and the harder it is to start writing.

"Writing comes more easily if you have something to say."
Sholem Asch

9 Do's and Don'ts of Giving Credit: Tips for Avoiding Plagiarism from the Purdue University Online Writing Lab

You've done your research, you're finishing your paper, and you're wondering exactly who and what you should credit. Follow these tips to stay safe.

You DO have to give credit...

1. when you are using or referring to somebody else's words or ideas from a magazine, book, newspaper, song, TV program, movie, Web page, computer program, letter, advertisement, or any other medium.

2. when you use information gained through interviewing another person.

3. when you copy the exact words or a "unique phrase" from somewhere.

4. when you reprint any diagrams, illustrations, charts, and pictures.

5. when you use ideas that others have given you in conversations or over email.

You DON'T have to give credit...

6. when you are writing your own experiences, observations, insights, thoughts, or conclusions about a subject.

7. when you are using "common knowledge"—folklore, commonsense observations, shared information within your field of study or cultural group. Material is probably common knowledge if:

   • you find the same information undocumented in at least five other sources

   • you think it is information that your readers will already know

   • you think a person could easily find the information with general reference sources

8. when you are compiling generally accepted facts.

9. when you are writing up your own experimental results.

13 Ways to Lighten Up at School

Humor in the classroom makes learning more fun. Share these ideas with your teacher and pick some to try.

1. Post cartoons or jokes on a class bulletin board.

2. Take a five-minute "laugh break" each day. Share jokes, tell funny stories, or practice tongue-twisters.

3. Create a Class Comics Yearbook. Each week, have someone in the class draw a cartoon about something that happened during the week, then sign and date the cartoon. At the end of the school year, collect the cartoons in a book and make copies for everyone.

4. Show a funny video during homeroom or study hall.

5. Decorate the classroom with silly props—toys, masks, rubber chickens, pink flamingos, wind-up toys, stuffed animals, action figures, etc.

6. Set aside a shelf for funny books and audios—"laugh break" materials.

7. Create a Humor Corner. Paper the walls with cartoons and funny posters. Cover the floor with a carpet remnant and pile pillows on it. Hang a mirror for making funny faces. Make this the place where stressed students can go to cool off and calm down.

8. Invite a clown to visit your school or class.

9. Write funny notes or quotes on Post-its and stick them all around the classroom—on walls, desks, boards, shelves, windows, globes, wherever.

10. Create a Humor First-Aid Kit. It could include such things as masks, colorful suspenders, a clown nose, cartoon character Band-Aids, joke books, etc.

11. Use a joke-a-day calendar for your classroom calendar. Start each day by reading the joke out loud.

12. Snap funny pictures of classmates. Have everyone make faces. Hang the pictures on the class bulletin board or outside the classroom.

13. Have a class contest to generate more ideas for bringing humor into the classroom.

20 Ways to Change the Social Scene at School

1. **Smile or say hello to someone new each day.** You'll be surprised at how easy it is and what it might lead to—new friends, for instance.

2. **Eat lunch with a different group at least once a week.** Maybe you eat lunch with the same people each day. Try eating with people from different classes or activities, or with people you'd like to know better.

3. **If you find you enjoy lunch with different people, start a Friendly Lunch Club.** Model it after the Friendly Supper Club in Montgomery, Alabama, where people gather once a month, and the only rule is to bring someone from a different culture or race for "honest interaction."

4. **Don't be afraid to be a leader.** A leader is a normal person who makes plans, helps organize events and activities, takes action, instigates change, and helps others. You can be a leader by acting on one or more of the ideas on this list or coming up with ideas of your own to work on.

5. **Start a SHiNE club in your school.** SHiNE (Seeking Harmony in Neighborhoods Everyday) is a group by and for teens that promotes

tolerance and diversity. SHiNE fights discrimination and school violence and helps teens build important skills for success, while getting them more involved in their schools and communities. To learn more, visit the SHiNE Web site: www.shine.com.

6. **Be a floater.** Don't limit yourself to one group or clique. Try seeing how many different places you can fit in.

7. **Combat cluelessness and cruelty.** If you hear someone saying something misinformed or bigoted about another group, call that person on it. Let him or her know that you don't appreciate those comments.

8. **Start or run student-led workshops on "obias" and "isms."** As in homophobia, racism, or sexism. Invite speakers from local awareness and tolerance organizations.

9. **Organize a multicultural event for your school and community.** Your event could be a film or music festival, an art show, a polyethnic potluck, or even a talent show. Spotlight the cultures of your school's diverse population.

10. **Take a stand against slurs.** When people use slurs and other forms of hate speech, don't let them get away with it. Make sure they know it's not acceptable. Talk with your teachers about using class time to raise awareness about these words. To learn more about hate speech, visit the Southern Poverty Law Center's Web site: www.splcenter.org. Or go to www.tolerance.org/teach, a great source of information about anti-bias activities in schools across the country.

11. **Tackle bullying in your school.** Work to get a formal complaint process in place, if there isn't one already. Talk to other students about their experiences and see if they have ideas for change. Let teachers know about bullying incidents in your school, instead of keeping quiet.

12. **Create a put-down-free zone at school.** Make a safe space where students can go—a hall, room, or lunch table. Everyone has to leave their insults and their labels (for themselves and others) behind when they enter the zone.

13. **Start (or participate in) a Gay-Straight Student Alliance.** Homophobia is all too common in schools, so help fight it. The alliance can combat discrimination with sensitivity training for students and teachers. Give students a safe place to talk about whether they feel threatened in school, are trying to come out, are questioning their sexual identity, or are confronting their own homophobia. For information on starting a Gay-Straight Alliance, visit the Gay, Lesbian, and Straight Education Network Web site: www.glsen.org.

14. **Encourage peer-to-peer mentoring.** Start a mentoring club in which older students help support younger ones (and vice versa). *Examples:* Sophomores could help freshmen get used to life in high school and find their way around. Students who have taken standardized tests could give advice and tips to those who need to take them. Students in any grade could help their peers by offering tutoring services. Peer mentors could also take responsibility for helping to welcome new students who transfer to the school midyear, or who have recently moved to the area and don't yet know many people. All of these efforts will help people in different grades and classes get to know each other better and respect each other more.

15. **Raise awareness about people with disabilities.** Look at your school through the eyes of someone who has a disability. How wheelchair accessible is it? Are there services for students who might be sight or hearing impaired? What changes need to be made? Talk to your principal about how you can help to make the necessary changes.

16. **Tutor other students at your school.** You could help ESL (English as a Second Language) students with their English and learn something about their culture in return. Or you could help tutor students in other grades. Are there ESL interpreters available at school events? If not, you could make this happen.

17. **Find an issue for activism that cuts across clique and group lines.** Choose an issue that affects everyone—the environment or human rights, for example—and get lots of students at your school involved. When working together to raise awareness or solve a problem, it's easier for people to forget about the social boundaries they're used to. Or how about joining together as volunteers for a community effort such as Habitat for Humanity, where you build houses for people in need? (For more information, visit www.habitat.org.) Service projects like cleaning up vacant lots, creating community gardens, or volunteering with the elderly are a great way to build unity and promote acceptance. Working together, you can be a force for positive change in your school and your community.

18. **Be a student/peer mediator.** Encourage peer understanding and help people resolve problems before they escalate. If your school doesn't have a student/peer mediator program, try starting one. Being a peer mediator is a role that lets you become directly involved in issues such as discrimination, bullying, and sexual harassment in your school.

19. **Raise awareness about sexual harassment.** Do you know what your school's policy and procedures are regarding this issue? If you don't, chances are many other students don't either. Work with a teacher or counselor to get the information out there. Perhaps you could help

create a pamphlet that addresses the issue, or organize workshops that use role-plays to demonstrate the different forms of sexual harassment and how to handle them.

20. **Start a Web site that promotes school unity and tolerance.** Create a peer-mediated discussion board where students can address issues and problems in a safe (and anonymous) online setting. Set up a regularly scheduled online essay contest on topics such as diversity, tolerance, and acceptance. Raise awareness about community events and problems as well. You could even start a pen-pal program on the site, giving students in different grades and from different groups a place to connect and correspond.

IO Ways to Build School Spirit

You may think that school spirit is corny, but it helps students care about their school. When you care about your school, you're more likely to do well and less likely to drop out. School spirit also helps create a sense of community. It links students who might otherwise have little or nothing in common.

1. **Does your school have a symbol, logo, slogan, song, fight song, and/or cheer?** If not, have a contest to generate ideas. Then have a vote so everyone (students, teachers, and administrators) can choose their favorites. *Tip:* If your school already has a symbol, logo, slogan, etc., but it's outdated, unpopular, or offensive, form a group of students who feel the same and lobby for change.

2. **Show your school pride.** Buy and wear T-shirts, sweatshirts, jackets, caps, or other clothing printed with your school's name or logo. Ask your parents to display a school bumper sticker or window sticker on the family car.

3. **Start a Spirit Club at your school.** Or join one, if it already exists. Plan events and activities to boost school spirit. Create inspiring banners or posters to display in the halls.

4. **Hold an annual Spirit Week at your school**. Schedule it for just after homecoming or during the February slump. Offer a variety of after-school activities and events. *Examples:* a mural contest, a student bake-off, a pie-eating contest, relay races.

5. **Put your school in the news.** Find out which reporters cover schools in your area and learn how to contact them. Keep them informed of important events and achievements at your school.

6. **Come up with fun and unique ways to attract community and media attention to your school.** Work with your class or club to plan projects and events. *Examples:* An all-school banquet featuring the world's largest submarine sandwich; a school play where admission is free to anyone who donates canned goods or other nonperishables for your local food shelf.

7. **Support your school's athletes.** Go to their games and matches and cheer them on. Have tailgate parties before football games. Post game schedules on school bulletin boards; if your school has a Web site, post them there, too. Use the morning announcements to recap recent games and encourage everyone to attend upcoming games. Support other school events, too—plays, concerts, musicals—by showing up and applauding.

8. **Honor all types of achievers at your school, not just the athletes.** What about awarding letters for academic achievement? For service? For the arts? Give monthly School Spirit Awards to the most caring, enthusiastic, and involved students, teachers, administrators, support staff members, and volunteers.

9. **Start a friendly rivalry with another school in your community.** Figure out ways to compete with each other that boost school spirit. *Examples:* Pit your school's best debaters against theirs; have an academic tournament (like College Bowl); see which school can generate the most volunteers for a local Habitat for Humanity project.

10. **Make a special effort to welcome incoming classes and new students.** Produce "survival kits" for newcomers. Each kit might include a school map, directory, calendar, and handbook, a list of activities and clubs at your school, descriptions of upcoming events (including dates and times), PTA/PTO information for parents, and...what else? What would be helpful? What would be fun?

The American Library Association's 12 Tips for Forming a Reading Habit

Reading is vital to your current and future success in life. The more you read, the easier it gets, and the more you enjoy reading. These tips from the world's oldest and largest library association can help you become a better reader.

1. Mix up your activities: read your email for awhile, read a book for awhile, do your homework for awhile. Repeat. Have snacks handy.

2. Learn while you read—the one does not exclude the other.

3. Read in small bites—10 minutes on the way to and from school, 15 minutes before bed, 10 minutes waiting for friends to pick you up. That totals 35 minutes—a good-sized Daily Reading Total (DRT).

4. Join a book discussion group at your school or public library, or online. Try the ALA's own group at www.ala.org/teenhoopla.

5. Realize that your reading speed increases the more you read.

6. Realize that time goes faster when you're reading for the fun of it.

7. Read what you are passionate about.

8. Find the right book or magazine for you.

9. Keep a list of what you read. Compare it to the ALA's lists of Best Books (www.ala.org/yalsa/booklists/bbya), Quick Picks (www.ala.org/yalsa/booklists/quickpicks), or Outstanding Books for the College Bound (www.ala.org/yalsa/booklists/obcb).

10. Write about what you read.

11. Realize that reading for the fun of it is a good way to relax.

12. Talk about your reading with friends and family.

Bonus tip: Each October, hundreds of public and school libraries, classrooms, and bookstores across the country celebrate Teen Read Week with special events including poetry readings, contests, workshops, author appearances, and more. Check your local library to learn what's planned for this year.

6 Ways to Find the Right Book to Read

When people say, "Reading is boring!" it's because they haven't found the right book. How can you find the right book? Forget about school projects, book reports, and teacher-pleasing reading. Try these ideas instead.

1. Start with your interests. Do you like music, fashion, computers, celebrities, sports? There are plenty of books on all of these topics.

2. No right book yet? Move on to your needs. Do you need to learn how to fix your bike? Redecorate your room? Research Colorado for your family vacation? You'll find tons of books on any and all of these.

3. No right book yet? Think about your favorite movie or TV show. You'll find novels based on movies, biographies of stars, books about how television shows and movies are made, and much more.

4. No right book yet? Try the Internet. Explore Web sites that interest you; often, they have recommended reading lists. Check out the book

reviews and book lists at Booklist (www.ala.org/booklist/index.html) and www.teenreads.com.

5. No right book yet? Visit an online bookstore to find out about interesting books. Try Amazon (www.amazon.com) or Barnes & Noble (www.bn.com).

6. Still no right book? Talk to your friends, an adult you share interests with, a teacher, or a librarian. They'll all have suggestions to pass on to you.

> "If you get lost in a book,
> everything that's bothering you just goes away."
> *Brandon Keefe*

10 Books Some People Don't Want You to Read

Free people read freely. Fight back against censorship by reading a book that's been banned or challenged. Banned books are those which have been removed from library shelves. Challenged books are those for which a formal, written complaint has been filed with a library or school about their content or appropriateness. Following is a list of the most frequently challenged books for 2001. Read one—or more. Let freedom read!

1. The Harry Potter series by J.K. Rowling.

2. *Of Mice and Men* by John Steinbeck.

3. *The Chocolate War* by Robert Cormier.

4. *I Know Why the Caged Bird Sings* by Maya Angelou.

5. *Summer of My German Soldier* by Bette Greene.

6. *The Catcher in the Rye* by J.D. Salinger.

7. The Alice series by Phyllis Reynolds Naylor.

8. *Go Ask Alice* by Anonymous.

9. *Fallen Angels* by Walter Dean Myers.

10. *Blood and Chocolate* by Annette Curtis Klause.

To learn about other banned and challenged books, visit the American Library Association's Web site, www.ala.org, and do a search for "banned books." Celebrate your freedom to read each September during Banned Books Week. Ask a librarian for details.

> "I don't want to be shut out from the truth.
> If they ban books, they might as well
> lock us away from the world."
> *Rory Edwards, age 12*

How to Start a Book Group

Reading is something you do on your own, whether you're alone or with other people. You start reading, and if it's something you enjoy, you literally "get lost" in your book. If you like to talk about books you read—to share your opinions and hear what other people think—start a book group. Here's how.

1. **Find friends who like to read.** Tell them you want to start a book group and ask if they'd like to be part of it.

2. **Schedule a planning meeting.** That's where you'll make decisions about your book group. Ask everyone to come with a list of ideas for books they'd like to read.

At your planning meeting:

3. **Decide how often you'll meet.** Many book groups meet once a month. That gives members time to read in between meetings. Instead of setting specific *dates,* try a specific *day*—like the first Tuesday of each month, or the third Friday. This will be easier for people to remember.

4. **Decide where you'll meet.** You might hold the meetings in your room at home, or rotate among members' houses. You could see about reserving a meeting room at your local public library or community center. Maybe you can meet in your school, a neighborhood coffee house, or a local bookstore. Find someplace comfortable, convenient, and reasonably quiet where you can talk.

5. **Decide how long your meetings will last.** Two to three hours is typical. That gives people a chance to arrive, settle in, and catch up with each other before the meeting officially starts.

6. **Decide what you'll read.** Invite people to share their ideas. Agree on the first several books you'll read. You might do this by letting each person choose one book, or voting as a group on different choices. No one person should choose all the books. *Tips:* Current bestsellers are fun, but they're usually available only in hardcover, so they're expensive to buy. Checking them out of the library can be hard because so many people want to read them. Think about last year's bestsellers (especially if they're in paperback), classics, or other books that seem interesting. If you need more ideas, ask a librarian, the media-center specialist at your school, or a helpful salesperson at your local bookstore. Check out the book lists and reviews at the American Library Association's Web site (www.ala.org) or YALSA, the Young Adult Library Services Association (www.ala.org/yalsa).

7. **Decide who will lead the meetings.** You might rotate this responsibility among your book group's members. But someone should be in charge of starting the discussion, keeping it focused on the book, making sure that everyone who wants to contribute has a chance to talk, and ending the meeting.

8. **Set a date for your first book-group meeting.** Have fun!

Helpful resources if you need them:

- Book groups are so popular that tons of books have been written about them—how to start them, how to run the meetings, what to read. Visit a library or bookstore to see what's available.

- Many bookstores publish monthly newsletters full of useful information for book groups. Check your local bookstores, find out if they publish newsletters, and get on their mailing lists.

- Many book publishers create "Reader's Companions" or discussion guides for their books. Ask a librarian or media-center specialist to help you find these, or go online and search publishers' Web sites. Some are available free at bookstores.

27 Clues That
You're a Remarkable Reader

If you're a remarkable reader, you'll see yourself in this list from the Young Adult Library Services Association. The experts at YALSA are eager to hear about your personal reading successes or problems. You can also ask them for more information about books and reading. Write to yalsa@ala.org.

Do you:

1. Read a book for enjoyment during class?
2. Have a parent who continually says, "Get your nose out of that book and go outside!"?
3. Have a parent who continually says, "You'll ruin your eyes because you read so much!"?
4. Read in the bathtub?
5. Read a book a day?
6. Read 2–3 books on the weekend?
7. Read in bed at night until a book is finished?
8. Wish some books would never end?
9. Reread favorite books?
10. Read while walking home from school?
11. Forget to eat while reading?
12. Eat while reading?
13. Get lost in a book?
14. Check out too many books at one time from the library because you want to make sure to have a book you will like?
15. Read while watching television, especially during the commercials?
16. Spend your entire allowance on books?
17. Prefer reading to rollerblading, swimming, or shopping?
18. Turn down the corners of pages to mark your place?
19. Read on planes, trains, and automobiles?
20. Read the first thing in the morning?
21. Read the last thing at night?

22. Read magazines and newspapers, as well as books?

23. Read the backs of cereal boxes?

24. Visit the school and public library regularly?

25. Read while the computer boots up?

26. Visit Amazon.com and BarnesandNoble.com regularly?

27. Have a favorite reading spot?

21 Ways to Learn Something New

1. Take an art class (painting, sculpture, collage) at a community center.

2. Find out what course offerings are available at a local writing center (poetry, creative writing, storytelling, mysteries, autobiography).

3. Look on the bulletin board of your local library or bookstore for upcoming events such as writers' workshops, readings, lectures, and book-club meetings. Start your own book club, if you'd like.

4. Get on the mailing list at a bookstore that holds readings. Come prepared with questions for the author or poet.

5. Use the library for research that you conduct on your own—just because you want to learn more about a topic that fascinates you.

6. See if a local recreation center offers yoga, self-defense, karate, judo, aerobics, or swimming classes.

7. Join a youth group through your faith community or another source. Activities may include social events, discussions, sports and fitness, or even trips.

8. If you've got a dog, take classes in basic or advanced dog training.

9. Sign up for acting classes or theater workshops.

10. Join a community choir or jazz band.

11. Enroll in dance classes at a local studio.

12. Ask someone who knows sign language to teach it to you.

13. Inquire if your local nature center offers any classes or nature walks.

14. See if a local cookware store features cooking classes, or team up with a friend and start your own.

15. In the summer, get into the art scene by checking out arts and crafts fairs. Talk with the artisans and find out how they started their

craft—pottery, jewelry making, handpainted clothing, woodworking, blacksmithing, glassmaking, photography, whatever—and how they do it. Inquire about classes that may be available in your area.

16. Plant a garden and find resources that will help you learn about different species of plants and how they grow. Nurseries and gardening centers can be great places to learn more about plant care.

17. Check out your local community center to find out what kind of community education programs are offered. (Foreign languages? Belly dancing? Weight lifting?)

18. Write a column or article for your community newspaper or a neighborhood newsletter. See how much you learn by interviewing people and trying out your writing skills.

19. Get out a telescope and look at the stars, along with a reference book on astronomy. Call a planetarium for show times and test your knowledge.

20. Volunteer at a local museum, or just visit one on a regular basis. Spend time learning about the history of different objects or peoples.

21. If you live near a college or university, attend lectures, concerts, or seminars open to the public. This is a great way to learn more about a topic you probably never would have heard about otherwise.

"You can learn new things at any time in your life if you're willing to be a beginner. If you actually learn to like being a beginner, the whole world opens up to you."
Barbara Sher

9 Things You Can Do If You Don't Have a Home Computer

1. Ask your teacher about using the classroom computer before or after school.

2. Check with your school computer lab or media center about using a computer before or after school.

3. Check your local public library. Many libraries have computers with Internet access for people to use.

4. Check community resources—like the Boys and Girls Clubs, YMCA, YWCA, or community centers. They may have computers you can use.

5. See if your community has a Community Access Center. CACs are designed to give all members of a community access to computers and the Internet. They are located in public libraries, schools, community centers, churches, and other public places.

6. Check local coffee shops. Many have computers with Internet connections available for customers to use.

7. See if there's an Internet café, cybercafé, or netcafé near you. You'll have to pay for access.

8. Ask your parents about talking to a neighbor or family friend about "bartering" to use a computer. *Examples:* You might offer to mow their lawn or baby-sit in exchange for computer time.

9. Start saving. Computers are becoming less expensive. Maybe your parents are willing to work out a cost-sharing plan. They pay for part; you pay for part.

II Signs That You're Web-Aware

You surf. You chat. You send instant messages. So you must be Web-aware, right? Only if all 11 of these signs are true for you.

1. I know how to protect my privacy on the Internet by not sharing personal details in chat rooms, newsgroups, or instant messaging. This includes my name, gender, age, address, email address, telephone number, picture, credit card information, or passwords.

2. I talk to my parents about what I'm doing online and who I chat with.

3. I read the privacy policies on Web sites before filling out online registration or contest forms to make sure they will not be sharing my information.

4. If I encounter disturbing material or harassing messages online, I don't respond. I tell a parent or other adult and my Internet Service Provider (ISP).

5. If I am planning to meet an online acquaintance in real life, I get permission from a parent first. I arrange the meeting for a public place and I don't go alone.

6. I try to confirm that online information is correct by finding out more about the author and by checking it against other sources.

7. I respect others. I never "flame" or insult others or spread gossip.

8. I know the following activities are illegal and I don't practice them: hacking, making physical threats, and downloading pirated software.

9. I respect copyright by not stealing from other Web sits or using plagiarized material for homework assignments.

10. I check with my parents before making financial transactions online, including purchasing, ordering, or selling anything.

11. I protect the home computer by always checking for viruses when using a disk or downloading from the Internet. I never open an attachment or file from someone I don't know, and that I didn't request.

IO Commandments of Email Etiquette

1. **Use a spell-check program.** Read every email at least two times before you send it. Even if you're just sending a brief note to a friend, wy luk like you kant' spel?

2. **Review your message carefully before you send it.** There's no such thing as truly "private" email. Is your message something you'd feel comfortable having total strangers read? What if the recipient decides to forward it to other people? (That's easy to do but not very polite. See #7 below.)

3. **Never use all capital or all lowercase letters.** CAPITALS SHOUT. lowercase whispers or makes it seem like you can't find the shift key. Find other ways to emphasize words you want to stand out. Try *asterisks* or _underlines_ to call attention to certain words.

4. **Avoid using special fonts or colors.** They may get lost in translation from your computer to your friend's computer. Or they may make your email unreadable.

5. **Use the subject line.** Give your reader a heads-up on what the email includes. Something like "Party on Saturday" or "Need homework help!" or "Busy? I'm bored" works.

6. **Be extra-polite in emails.** Brief, curt messages can seem crabby or impatient. Take the extra few seconds to add "Please" or "Thank you."

7. **Don't forward email without permission.** Email sent to you is meant just for you. If you want to forward a really interesting or useful email to someone else, ask the sender first if it's okay.

8. **If you get an email that upsets you, don't answer it right away.** Take time to think about it. Maybe the sender didn't mean to upset you. Maybe you misread the message or took it the wrong way. Don't immediately bang out a hasty, angry response and punch "Send." Instead, pick up the phone and call your friend, or arrange to meet and talk face-to-face.

9. **Use emoticons to communicate emotions.** Email can be flat and blah. It's just letters on a screen, without the little touches (colors, fancy letters, underlines, drawings, etc.) you might add to a personal handwritten letter, and without the visual and vocal clues (facial expressions, tone of voice, body language) you get in face-to-face conversations. Emoticons can be silly, and you don't want to clutter your email with zillions of them, but an occasional :-) (smiley) or :-((frowny) or ;-) (winky) or =:-O (surprised! shocked! amazed!) can help your reader know how you feel.

10. **Be patient.** Not everyone checks their email every second or even every day. If your friend doesn't respond immediately, this doesn't mean he or she doesn't care. Wait a day or two before asking, "Hey, did you get my email?" Or, if it's really important, pick up the phone and call.

7 Things You Should Know
About Online Privacy
from the American Bar Association

1. According to the Federal Trade Commission, 93% of Web sites collect personal information. Only 44% post privacy notices. Just 10% comply with all fair information practices recommended by the FTC.

2. Any personal information about you that is stored on your computer—your name, address, phone number, family history, medical history, lifestyle, shopping habits, email, chats, and so on—may be accessible to strangers.

3. Anything you do on the Web, even if it's just browsing a Web page, transmits information that can identify you and be tracked. This information can be collected to produce profiles of what you do online and who you associate with. The technology that makes cyberspace possible also makes detailed, cumulative, invisible observation of us possible.

4. There are few laws that limit what the private sector can do with information collected in cyberspace. Information collectors can largely do what they want with most of the information they collect. Commercial sites use this information to develop profiles of individual customers to sell more effectively.

5. Many Web sites put "cookies" on computers that visit their sites, which identify the computer when it comes to the site again. Some sites put a "tag" on your computer that tracks you from site to site as you surf the Web.

6. Deleted email isn't really deleted. Backup copies may exist on your computer, or on the computer of the person you sent the email to. If your email was sent through a commercial service or the Internet, it may have passed through several computers, and each of those computers may have a copy. Unless your email is encrypted, it can be accessed and viewed on intermediate computers between you and the receiver. *Tip:* Think of an email as a postcard.

7. You can limit how much information is collected about you, and limit the chance of others getting access to your information without your knowledge. Here's how:

   • Never give your Social Security Number as an identifier.

   • Use passwords at least 6 characters long, with a mix of letters and numbers. Change your passwords frequently.

- Conceal your identity as you surf the Web. Surf through a site like www.anonymizer.com.

- Don't use your regular email account when you post to newsgroups or mailing lists. Open a second email account using a pseudonym, and use that instead.

- Configure your Web browser to warn you when a site tries to place a "cookie" on your computer. Then you can decide to accept it or not.

12 Ways to Can Spam

If you have email, you get spam—annoying, unsolicited junk email. Lose Weight! Save Money! Earn Millions Working from Home! Lower Your Mortgage! Enhance Your (name-of-body-part-here)! And so on. You probably can't stop spam, but you can fight back against it. Here's how.

1. **Use a unique email address.** Spammers use "dictionary attacks" to sort through possible name combinations at large Internet service providers (ISPs) or email services. A common name like jdoe may get more spam than a name like jd51x02oe.

2. **Try not to display your email address in public.** Don't post it in chat rooms, on Web sites, or in newsgroups unless it's required for registration.

3. **Check the privacy policy when you submit your email address to a Web site.** See if it allows the company to sell your address. Don't submit your address to sites that won't protect it.

4. **Consider using two email addresses—**one for personal messages, and the other for chat rooms, Web sites, and newsgroups. If a Web site asks if it's okay to send you news or information, check the box that says "no." Or you may have to uncheck a box that says "yes." *Tip:* This isn't a generous offer by the site to keep you informed. It's a way to get your permission to sell your email address.

5. **If your online service has a member directory, opt out.** Spammers use these directories to harvest email addresses.

6. **Use an email filter.** Check your email account to see if it provides a tool to filter out potential spam, or a way to channel spam into a bulk email folder.

7. **Don't try to unsubscribe from something you didn't subscribe to.** Many spam messages end with something like "If you wish to be unsubscribed from this list, please Click here" or "If you have

received this mailing in error, <u>Click here.</u>" Replying lets the spammer know that your email address is valid, and you may end up getting even *more* spam.

8. **Send copies of unwanted or deceptive messages to the Federal Trade Commission (uce@ftc.gov).** The FTC uses the unsolicited emails stored in this database to pursue law-enforcement actions against spammers.

9. **Send copies of the spam to your ISP's abuse desk.** Often, the email address is abuse@yourisp.name.com or postmaster@yourispname.com. Make sure to include the full email header on the spam. At the top of the message, say that you're complaining about being spammed.

10. **Join the fight against spam.** Check out the Coalition Against Unsolicited Commercial Email (CAUCE), a grass-roots, all-volunteer group of Netizens at www.cauce.org.

11. **Can't tell if an email is spam or not?** Maybe it's your long-lost Uncle Phil trying to contact you. You may want to peek at the email to find out—but be warned: a lot of spam is porn. Never, *never,* NEVER open an attachment unless you're absolutely, positively, 100 percent sure where it came from. It could contain a virus.

And here's the simplest way of all to deal with spam:

12. **If you don't recognize the sender, delete the email without reading it.** Then empty your email trash.

2 Things to Do When You Get an Email Chain Letter—and 6 Reasons Why

What to do:

1. **Delete it and empty your email trash.** Or:

2. **Forward it to the FTC's database of unsolicited spam emails at uce@ftc.gov.** The FTC uses the database in its law-enforcement efforts. Then delete it and empty your email trash.

Why:

1. **Many chain emails are illegal scams.** If they involve money or valuable items and promise big returns, watch out. If you start one or send one, you're breaking the law. If you send money, you'll probably

lose it. *A chain letter will never make you rich.* Any claim that a chain email is "legal" or "endorsed by the government" is a lie.

2. **Many chain emails are hoaxes.** A typical hoax email starts with a *hook* to catch your interest. A hook might be something like "Earn cash fast!" or "Save a dying child!" or "Virus alert!" The next part is a *threat*—a warning of something terrible that will happen to you (or the dying child, or your computer) if you don't pass the email on. Then comes the *request,* which usually goes something like this: "Send this to everyone on your email list!" or "Distribute this letter to as many people as possible!"

3. **Many chain emails spread urban myths or legends, or false virus alerts.** Bill Gates does not want to give you money. Sending email to a "dying child" will not save his or her life. No genuine virus alert asks you to "forward this to everyone you know."

4. **Email petitions are pointless.** Most email petitions are armchair activism—a lazy way to try to make a difference in the world. They have no legal power. Plus, when you sign your name and email address, you expose yourself to spammers.

5. **Forwarded email is annoying.** Did you ever receive an email that
   >>>>>>>looks
   >>>>>>>like
   >>>>>>>this?
   Chances are, it came from someone (a friend or family member) who got it from someone, who got it from someone else, who got it from.... Get it? Forwarding jokes, sob stories, "inspiring" stories, prayer chains, friendship letters, etc., is a lazy way to stay in touch with people you care about.

6. **All chain emails waste bandwidth, time, and money.** They can slow down or crash email servers. They clog the Internet with useless junk. Imagine if you forward an email to 10 people. Those 10 people each forward it to 10 more. Seven steps later, that email is on its way to 1 million people!

Learn more about chain email:

- www.ftc.gov/chainmail

Learn more about email hoaxes, urban myths, urban legends, and bogus virus alerts:

- hoaxbusters.ciac.org

- www.symantec.com/avcenter/hoax.html

- www.snopes.com

6 Clues to Decoding a URL

Those long, complicated Web site addresses, or URLs (for Universal Resource Locators), can be confusing. What do they mean? And what can they tell you about a site? Here's a short course on decoding URLs.

http://www.media-awareness.ca/eng/sitemap.html

1. **http** means that this is a hypertext document. Most online documents are.

2. **www** is short for "World Wide Web," where all Web sites reside.

3. **media-awareness.ca** is the domain name of the person or organization hosting the site—in this case, media-awareness. The **.ca** indicates that the site is hosted by a Canadian institution. For a list of country codes, go to www.iana.org/cctld/cctld-whois.htm. *Tip:* Most U.S. site domain names do not end in **.us.** *Examples:* http://www.factmonster.com and http://www.amazon.com.

4. **eng/sitemap.html** maps out the pathway of directories and subdirectories leading to the page you are on. For this particular page on the Media Awareness Network site, **eng/** indicates that you are on the English part of the site. (Many Canadian sites are in both English and French.) The **sitemap** is the name of the page or document you have arrived at. Finally, **html** indicates the code or format that it has been created in.

5. Sometimes (not in this case) you might see a "user" reference, or tilde (~) symbol in a subdirectory, followed by a name. This indicates that you may be on a personal Web page that is being hosted by an ISP (Internet Service Provider).

6. The type of organization behind a Web site can give some clues to its credibility. These are indicated by top-level domain (TLD) codes. Some examples:

   - **.gov** In the U.S., **.gov** applies to federal departments. In Canada, provincial governments use **.gov** followed by a provincial abbreviation and **.ca.**

   - **.edu** In the U.S., **.edu** indicates American colleges and universities offering 4-year degree programs.

   Tip: URLs with **.gov** and **.edu** are often good sources of factual information.

   - **.org, .com,** and **.net** In the early days of the Web, **.org** indicated a wide assortment of groups, including nonprofit organizations; **.com** indicated commercial organizations; and **.net** was intended for organizations directly involved in Internet operations, such as ISPs. Now anyone can apply for and use these letters in their domain names.

In 2000, new TLDs were added to the Internet's domain-name system. They include **.aero** (for the air-transport industry), **.biz** (businesses), **.coop** (cooperatives), **.info** (all uses), **.museum** (museums), **.name** (individuals), and **.pro** (professions).

Note: These clues are just the tip of the iceberg when it comes to decoding URLs. If you're really into this sort of thing and you want to know more, visit your local library and get the latest edition of a book that explains the Internet (examples: *How the Internet Works, The Complete Idiot's Guide to the Internet, The Internet for Dummies*). Or ask the director of the computer lab at your school. Or go to the "How to Read a URL" page at navigators.com/url.html for basic information and links. This page has not been updated for quite some time, so some of the information may be out of date.

6 Ways to Tell if a Web Site is Trustworthy

Anyone can put anything on the Web. Facts and fiction. Truth and lies. Fiction pretending to be facts, and lies presented as truth. How can you tell if a Web site is trustworthy—if the information you find there is credible? Journalists, police, and researchers use five Ws and one H to get the "full" story. You can use them in cyberspace.

1. **Ask yourself: WHO is the source of the information?**

   • Has someone taken responsibility for the content of this Web site?

   • Is information about the author or organization clearly stated?

   • Are there any links to in-depth information about the author or organization?

   • Can you contact the company or author through a real-world postal address or phone number?

   • Can you confirm that the company or author is a credible, authoritative source of information?

   • Can you verify the authority of any of the site's content that is attributed to other sources?

2. **Ask yourself: WHAT are you getting?**

   Is the information biased in any way?

   - Does the site rely on loaded language or broad, unsubstantiated statements?

   - Is emotion used as a means of persuasion?

   - Does the site offer more than one viewpoint?

   - Are there links to other or alternative viewpoints?

   Does the site's information seem thorough and well-organized?

   - Does the site clearly state the topics that it intends to address?

   - Does it follow through on the information it has promised?

   - Does the information seem complete? Consistent?

   - Is the information well-written and easy to understand?

   - Does the Web site offer a list of further in-depth resources or links to such resources?

   - What's the copyright status of material found on the site?

3. **Ask yourself: WHEN was the site created?**

   - Is it important that the information you are seeking be right up to date?

   - Is a reference date provided to show when the material was put online, or when it was last updated?

   - Do the links work?

4. **Ask yourself: WHERE is the site?** Not the real physical location, but the meaning of the URL (Uniform Resource Locator)—the site address. See "6 Clues to Decoding a URL" on pages 163–164.

5. **Ask yourself: WHY are you here?** Before you saddle up and ride into cyberspace, it's a good idea to stop and consider whether the Internet is even the best place to go. Ask yourself:

   - Can I get the information faster off-line?

   - Does the online material I'm finding suit my needs?

   - Am I able to verify this information?

6. **Ask yourself: HOW can you tell what's what?**

   - When in doubt, doubt. Skepticism should be the rule of thumb on the Internet.

- Apply the five W's of cyberspace to the Web sites you visit.

- Double-check your facts and sources—and then check them some more!

- Use Meta-Web information searches to assess the credibility of Web sites. Enter the author's name into a search engine to conduct a quick background check. Or find which sites link to a specific site by going to a search engine like google.com and entering a "link:" command in the Search box, followed by the page's URL.

3 Rules for Doing Internet Research

1. **Know how to use search engines to find what you're looking for.** Search engines sort through millions of Web sites so you don't have to.

   - Teachers, media specialists, librarians, and Web-smart friends and family members can help you learn how to use search engines.

   - If you want to learn on your own, most search-engine Web sites (like google.com and yahoo.com) have special sections with search tips and tutorials.

   - The Search Engine Watch site (www.searchenginewatch.com) lists and describes all of the major search engines and explains how to use them.

2. **Don't be a cybercheat.** Information you find on the Internet is easy to access and copy, but that doesn't mean it's in the "public domain." It belongs to whoever created it.

   - Cutting-and-pasting sentences, paragraphs, or documents from Web sites and other Internet sources (newsgroups, chat rooms, email, etc.) without giving credit is plagiarism.

   - Copying a paper from a "free term paper" site is plagiarism.

   - Buying a paper from a "paper mill" is plagiarism.

   - Although many students cheat, many get caught. If you can find information on the Web, so can your teacher.

   - Many educators subscribe to services that check student papers for plagiarism.

3. **Know how to cite Internet resources.** Give proper credit to any information, ideas, words, or work you find on the Internet and use in your paper.

- Check with your teachers first. They may have specific guidelines they want you to follow.

- Some Web pages have a "Cite This Page" icon or link. Click on it to get a customized citation. Go to factmonster.com for examples.

- Visit your library's reference and look at the latest edition of the *MLA Handbook for Writers of Research Papers, The Columbia Guide to Online Style,* or *Online! A Reference Guide to Using Internet Sources.*

- The publishers of *Online!* host a Web site that includes detailed instructions and examples of citation styles. Go to www.bedford stmartins.com/online/ and click on Citation Styles.

- If you don't have guidelines close at hand, record information about each source now and worry about style later. The more information you have, the better. Here's a list of basics:

  —The name of the author (if available) or source.

  —The title of the document.

  —The date of publication on the Internet. Sometimes this won't be available. Look for a copyright statement instead.

  —The URL (Internet address) of the page where you found the document.

  —The date you accessed the site and read or downloaded the document. (Why? Because many Web sites are updated often, and their content changes.) This is called the "retrieval date."

6 Web Sites That Won't Insult You

www.teencentral.net
An anonymous, password-protected, safe cyber-space for teens to work out their issues. Developed by experts in teen counseling and psychology; professionally monitored; sponsored by KidsPeace, specialists in teen crisis counseling.

www.freevibe.com
Bulletin boards, celebrity interviews, games, polls, and facts about drugs from the National Youth Anti-Drug Media Campaign.

www.shine.com
Promotes activism, cultural harmony, nonviolence, and self-esteem. SHiNE (Seeking Harmony in Neighborhoods Everyday) is the designated youth component of the White House's National Campaign Against Youth Violence.

www.teenadvice.org
Teens ages 13 & up from around the globe help other teens solve problems and deal with life's challenges. This site has been recognized by journalists, Internet guides, educational institutions, and county health departments.

www.teenwire.com
Factual, nonjudgmental sexuality and relationship information from Planned Parenthood of America.

www.youthnoise.com
Invites teens to speak out and take action against gun violence, youth rights, child exploitation, hunger, homelessness, HIV/AIDS, child abuse, hate crimes, intolerance, and more. An initiative of Save the Children Federation, Inc.

12 Ways to Prevent Eye Strain

Staring at a computer screen for long periods of time can cause tired, dry, aching eyes, trouble focusing, and headaches. This collection of symptoms has an official name: Computer Vision Syndrome (CVS). Try these tips to ease your eyes during extended surfing sessions.

1. Take 15-minute breaks every hour or two. Rest or do something away from your computer.

2. Make a conscious effort to refocus your eyes every 10–15 minutes. Look away from the screen and across the room or out the window.

3. Blink more often. Some studies show that people who work at computers blink five times less than normal.

4. Put reference materials (dictionaries, books, etc.) beside and as close to the computer screen as possible. Avoid frequent head and eye movements and focusing changes. Use a copy stand to hold printed pages you need to look at often.

5. Adjust the brightness control or contrast knob on your screen to a comfortable setting. Experts recommend matching the screen to your environment: bright in a bright room, dimmer in dim lighting.

6. Use a computer light that provides indirect lighting on your computer screen.

7. Minimize reflected glare from windows. Use shades, drapes, or blinds.

8. Use a glare filter screen or computer hood. If you wear glasses, ask your optometrist about glare-reducing lens tints and coatings.

9. Put a dimmer on your overhead light switch so you can control the brightness. Reduce the light level in the computer area to about half of the usual level. Use desk lamps for other work.

10. Change the default background color on your browser(s) from bright white to off-white.

11. If a Web site is hard to see, don't squint. Change the colors and/or font sizes—or exit that site and go somewhere else.

12. Have your eyes examined once a year.

Life Lists

Planning Ahead

5 Keys to Success in Life

No matter what your hopes and dreams for the future may be, five key traits are essential to your success. These traits are also the keys to unlocking your potential and reaching your goals.

KEY #1: IMAGINATION

Imagination is: the ability to dream big dreams • creating a vision of how you'd like things to be • believing that all things are possible • finding a way to use obstacles to your advantage • not putting limits on your potential • figuring out how to turn "no" into "yes."

Try this: Give yourself permission to daydream. Keep a journal of your imaginings. Promise yourself to turn at least one dream into reality.

KEY #2: CONFIDENCE

Confidence is: knowing that you have what it takes to reach your goals • a willingness to tackle new challenges • having faith that even things that seem beyond your reach now will someday be attainable • a commitment to keep going, even when times get tough • believing that you can do practically anything you set your mind to • recognizing that your talents and skills are special • putting one foot in front of the other and going for it • knowing you can make mistakes and learn from them, without seeing them as a sign of failure.

Try this: Think about an area of your life where you lack confidence. What steps can you take to improve your confidence? Write these steps down. Take the first step today.

KEY #3: WILLINGNESS TO TAKE RISKS

Being a risk taker is: doing something despite a fear of failing • being honest about your feelings, wants, and needs • enjoying your individuality

170

• going for a goal even though it seems out of your reach • challenging yourself, either physically or mentally • trying something new or different.

Try this: Is there a healthy risk you're thinking about taking? Make two columns on a sheet of paper. Label them "Pros" and "Cons." Write down every reason you can think of for taking the risk—and every reason you can think of for not taking the risk. One list may be so much longer that your decision is obvious. Or the shorter list may have more crucial factors on it. Decide what you'll do.

KEY #4: COURAGE

Courage is: standing up for yourself and others • owning and applying your strengths when facing a difficult situation • doing the right thing, especially when the wrong thing would be easier and more fun • standing apart from the crowd • confronting your problems and asking for help • facing adversity and coming up with a plan to get through it • a willingness to make mistakes • taking a step toward your goal.

Try this: Was there ever a time when your courage failed you? What happened? Knowing what you know now, what would you do differently? Plan to be courageous the next time this (or something similar) happens.

KEY #5: DETERMINATION

Determination is: going for a goal even when some people doubt you • coming back and trying harder at something you've failed at before • persisting with your goals despite the obstacles • revising your plans as needed to adjust to changes and challenges • never giving up.

Try this: Do you know someone who has shown determination in his or her life? What did this person face, and what did he or she do to persevere? How can this person's determination serve as a role model for you? Tell the person—in writing or face-to-face—how much he or she means to you.

12 Ways to Get Control of Your Time

1. **Use a planning calendar.** Write down due dates (homework, projects, long-term assignments), appointments (doctor, dentist), practices, lesson times, birthdays, holidays, school events, special events, vacations, and anything else you don't want to or shouldn't forget. Some people prefer paper calendars; others like handheld computers or PDAs. Use whatever works for you and whatever you can afford. Some businesses and schools give away free planning calendars.

2. **Make a daily Things-to-Do list.** Ideally, your planning calendar should have room for this. If it doesn't, you can use a big sticky note and put it on the page.

   - Write down everything you're supposed to do today.

   - Write down anything you were supposed to do yesterday but didn't get around to.

   - Write down anything you need to do to get ready for the next few days.

   - Prioritize your Things-to-Do list. Rank each task in 1-2-3 or A-B-C order. Do the 1 or A task first, then the 2 or B task, and so on down through your list.

   - Check off each task you complete.

3. **Start each day with planning time.** This shouldn't take more than 10 minutes. Review yesterday's Things-to-Do list for anything you missed. Make today's Things-to-Do list. Look ahead to the next few days; is there anything you should do today to get ready for something coming up? *Tip:* If you fail to plan, you plan to fail.

4. **Include your personal values and goals in your planning.** What's important to you? More time with your family? More time with your friends? Getting fit or staying fit? Volunteering? Learning a new language? Turn hopes and dreams into realities by building them into your daily Things-to-Do list.

5. **Be flexible.** Things change. Give yourself room to adapt to new circumstances and take advantage of new opportunities.

6. **Eliminate tasks you don't need to do, or tasks it's too late to do, or tasks you don't really care about.** Don't clutter your Things-to-Do list with trivial things. Cross them out and forget about them.

7. **Try not to overschedule yourself.** Too many things to do? Review your tasks and activities. Which ones can you live without?

8. **Learn to say no.** Stay focused on your own goals and priorities. What matters most to you? Pleasing other people should not be at the top of your list.

9. **Find and use little chunks of time.** Waiting for a bus, in between classes, just before your favorite TV show—these are all little chunks of time you can put to good use. Choose something small, get it done, and get it out of the way.

10. **Identify time stealers.** What's keeping you from getting things done? Are you spending too much time on the telephone or in chat

rooms? Instant-messaging or emailing your friends? Surfing the Web? Watching TV? Trying to find things in your messy room? Procrastinating? Staring into space?

11. **Conquer procrastination.** Putting things off steals your time and your energy. If there's something big you've been avoiding, break it into smaller steps. Add these steps to your Things-to-Do list and tackle them one at a time.

12. **Plan some time just for fun.** But get your work done first. Free time feels freer when you don't have unfinished business.

> "Time is life. It is irreversible and irreplaceable.
> To waste your time is to waste your life,
> but to master your time is to master your life
> and make the most of it."
> *Alan Lakein*

10 Tips for Procrastinators

1. Allow more time than you think a project will take. For example, if you think writing an essay will take two hours, plan three or even four hours to do it.

2. Set realistic goals, but don't set them in stone. Stay flexible.

3. Divide and conquer. Break down big, intimidating projects into smaller, more manageable steps.

4. Start something *right now* instead of waiting until you feel thoroughly prepared.

5. Make a conscious effort to realize that your paper, project, or whatever can't be perfect. Grasping this fact helps deflate the fear of failure.

6. Begin your day with your most difficult task or the one you enjoy least. The rest of the day will seem easy by comparison.

7. Plan to have fun without feeling guilty. Start with the things you most enjoy doing—the things you usually save for last and don't get around to at all. Then add the things you're supposed to do.

8. Keep a diary of your progress. List the things you accomplish each day. Read it over from time to time and feel proud of what you've done. Reward yourself.

9. Remove distractions from your workspace. Keep food, TV, magazines, games, the Internet, and other temptations out of your way. Don't go to the library and get lost in a book on ancient Egypt when you're looking for information on civil rights.

10. Keep a list of backup projects—things you mean to do when you have time. Once you've tackled your procrastination, you'll have the time to do them.

> "He who hesitates is last."
> **Mae West**

10 Goal-Setting Steps

Yogi Berra once said, "If you don't know where you are going, you might wind up someplace else." Goals help us get where we want to go, do what we want to do, and be what we want to be. Goal-setting is one of the most important life skills you can have. Try this step-by-step process for setting— and reaching—your goals.

1. **List your hopes, dreams, and wishes.** What do you really want? What inspires you? What do you daydream about? If you could do anything, what would it be?

2. **List your values.** What matters to you? What do you care about most? What gives meaning and purpose to your life? What's really important? Think about people who model your values—people you look up to and admire.

3. **List your talents, strengths, and skills.** What are your gifts? Where do you shine? It's okay to list talents, strengths, and skills you're just starting to develop.

4. **Define a goal.** Your goal should relate to your dreams, values, and strengths. In other words, it should be something you want, some- thing that matters, and something you think you can do.

   Give your goal the power of the Three Ps:

   • Keep it *positive*.

   • Make it *personal*.

   • Know it's *possible*.

Make it "SMART":

- <u>S</u>pecific. Nail down the details of your goal.

- <u>M</u>easurable. Define exactly what you intend to accomplish. When a goal is measurable, you know when you have succeeded.

- <u>A</u>ttainable. Your goal should be challenging, but also within your reach. Otherwise, you won't be motivated to strive for it.

- <u>R</u>elevant and <u>R</u>ewarding. Your goal has to mean something to you. It has to be something you want. Otherwise, don't waste your time.

- <u>T</u>imed. Set a date when you'll start working on your goal, and a date when you'll be able to say, "I did it!" These deadlines give you something to aim for and look forward to. If you're going for a long-term goal, you'll need to break it into a series of smaller goals and set deadlines for those, too.

5. **Plan it out.** Some people find that it helps to work backwards, starting with the date you want to reach your goal. Think first in big steps. Break big steps into smaller steps. Make a one-day plan, a one-week plan, a one-month plan, a one-year plan. Brainstorm anything and everything you'll need to reach each step—skills, resources, time, knowledge, information, help from others. What problems might you face? What might prevent you from reaching your goal? Anticipate setbacks and solutions.

6. **Think *performance,* not *outcome.*** Use active words ("do," "learn," "ask," "begin," "attend," "search," "call," "complete") to keep you moving forward. Focus on your own performance. This you can control. The actual outcome might be affected by reasons you can't control. If this happens, and if the outcome is all you care about, you'll feel like a failure.

7. **Write it all down.** Put your plan on paper. Fill in as many details as you can, and leave room for adding more details later. Sign your plan. Now you've made a contract with yourself.

8. **Track your progress.** Each day (or each week, or each month, depending on your goal and how long-term it is), check to see where you are. Have you followed your plan? Are you taking the necessary steps toward your goal? What have you skipped? What have you forgotten? Are you farther along than you thought you would be?

9. **Be flexible.** Revise your plan if needed. It's *your* goal. You can decide how to reach it. Make your plan work for you, not against you.

10. **Reward yourself at each step along the way.** Vary your rewards. Small steps deserve small rewards. Big steps deserve larger rewards.

25 Quotes on Goal-Setting

1. "A goal is a dream with a deadline."—Napoleon Hill

2. "I don't know what the future holds, but I do know who holds the future."—Oprah Winfrey

3. "Your imagination is your preview of life's coming attractions." —Albert Einstein

4. "To fail to plan is to plan to fail."—Benjamin Franklin

5. "A goal properly set is halfway reached."—Zig Ziglar

6. "You don't have to be great to get going, but you have to get going to be great."—Les Brown

7. "It's the possibility of having a dream come true that makes life interesting."—Paulo Coelha

8. "Anything inside that immobilizes me, gets in my way, keeps me from my goals, is all mine."—Wayne Dyer

9. "The ultimate goal should be doing your best and enjoying it." —Peggy Fleming

10. "Obstacles are those frightful things you see when you take your eyes off the goal."—Hannah Moore

11. "Choosing a goal and sticking to it changes everything."—Scott Reed

12. "To accomplish great things, we must not only act, but also dream."—Anatole France

13. "The more you love and accept yourself, the sooner you'll be able to reach your goals."—Florence Griffith Joyner

14. "You have to have a dream so you can get up in the morning." —Billy Wilder

15. "Aim at nothing and you'll succeed."—Anonymous

16. "I've always believed that you can think positive just as well as you can think negative."—Sugar Ray Robinson

17. "Without goals and plans to reach them, you are like a ship that has set sail with no destination."—Fitzhugh Dodson

18. "The purpose of life is a life of purpose."—Robert Byrne

19. "Reach high, for stars lie hidden in your soul. Dream deep, for every dream precedes the goal."—Pamela Vaull Starr

20. "Circumstances may cause interruptions and delays, but never lose sight of your goal."—Mario Andretti

21. "An aim in life is the only fortune worth finding."—Jacqueline Kennedy Onassis

22. "If you're bored with life—you don't get up every morning with a burning desire to do things—you don't have enough goals." —Lou Holtz

23. "When we are motivated by goals that have deep meaning, by dreams that need completion, by pure love that needs expressing, then we truly live life."—Greg Anderson

24. "The achievement of your goal is assured the moment you commit yourself to it."—Mack R. Douglas

25. "One day Alice came to a fork in the road and saw a Cheshire cat in a tree. 'Which road do I take?' she asked. 'Where do you want to go?' was his response. 'I don't know,' Alice answered. 'Then,' said the cat, 'it doesn't matter.'"—Lewis Carroll, *Alice in Wonderland*

10 Reasons Why Goals Are Worth Having

1. **Goals help you be who you want to be.** You can have all the dreams in the world, but if you don't act on them, how will you get where you want to go? When you know how to set a goal and go for it, you chart a path of action that takes you step-by-step toward the future you want.

2. **Goals stretch your comfort zone.** In pursuit of a goal, you may find yourself talking to new people, trying out for a team, performing on stage, making a speech, or doing something else that draws people's attention. Pushing yourself past your normal comfort zone is a great way to grow.

3. **Goals boost your confidence.** When you set a goal and reach it, you prove to yourself and others that you've got what it takes to get things done. Goals not only make you stronger; they also help you feel good about yourself.

4. **Goals give your life purpose. Goals show you—and the world— what you value.** They also give you a sense of direction. When you're going after your goals, you're less likely to spend your days feeling bored or wasting your time.

5. **Goals help you rely on yourself.** You don't have to let other people decide your life for you. You can take charge of your life by setting goals and making a plan to reach them. Once you get into the goal-setting habit, you'll notice that you feel a lot more independent. And the people around you will notice your new independence.

6. **Goals encourage you to trust your decisions.** You're at a point in your life where you're making more decisions at home and at school. Sometimes it's easy to go along with the crowd or be swayed by what other people want you to do. But when you keep your goals in mind, your choices become clearer. You learn to trust your decisions because they're right for *you*.

7. **Goals help you turn the impossible into the possible.** Goal-setting breaks down seemingly out-of-reach dreams into small, manageable, and practical steps. You can turn your "someday" dreams into real-life accomplishments.

8. **Goals prove that you can make a difference.** Are your goals about changing your own life? Are they about changing the lives of others and improving the world? Whether you want to make a difference in your own life or someone else's, goal-setting helps you achieve what you set out to do—one step at a time.

9. **Goals improve your outlook on life.** Goals help you move forward— a positive direction to be going. (Much better than sitting still or getting nowhere at all.) This momentum is a real energizer. You'll feel more positive, guaranteed.

10. **Goals lead to feelings of satisfaction.** Studies have shown that people who set and reach goals perform at higher levels, are more satisfied with themselves, and achieve more. In fact, if you look at the goal-setters you know or admire (friends, family members, teachers, business owners, community leaders, athletes, celebrities), you'll probably see people who are proud of their success and eager to keep aiming for more in life.

"If there's something you want out of life,
you have to go after it.
Can't nobody stop you except yourself."
Kobe Bryant

My Life List

When John Goddard was 15 years old, he thought about all the things he wanted to do and experience during his lifetime. He wrote a "Life List" of 127 goals. Then he set about accomplishing them—more than 100 so far. He has explored the Nile River, become an Eagle Scout, climbed Mt. Kilimanjaro, learned to fly a plane, written a book, read the Bible from cover to cover, and circled the globe four times, to name just a few. A world-renowned explorer and motivational speaker, Goddard is proof that you can do whatever you want—if you set goals. You might use this page to start your own "Life List." Be wild. Be crazy. Don't limit yourself. Goddard didn't, and he has lived a rich and fascinating life.

1. _____
2. _____
3. _____
4. _____
5. _____
6. _____
7. _____
8. _____
9. _____
10. _____
11. _____
12. _____
13. _____
14. _____
15. _____
16. _____
17. _____
18. _____

≡ Who Wouldn't Listen

er people try to set limits for us. They tell us what we can and can't do, and especially what we aren't any good at. Read these examples, then think about people who try to set limits for you. Maybe they're right...but more likely they're wrong.

1. After **Michael Jordan** lost the chance to be North Carolina High School Player of the Year, he was told by his teachers to go into math, "where the money is." Jordan is now a basketball legend and one of the world's wealthiest men.

2. The editor of the *San Francisco Examiner* told a young writer, "I'm sorry, Mr. Kipling, but you just don't know how to use the English language." In 1907, **Rudyard Kipling** was awarded the Nobel Prize for Literature.

3. The head of a drama school advised an aspiring actress to "try another profession. *Any* other." The actress's name was **Lucille Ball.** She went on to star in movies, radio shows, and the hit TV series *I Love Lucy,* which won five Emmy Awards.

4. The manager of the Grand Ole Opry in Nashville, Tennessee, fired a singer after one performance, saying, "You ain't goin' nowhere...son. You ought to go back to drivin' a truck." The singer was **Elvis Presley.**

5. A young newspaper staffer was fired by his editor because he had "no good ideas" and he "doodled too much." His name was **Walt Disney.**

6. When **Robert Jarvik** was rejected by every American medical school he applied to, he went to Italy and attended medical school there for two years. He later returned to the States, earned his M.D. from the University of Utah—and designed the first permanent, totally artificial heart to be implanted in a human.

7. **Madeleine L'Engle's** book *A Wrinkle in Time* was rejected by almost every major publisher before Farrar, Straus, and Giroux agreed to take it—after warning that the book would probably not sell. It won the Newbery Medal in 1963 and is now one of the most beloved children's books of all time.

"Leaders are visionaries with a poorly developed sense of fear and no concept of the odds against them."
Dr. Robert Jarvik

12 Keys to Your Future Career

An old saying goes, "If you don't figure out what you want to do with your life, someone else will." You don't have to decide right this second, but you can start making plans and exploring options. Try these ideas. Some you can do right now; others you may have to wait to do until you're older. Put them on your "to-do" list for the future.

1. **Stay in school.** Sticking it out can sometimes be tough, but don't give up. Get the help you need from teachers, counselors, and advisors. Your future will be very limited if you don't finish high school— and you should plan for college, too.

2. **Meet with your school counselor.** He or she is a good resource for figuring out where you want to go in life. Guidance counselors can give you valuable information about college and university programs, trade and technical schools, scholarships, internships, potential mentors, and leads on part-time jobs. They can also help you plan which classes to take and which extracurricular activities will boost your chances of getting into the college or trade school of your choice.

3. **Open your mind.** Try new things. Experience life. Explore as much as you can. Discover your talents. Learn a new skill. Volunteer. Be curious, and set your sights high.

4. **Read, read, read.** Books open up a world of knowledge. Read biographies of people you admire, and autobiographies of people you find inspiring. Read books on topics that interest you, even if they don't seem to have any direct connection to your future. You may be surprised. Read magazines and newspapers. Keep up with late-breaking news and information.

5. **Surf the Web.** The Internet is an electronic universe loaded with a wealth of information that didn't exist when your parents were thinking about careers. It's a fast and fun way to learn about any topic you can think of.

6. **Get real-world experience.** The only way to find out for sure what you like or what you're good at is to get out in the world and try things. Join a club, participate in student government, volunteer, try out for a sports team, play an instrument, be active in your community. You'll develop confidence, improve your interpersonal skills, and have plenty of things to list on your college applications and résumés when the time comes.

7. **Volunteer.** Offer your time and services to those who need them. Volunteering is good for the spirit, it gives you a chance to make a

positive contribution to your community, and it looks good on college and job applications. Volunteering is also a great way to explore potential careers.

8. **Find a mentor.** A mentor is someone who can offer you guidance in some or all facets of your life. A mentor is someone who can teach you, provide emotional support, help you with moral dilemmas, help you meet challenges and tackle obstacles, give advice, guide you with personal decisions, and impart wisdom. A mentor can be a teacher, a relative, a spiritual leader, a friend of your parents, a senior citizen, an older student, a coach, a neighbor, or anyone else who has time to offer you direction and encouragement. For more information, visit the National Mentoring Partnership's Web site: www.mentoring.org.

9. **Network.** Networking is all about talking to people who can point you in the right direction on your career path. It's an incredibly valuable skill. Put the word out to anyone you can think of—relatives, friends, classmates, teachers, neighbors—that you're interested in learning about a particular topic. They may know someone who knows someone, and before you know it, you've started your own network of connections.

10. **Find an internship.** An internship gives you hands-on experience in a real work environment. It gives you contact with people who could become mentors, references, or future employers. Some internships offer a small salary called a stipend; most don't. Your guidance counselor can help you find something in an area that interests you. Or go to a library and look at the latest edition of *The Internship Bible,* published by the Princeton Review.

11. **Become an apprentice.** An apprenticeship is very similar to an internship. The main difference is that apprentices usually get paid to learn a trade or craft by working side by side with a master craftsperson, technician, or supervisor. Especially if you don't plan to attend a four-year college, this type of experience can give you a head start into a better paying career. For more information about apprenticeships, talk with your guidance counselor. Or go to the library and look at the latest edition of *Ferguson's Guide to Apprenticeship Programs.*

12. **Get a part-time job.** If you're not old enough to do this officially, you can do it unofficially. Baby-sit or mow lawns in your neighborhood. Work after school, on the weekends, during breaks. You'll gain valuable work experience and job skills.

How to Find a Mentor: Tips from the National Mentoring Partnership

A mentor is a wise and trusted friend; a good listener; someone who cares; someone who has been there; someone who can help you get where you want to go. A mentor can help you find a job, prepare for college or other training, explore career possibilities, meet successful people, stay focused on your goals, succeed in school, pursue sports interests, learn how to type and use a computer, and help you deal with problems at home or school...to name just a few reasons why you might want one. To learn more about mentors and mentoring, visit www.mentoring.org. Take the online course on finding a mentor and building a strong relationship with your mentor.

First, think!

1. Think about all of your different needs. Maybe you need help with schoolwork. Maybe you're ready to think about a career or explore college options. Maybe you just need someone to talk to, someone neutral, who will be able to give you good advice.

2. Make some notes about what you'd like to get out of a mentoring relationship. It is easier to ask someone for help if you yourself know what you are asking for.

3. Make a list of all the people you know who might be able to be your mentor or to help you find a mentor. Be sure to consider the full range of possibilities, including family, friends, neighbors, teachers, coaches, club leaders, ministers, and others. Think about what things different people can help you with.

4. Think about how you might approach them. You may want to call on the telephone and arrange a time to meet and talk in person. Or you may want to stop by in an informal way. Ask if this is a convenient time to talk to them for a few minutes and ask for their help.

Next, ask!

Ask the person to be your mentor or to help you find a mentor. Do it! Follow these steps.

1. Tell them what you want from a mentor.

2. Tell them why you thought they would be a good mentor.

3. Ask if they would be willing to be your mentor or to help you find a mentor.

4. If they say "no," they don't have the time, you should say thanks anyway, but perhaps they could suggest someone else to whom you might turn.

5. If they say "yes," set up a time for the two of you to have your first meeting.

If at first you don't succeed, try again. ***Don't give up, and don't get discouraged.*** You may hear a "no" from four different people before you hear that magical "yes" from person number five. Babe Ruth struck out 1,330 times, but he also hit 714 home runs. Jackie Joyner-Kersee overcame chronic asthma to become a double gold medalist at the Olympics in track and field. Don't worry about failing. Worry about the chances you miss when you fail to try.

8 Ways to Make the Most of Your Mentorship

1. **Set goals for your mentorship.** At your first meeting, you may want to take the lead and let your mentor know what you hope to accomplish. Do you want help with your French? Do you want to learn about your mentor's career? Do you need help preparing your college application? Do you just want to talk about life?

2. **Show up for your appointments.** Mentors are busy people, just like you. They're taking time out from their schedules to meet with you, so be sure to respect that. If you're going to be late, or if you'll have to miss a session, be sure to call ahead of time. Treat your mentorship like a job or an important appointment, and you'll be treated as an adult accordingly.

3. **Be assertive.** Practice talking and asking questions in a direct, straightforward way. Don't ask vague questions or make your mentor try to guess what you want or need.

4. **Practice your conversation skills.** Avoid answering questions with "yeah" and "uh-huh." Instead, offer as much information as you can, and be sure to ask questions that will show interest in your mentor.

5. **Listen actively.** Pay attention to what your mentor is saying; avoid letting your mind wander. Nod your head to show that you understand.

6. **Keep an open mind.** If your mentor suggests an activity that you've never tried or you don't think you'll like, give it a try anyway. What's the worst that could happen? Next time, you can suggest an activity

you'd enjoy more. Be open to new experiences; you may be surprised by what you learn.

7. **Be persistent.** Don't give up on your mentorship if things aren't as you imagine right away. Like all worthwhile pursuits, mentorships require time and effort. If the mentorship isn't working out in the beginning, stick it out for a few more meetings and talk to your mentor about how to improve the relationship. Be sure to give it your all before even thinking about calling it quits.

8. **Be appreciative.** Let your mentor know how much the time you spend together means to you. Every so often, write your mentor a note of appreciation or send a thank-you card.

Follow Your Muse: 4 Steps to Success

Maybe you dream of acting in a play someday, or performing in a band, or seeing your paintings in a gallery or museum. Can you make your dream come true? It's up to you.

1. Write down something creative you've always dreamed of doing. Would you like to paint a mural? Write a screenplay? Play the guitar? What?

2. List all the reasons you haven't yet pursued your dream. Be as detailed and complete as you can.

3. Examine your list. How many of the obstacles are *practical* (lack of money or time, no place to work) and how many are *motivational* (afraid to try, haven't looked for a teacher)? Identify each type. Are you standing in the way of your own dream? Even factors seemingly "outside" of you, such as a lack of money or equipment, are surmountable.

   Example: You want to take piano lessons, but you can't afford it. If it's really your dream, you can make it happen. Here are some starter ideas:

   • Find a student at your school who already plays piano and ask him if he'll teach you. His rates will be a fraction of those of a professional teacher.

   • Contact music schools in your area. See if they offer scholarships.

   • Talk to people until you get the names of accomplished amateurs who play piano for enjoyment. They may teach you for free.

- Make a list of all the piano teachers in your area. (You can get names by calling music schools, asking musicians you know, and/or talking to your own school's orchestra, band, or choir leader.) Call every teacher on the list. Explain your situation and offer to barter for lessons. You could care for their lawn, shovel snow, wash cars, baby-sit, or do carpentry, housecleaning, shopping, or laundry.

Adults are impressed by teenagers who are motivated and eager to learn. If you're persistent, you *will* find someone who wants to help.

4. Go over your list of obstacles and brainstorm ways to overcome them. If you *really* want to do something, you can. It's just a question of how much you want it.

"Success breeds confidence."
Beryl Markham

Saving the World

10 Myths About Teens—
and How to Set the Record Straight

Ever walk into the mall with your friends and notice how the sales clerk is watching you like a hawk? Are you sick of articles, books, and so-called "news" about how bad, dangerous, irresponsible, self-absorbed, and lazy teens are today? What about movies that portray teens as sex-crazed party animals dying to be popular? Maybe you've heard these myths about teens...

1. Teens can't handle responsibility, or complex and serious issues like sex, drugs, death, or illness.

2. All teenage girls are boy-crazy.

3. Teens can't form a complete, like, sentence.

4. Every new interest you decide to explore is "just a phase."

5. All teens believe the world revolves around them, and their favorite words are "me," "my," and "I."

6. Teenage girls are either rolling their eyes, snapping their gum, or flipping their hair.

7. All teens have a telephone glued to their ear at all times.

8. All teenage guys have raging hormones.

9. All teens are troublemakers and juvenile delinquents.

10. The biggest problem you have is deciding what to wear.

How can you set the record straight and prove the world wrong? Try these ideas:

Speak out. If you see teens being stereotyped in a newspaper or magazine article, write a letter to the editor. Let them know why you think they are making unfair assumptions about teens.

Get involved. Make your own media! Write a zine, read at a poetry slam, do a public access television show, or publish your opinion in your school or local newspaper. Be a positive contributor to your community. Join volunteer activities, or start an activist group of your own.

Take a stand. Defy the stereotypes. Show your individuality, and nurture your unique talents. Don't be one of the numbers, and avoid people who treat you like one.

10 Ways to Handle Hate Words and Slurs

1. **Stand up for yourself.** If someone uses a slur, calls you a name, teases you, or harasses you, you might say, "It's not okay to say that. I'm not going to listen to you anymore."

2. **Confront someone with confidence.** If someone calls you a name, ask the person what he means by that or why he talks that way. His response will probably sound stupid to you and everyone else. Look the person in the eye to show that you're not backing down.

3. **Stand up for someone else.** If you see someone being slurred, teased, or harassed, stand up to the person who's doing it and tell her to stop. Let her know that you don't agree with her words or actions.

4. **Support the victim.** Ask the person to walk with you or sit with you at lunch. Talk with him about the incident. If he feels threatened by it, offer to go with him to tell a teacher, the principal, or another adult what happened.

5. **Know when to walk away.** If someone picks on you and you sense you're in danger of being physically hurt, have the courage to walk away. Immediately walk toward other people or a classroom, so you're less likely to be followed.

6. **Talk with your friends to get some perspective.** Your friends can let you know that it's not just you who's insulted or angered by hurtful words. Friends can also boost your confidence enough to confront someone or report an incident, or even help you do those things.

7. **Report the incident.** The adults at your school need to know what's going on. Go to a teacher, a guidance counselor, a school administrator, or the principal. Whether you file a formal report or not, these people can help you—and you'll be helping them by letting them know what's really happening in school.

8. **Tell your parents or guardians.** By talking to them about these incidents, you'll get the benefit of an adult perspective, while warning them about any dangers you're facing at school. If needed, a parent or guardian can step in and talk to school personnel.

9. **Spread the word.** Look at the entire culture of your school to see if it supports the use of slurs. If it does, do something about it. Work to promote tolerance and social change at school and in your community.

10. **Remember that you're not alone.** When you're the victim of hate words or slurs, you may feel singled out and alone. But you're not. Nearly every teen is slurred or labeled at some point. Knowing this may give you the strength to believe in yourself.

> "People hate what they don't understand."
> *Eva Le Gallienne*

5 Tips for Talking Nice

This week, get your friends together and pick one day to go 24 hours without saying anything mean to or about anyone else. Not one mean thing! Think you're up to the challenge? It's easier than it sounds. These tips will help.

1. Don't judge people by the way they dress, the music they listen to, the hobbies they have, or the sports they do—or don't—play. Judge them by what really matters—how they act and what they say. Better yet, don't judge them at all.

2. You don't have to like everyone you meet, but you can only dislike people you actually get to know. Every time you meet someone, give him or her a chance. Treat the person as you would want the person to treat you. You might be surprised by how many people will do the same with you.

3. When you need to express your feelings, make sure you do it in a non-blaming way.

4. When a problem occurs, make sure you attack the problem, not the person.

5. When a problem occurs, stop for a second and recognize what role you played in creating the conflict.

8 Ways to Combat Hate from the Anti-Defamation League

Did you know that most hate crimes in America are committed by people under the age of 20? Fight back against hate. Take the "Close the Book on Hate" Campaign Pledge from the Anti-Defamation League, an organization that's been combating anti-Semitism and bigotry of all kinds since 1913. Learn more about the ADL at www.adl.org.

1. I pledge from this day onward to do my best to interrupt prejudice and to stop those who, because of hate, would hurt, harass, or violate the civil rights of anyone.

2. I will try at all times to be aware of my own biases against people who are different from myself.

3. I will ask questions about cultures, religions and races that I don't understand.

4. I will speak out against anyone who mocks, seeks to intimidate or actually hurts someone of a different race, religion, ethnic group, or sexual orientation.

5. I will reach out to support those who are targets of harassment.

6. I will think about specific ways my school, other students and my community can promote respect for people and create a prejudice-free zone.

7. I firmly believe that one person can make a difference and that no person can be an "innocent bystander" when it comes to opposing hate.

8. By signing this pledge, I recognize that respect for individual dignity, achieving equality and opposing anti-Semitism, racism, ethnic bigotry, homophobia, or any other form of hatred is a non-negotiable responsibility of all people.

_____

My Signature

_____

Witness Signature

_____

Date

12 Ways to Become More Tolerant from the Southern Poverty Law Center

The more we learn about people who are different from us, the more tolerant, accepting, and welcoming we become. It's easy to dislike or even hate someone we don't know and may fear. It's hard to dislike or hate someone we know as a friend. Try these ideas from the Southern Poverty Law Center, a nonprofit organization that combats hate, intolerance, and discrimination. For more ideas, visit their Web site: www.tolerance.org.

1. Attend a play, listen to music, or go to a dance performance by artists whose race or ethnicity is different from your own.

2. Volunteer at a local social services organization.

3. Attend services at a variety of churches, synagogues, and temples to learn about different faiths.

4. Ask a person of another cultural heritage to teach you how to perform a traditional dance or cook a traditional meal.

5. Learn sign language.

6. Take a conversation course in another language that is spoken in your community.

7. Speak up when you hear slurs. Let people know that bias speech is always unacceptable.

8. Research your family history. Share information about your heritage in talks with others.

9. List all the stereotypes you can—positive and negative—about a particular group. Are these stereotypes reflected in your actions?

10. Think about how you appear to others. List personality traits that are compatible with tolerance (*examples:* compassion, curiosity, openness). List those that seem incompatible with tolerance (*examples:* jealousy, bossiness, perfectionism).

11. Create a "diversity profile" of your friends and acquaintances. Set the goal of expanding it by next year.

12. Read a book or watch a movie about another culture.

3 Reasons to Become More Tolerant

1. **The more you learn, the less you fear.** Have you ever had a precon-
   ceived notion about a person, then found out you were wrong once
   you got to know him or her? That's how tolerance begins. Once you
   learn you have nothing to fear, you become willing to try more new
   things, ideas, and people. As you practice tolerance and become more
   comfortable with differences by experiencing them firsthand through
   relationships, curiosity replaces fear. Your mind opens. You start
   respecting other people's opinions, practices, and behaviors. You gain
   a deeper understanding of yourself and others. It's easy to hate a
   stereotype, hard to hate someone you know and understand.

2. **Tolerant people are more self-confident and comfortable in all
   kinds of situations.** Who wouldn't like to feel safer and more
   secure anytime, anywhere? Studies have shown that people who get
   along with different kinds of people are emotionally and physically
   healthier—and more successful in their careers—than those who
   don't.

3. **Tolerance makes life more interesting.** What if you were allowed to
   read books by only one author? If you had to wear blue jeans, white
   T-shirts, and black sneakers every day? What if you were never allowed
   to try anything new, not even a new soft drink or video game? What
   if all of your friends looked, thought, and behaved exactly alike?
   What if they all had to be the same age, religion, gender, and race?
   Bo-ring. That's what life without diversity would be like.

"The highest result of education is tolerance."
Helen Keller

13 Things You Can Do to Promote Diversity

Help promote diversity with this starter list of ideas. Some require only individual action; some require concerted effort. Consider this list a launching pad—there is a lot more that can be done.

1. Don't ignore it! Do not let a racist incident pass without remark. To do so sends the message that you are in agreement with such behaviors and attitudes. The intervention may not always take place at the exact time or place of the incident, but it must be brought up as soon as appropriate.

2. Look inside yourself for prejudices and stereotypes and pledge to keep an open mind.

3. Be a leader. Welcome new students to your school. Cross any racial or ethnic lines to make students feel safe and be an example for others.

4. Educate yourself. Expose yourself to new information and experiences.

5. Be aware of your own hesitancies to intervene in uncomfortable situations. Confront your own fears about interrupting discrimination, set your priorities, and take action.

6. Show a different movie each week after school about another culture to both highlight similarities and celebrate differences among all cultures.

7. Create a diverse coalition. Gather together students, teachers, counselors, and administrators for a forum discussing racism within your school—its effects and possible solutions. Communication is the key to growth and change.

8. Bring ethnic art to your school for a show to encourage diversity and awareness. Have your newspaper run a story to promote it as a celebration of harmony and unity.

9. Report hate crimes immediately to a teacher or police officer.

10. Throughout the school year, choose one day a month to celebrate a different culture at an after-school fair. Contact administrators for permission and help. Get your newspaper to print stories and information on the culture of that day. Celebrate diversity with ethnic foods, music, and dance.

11. Acknowledge and appreciate differences in people and groups.

12. Remember that issues of human dignity, equality, and safety are non-negotiable.

13. Recognize that fighting the "isms" is a long-term struggle, so try not to get too frustrated. The "isms" won't be eradicated in a day or from one "multicultural presentation." It is a constant process of change and growth.

11 Ways to Remember 9/11

Our world changed forever on September 11, 2001, when thousands of people died at the World Trade Center, the Pentagon, and in Pennsylvania onboard United Airlines Flight 93. September 11 is now a national day of remembrance. You may have your own ways to remember, or you may want to try one or more of these ideas.

1. Get together with your family, friends, or neighbors, or take time alone to reflect.

2. Light a candle. The flame of the candle symbolizes the light of hope, liberty, and remembrance. Your personal candlelight vigil can be formal or informal.

3. Ring a bell. The ringing of the bell three times represents the three sites that were attacked. If you don't have a bell, you can tap a glass as you say: "With honor and respect, we remember those who died at the World Trade Center." (Bell rings.) "Those who died at the Pentagon." (Bell rings.) "Those who died on United Flight 93 in Pennsylvania." (Bell rings.)

4. Gather with loved ones for dinner.

5. Say a prayer for the families who lost loved ones.

6. Say a prayer for our nation.

7. Tell a family member, "I love you."

8. Tell your friends that you appreciate them.

9. Heal a rift with a family member or friend.

10. Display your American flag.

11. Send a donation to your favorite charity in honor of those who died, the families who grieve, and the ordinary Americans who responded with extraordinary courage.

A Kind Act I Can Do

Use this list to plan something kind to do for someone else. You'll feel better, the other person will feel better, and your action, no matter how small or simple it seems, will help make the world a better place.

1. The person's name:

_____

2. What I'll do:

_____

3. What (if anything) I'll need:

_____

4. When I'll do it:

_____

5. Where I'll do it:

_____

After you do the kind act, write down what happened, how you felt, how you think the other person felt, or anything else you want to remember about your action and the results.

_____

_____

_____

Will you do something like this again? YES ❐ NO ❐ Why or why not?

_____

_____

"You cannot do a kindness too soon,
for you never know how soon it will be too late."
Ralph Waldo Emerson

5 Ways to Fight Ad Creep

Americans are drowning in advertising. According to John Forde, host of public television's Mental Engineering, *"The average American kid sees half a million commercials between birth and age 18." It's estimated that we see up to 3,000 advertisements each day. What can you do? More than you think.*

1. Refuse to be part of ad creep. How many logos are you wearing right now? Who's paying you to be a walking billboard?

2. The next time you go shopping for a basic—like a black T-shirt—find one with your favorite logo. Then find one with *no* logo. Compare prices. Chances are, the logo-free shirt costs less. Do you really want to pay for the privilege of advertising a company's products? What's in it for you?

3. Try this idea from the Center for Commercial-Free Public Education (www.commercialfree.org): Get a group together and walk through your school. Look for sponsored educational materials, posters and textbooks with company names and ads, banner ads on computers, Channel One, soda machines, etc. Take pictures, collect examples, and write it all down. Use this information to show your local school board members how much commercialism is in your district.

4. Tired of ads before movies, at the ATM, on your computer, on the sidewalks, on lampposts, on blimps, on buses, in the bathroom at your favorite restaurant? If you are, complain. Write to the advertisers and tell them what you think. Visit the BadAds Web site (www.badads.org) for tons of ideas and helpful links.

5. Keep up with current anti-ad-creep actions by Commercial Alert, a nonprofit organization whose mission is "to keep the commercial culture within its proper sphere, and to prevent it from exploiting children and subverting the higher values of family, community, environmental integrity and democracy." Visit www.commercialalert.org to learn about the latest corporate shenanigans—and what you can do.

35 Possible Places to Volunteer

You'd like to volunteer, but you're not sure where to go or what to do. Start by deciding what you like, then go from there. These lists will help you head in the right direction.

If you like being around people, consider volunteering at:

1. a place of worship
2. a nursing home
3. a childcare center
4. a retirement center
5. a day camp
6. an elementary school
7. the Boys and Girls Clubs
8. the YMCA/YWCA
9. the Girl Scouts or Boy Scouts of America
10. a hospital
11. a recreation or community center

If you like animals, consider volunteering at:

12. a veterinary clinic
13. an animal shelter
14. a zoo
15. an aquarium
16. a ranch or farm
17. an equestrian center
18. an animal training facility
19. a grooming salon

If you love being outdoors, consider volunteering at:

20. a botanical society
21. a national or local park
22. a ranger station
23. a beach or other environmental clean-up area
24. the conservation corps
25. an environmental organization
26. an outdoor educational facility
27. a nature center

If working to better humanity is your calling, consider volunteering at:

28. a place of worship
29. a food bank
30. a homeless shelter
31. a hospital or clinic
32. a blood drive
33. a community recycling center
34. a political fundraising event
35. a childcare center

18 Great Reasons to Serve Others

Serving others—for example, by getting involved in a service organization—helps you, too. When Independent Sector, a coalition of leading nonprofits, foundations, and corporations, surveyed youth who serve, the students reported 18 benefits of their volunteer experience. Which ones would you like to have in your life?

1. I learned to respect others.
2. I learned to be helpful and kind.
3. I learned how to get along with and relate to others.
4. I gained satisfaction from helping others.
5. I learned to understand people who are different from me.
6. I learned how to relate to children.
7. I'm a better person now.
8. I learned new skills.
9. I developed leadership skills.
10. I'm more patient with others.
11. I understand more about how voluntary organizations work.
12. I understand more about good citizenship.
13. I explored or learned about career options.
14. I did better in school/my grades improved.
15. I've developed new career goals.
16. I'm more aware about programs in my community.
17. I learned how to help solve community problems.
18. I understand more about how government works.

5 National Days of Service

Volunteering is cool—so cool that nearly three out of five American teenagers volunteer. Teens today are more tolerant and thoughtful than ever, and less self-centered; they want to help others. Millions of teens take part in these national days of service.

National Youth Service Day
www.ysa.org/nysd
Held each April. The largest service event in the world.

Make a Difference Day
makeadifferenceday.com
Held the fourth Saturday of every October. A celebration of neighbors helping neighbors, during which millions of people accomplish thousands of service projects.

Martin Luther King, Jr. Day of Service
www.mlkday.org
Held on the third Monday of every January—on Martin Luther King, Jr. Day, a national holiday. Thousands of Americans remember Dr. King by making this "a day *on,* not a day off" and serving in their communities.

Global Youth Service Days
www.gysd.net
Held each April. The world's largest celebration of young people making a difference.

Join Hands Day
www.joinhandsday.org
Held on the third Saturday of every June. This day brings youth and adults together to improve their own neighborhoods and communities.

> "Everybody can be great,
> because everybody can serve."
> Martin Luther King, Jr.

IO National Programs That Promote Youth Service

When you're ready to start serving others, contact one or more of these programs.

SERVEnet
www.servenet.org
The premier Web site on service and volunteering. Enter your ZIP code, city, skills, interests, and availability, and be matched with organizations that need help. You can even be a "virtual volunteer," working from home on your computer.
See also: www.networkforgood.org; www.volunteermatch.org.

Youth Service America
www.ysa.org
A resource center and premier alliance of 300+ organizations committed to increasing the quantity and quality of opportunities for young Americans to serve locally, nationally, or globally.

USA Freedom Corps
www.usafreedomcorps.gov
Launched on January 29, 2002, as part of President George W. Bush's State of the Union Address, USAFC is a clearinghouse of volunteer opportunities.

Do Something!
www.dosomething.org
Funds and trains teens to be leaders in their communities. The Web site allows you to apply for grants and awards, get new volunteering ideas, and read inspiring stories of other young volunteers.

Points of Light Foundation and Volunteer Center National Network
www.pointsoflight.org
A national, nonpartisan, nonprofit organization that promotes volunteerism. Points of Light advocates community service through a partnership with the Volunteer Center National Network. Enter your ZIP code at the Web site to find the Volunteer Center nearest you, or call 1-800-VOLUNTEER (1-800-865-8683).

Corporation for National and Community Service
www.nationalservice.org
Engages Americans of all ages and backgrounds in service to help strengthen communities. The home of AmeriCorps, Senior Corps, and Learn and Serve America.

Participate America Foundation
www.participateamerica.org
Organizes and coordinates National Civic Participation Week in September,
created by the United States Senate as a way to honor those who lost
their lives on September 11, 2001.

Youth as Resources
www.yar.org
Community-based YAR programs, governed by a board of youth and adults,
provide grants to young people to design and carry out service projects.

Youth Volunteer Corps of America
www.yvca.org
The only national youth service program dedicating to providing volunteer opportunities for kids ages 11–18.

National Youth Leadership Council
www.nylc.org
Works with adults and youth to support service learning.

> "There is nothing to make you like other human beings
> so much as doing things for them."
> Zora Neale Hurston

8 Steps to Volunteering as a Family

*Volunteering as a family will bring your family closer. You don't have to com-
mit to a large project. Service can be as simple as visiting someone who's
homebound, picking up litter in a park, shoveling snow for an elderly neighbor, or baking cookies for the family across the hall. When you're ready for a
bigger commitment, try these suggestions from Susan J. Ellis, president of
Energize, Inc., an international training, consulting, and publishing firm spe-
cializing in volunteerism. Find them on the Web at www.energizeinc.com.*

1. Have a family meeting to consider this whole idea. Make sure everyone, no matter how young, participates in the discussion.

2. Make a list of all the volunteering each member of the family is doing
   now. Would the others like to help with any of these activities?

3. What causes interest you? Allow everyone to suggest a community
   problem of concern to him or her. If some of the ideas intrigue the

whole family, start exploring what organizations in your community are already working on these. Use the Yellow Pages, go to the library, search the Internet, or visit the Volunteer Center. To find the Volunteer Center nearest you, visit www.pointsoflight.org and enter your ZIP code, or call 1-800-VOLUNTEER (1-800-865-8683).

4. Consider what types of work everyone wants to do. Make two lists: one for Things We Know How to Do and one for Things We Would Like to Learn How to Do. Make sure something is listed for each member of the family. (This is a great opportunity to acknowledge each other's talents. The lists will also prove helpful when you interview with an agency.)

5. Call several organizations for appointments and screen your options. See whether the agency representatives are comfortable talking to children and teens as well as to adults. Ask if the agency has something meaningful for you to do as a group.

6. You may want to begin with a one-time activity. This will test the water to see how everyone likes volunteering together.

7. Once you commit to a volunteer project, take it seriously. Talk about it during the week and plan ahead to do it, even when things get hectic.

8. Enjoy the many benefits of volunteering as a family: spending quality time together, getting to know each other in new ways, demonstrating skills and learning new ones (which builds mutual respect), working together toward the same goals—and having something to talk about all week!

7 Ways to Connect with Others Who Care

The Web is home to vast amounts of information, links, tips, advice, contacts, stories, and more about service and volunteering. Surf these sites to learn, network, and discover projects and causes that interest you.

EarthYouth.net
earthyouth.takingitglobal.org
A network of young people taking action for a more sustainable planet.

Global Youth Connect
globalyouthconnect.org
A global movement of youth acting together for compassion, human rights, and responsibilities.

Idealist
www.idealist.org
A huge directory of nonprofit and volunteering resources. Search or browse over 29,000 nonprofit and community organizations in 153 countries; find volunteer opportunities in your community and around the world.

iEarn
www.iearn.org
A global network that enables young people to use the Internet and other new technologies to learn and make a difference in the world. iEarn stands for International Education and Resource Network.

TakingITGlobal
www.takingitglobal.org
An international network of youth, organizations, mentors, and initiatives working toward common goals.

UNICEF Voices of Youth
www.unicef.org/voy
An electronic discussion about the future. Give your views on current global issues; look at ways to take action in your own community.

YouthActionNet
www.youthactionnet.org
A virtual space where young people can share lessons, stories, information, and advice on how to lead effective change.

8 Steps to a Service Project from the Points of Light Foundation

You, too, can be part of the solution. Follow these steps to make a difference in your community. For more information, visit www.pointsoflight.org.

1. **RECRUIT** other young people who want to help plan the project. Find allies. Remember that you are not alone. There are all kinds of people and groups who are already trying to create change in your community. Connect with them:

   Volunteer Centers—are a key resource for volunteer involvement in a community. They promote volunteerism, train and assist nonprofit organizations, recruit and refer volunteers to opportunities, recognize volunteers, and implement numerous programs designed to help solve specific community problems. Find a Volunteer Center near you. Visit www.pointsoflight.org or call 1-800-VOLUNTEER (1-800-865-8683).

Schools—Aside from being a great resource for potential allies like teachers and administrators, schools also promote service either through extracurricular clubs or through service-learning (the connection between service and classroom curriculum). Schools also have available supplies, space, phones, computers, and other resources.

Community-Based Organizations—Community-based organizations can range from a council on aging, to a local hospital, environmental agency, or a homeless shelter. As you look at these organizations, keep in mind their purpose and how the issue you identified connects with that purpose. Research the Yellow Pages or contact your town/city hall, Volunteer Center, or United Way for information about these organizations.

Government Agencies—This may include local elected officials or the departments that provide the services. If, for example, you are interested in coaching little league or soccer, the city or county parks and recreation department often run these programs. Or, if you are interested in starting a recycling program in your school, your city or county government solid waste department may be responsible for recycling in the city.

Businesses—Many businesses are taking an active part in revitalizing communities. Some even have their own employee volunteer and philanthropy programs. You can ask local businesses for help in providing materials, money, people-power, and know-how. Don't ignore large companies who may have offices or factories in your area.

2. **GET TO KNOW EACH OTHER.** Use team-building activities to get to know the people you are working with. Your team will be working closely together for a significant period of time, so make sure your team knows each other.

3. **IDENTIFY ISSUES** that you and others want to change, or issues that are confronting your community.

To focus your interest:

- Examine what you see and talk to other people. Is the water undrinkable? Are there few jobs or activities for young people? Are AIDS cases among teens in your community on the rise? Ask what causes these problems. Talk to other young people, parents, and teachers about the issue and why it exists.

- What interests and abilities do you have? Look inside yourself. Think about who you are and what you love to do. Perhaps you're an outgoing person, or have a passion for music, or like using your hands. If you connect your vision to your personal life it will make your work fulfilling. If you're athletic, for example, you may use your abilities to organize and train youth with disabilities in a Jr. Special Olympics.

To help you get started:

- Write down all of your talents, hobbies, and interests.

- Pick a social issue and see if you can invent a way for your personal interest to be used in a campaign or project with this issue.

4. **ANALYZE WHY** this is a need. Figure out why this problem is an issue. What's the cause of the problem you choose to solve? Research who else is working on the issue. They might be able to help you by giving you resources or even by joining your team.

Do some research and ask yourself and your community:

- If resources were unlimited, what would you like to see in your community?

- What are the problems that present a great danger?

- What are some of the root causes of these problems?

- What are some action steps that can be taken?

5. **SELECT A PROJECT.** Consider how much time you will need and how much time you have. How many people will be involved? Where will the project take place, and how will you get to the project site? Who will supervise?

6. **DEVELOP AN ACTION PLAN.** While you may be able to work with others who are already involved in a project, you may have to start something on your own. Below are some things you should think about when planning a project on your own:

What is the goal of the project? Think about what you are trying to achieve.

Who is the project leader? It is always important to have a point person and a clear understanding of who is in charge. Think about any help you might need from adults you know to lead the project.

Who else do you need to help you? Think about adult help you will need or other volunteers you might need.

Where will the service project take place? If, for example, you are organizing a group to work with a community-based organization, make sure you provide directions to get there. If you are conducting a project that requires you to get a collection spot, try asking your school, local community center, or place of worship for available space.

What supplies do you need? Will the project require any supplies? If so, think of who can donate them. If, for example, you are making books for children in the local homeless shelter, see if the art class can donate leftover materials such as paper, paint, markers, scissors, or other craft items. If you are painting an elderly person's house, you may need paint, paint brushes, plastic sheeting, and tape. Check to see if the local hobby store would be willing to donate supplies.

What money do you need? Be creative in finding the funds you will need. This may be to cover supply costs or to help transport volunteers to the service project location. Aside from getting donated items, have a car wash to raise money, or ask local businesses to help you out in exchange for sponsorship.

How will you get there? Public transportation and car pools are the two most common solutions. You can also approach bus or van services, senior citizens' groups, schools, and local civic groups for help.

Liability and safety issues. Think about the safety issues involved.

- Have your volunteers sign a permission slip, if needed.

- Make sure you have names and phone numbers of who to contact in case of an emergency.

- Make sure you have a first aid kit.

- If you are using equipment, make sure to provide training on how to use it.

- Make sure you also have some adult help in case something goes wrong.

7. **CONDUCT THE PROJECT.** Put into action the plan you have selected and carefully planned. Remember, you are working to solve a problem or an issue confronting your community, so keep in mind safety first, fun second!

8. **REFLECT AND CELEBRATE** your service and what you accomplished.

    Celebration and Recognition. Make sure to recognize and celebrate the service effort of all your volunteers. You can do this through a simple "thank you," or an event like a pizza party. People like to feel appreciated for their efforts and to know that such efforts were important and of value to the community.

    Reflection and Evaluation. It is important to understand what you did through your service, both for yourself and for your community. Think about what you learned about the issue and yourself. For instance, has your attitude about homelessness changed after working in a soup kitchen, or did you know you could teach before tutoring a younger child?

8 Do's and Don'ts of Successful Volunteering from the Prudential Spirit of Community Awards

Each year, the Prudential Spirit of Community Awards recognize young people ages 11–18 for outstanding community service. Learn more on the Web at www.prudential.com (type "Spirit of Community Awards" in the Search window).

1. **DO** be flexible. It is rare to find the "perfect" fit right away. Keep an open mind—you might discover something new that interests you.

2. **DO** be persistent. Volunteer coordinators are often busy, so don't assume they're not interested in you if they don't call you right away.

3. **DO** attend orientation meetings. Keep in mind that informed volunteers are the best volunteers. These meetings will help you do the best job possible.

4. **DO** take necessary training classes. Ask about them before you decide to get involved and be prepared to learn what will be needed.

5. **DO** be responsible. Show up on time and follow through with your commitments. People will be depending on you.

6. **DON'T** expect to start at the top. You have to work hard and prove your worth before you are given more responsibility.

7. **DON'T** think that volunteering has to be a group effort. You can start your own volunteer program and do it on your own time.

8. **DO** expect to get plenty of personal enjoyment and satisfaction from your volunteer experiences.

> "I slept and dreamt that life was joy.
> I awoke and saw that life was service.
> I acted and behold, service was joy."
> *Rabindranath Tagore*

11 Ways to Make Service Last from Youth Service America

Service is a great way to participate in your community. But what good is today's project if the next generation of volunteers has to clean up the same dirty river or tutor in the same substandard schools? Follow these tips to increase the impact of volunteer work in your community.

1. Work for government policies that support volunteer service. Urge officials to change old laws and policies or write new ones. Write letters to the editor of your local paper about the issues and potential solutions.

2. Invite local officials to participate in your service activities. Educate them about your perspective on the issue and ask for their support.

3. Invite the local newspaper, television station, or radio station to cover your volunteer project.

4. Create a Web site. Educate your school or community about an issue.

5. Organize a debate, town hall meeting, or youth forum to engage local leaders and young people in discussion about youth issues.

6. Map your community's problems and assets. Share the results with local officials.

7. Volunteer for an issue or for a candidate's campaign.

8. Ask your teacher or school to offer class credit for volunteer work at a local government or nonprofit agency.

9. Launch a letter-writing campaign to your local or national government officials in support of legislation that empowers youth.

10. Work with local officials to increase funding for youth activities in your community.

11. If you are old enough to do so, REGISTER AND VOTE in the next election.

Focus on You

10 Reasons Why You Need Self-Esteem

Positive self-esteem is not about being stuck-up or feeling superior to other people. It's about being proud of yourself for who you are—your values and beliefs, actions and accomplishments. It comes from the inside, not the outside. Positive self-esteem is an important psychological skill. Here's why.

When you have self-esteem:

1. You're more likely to take positive risks. You know you might fail, but you also know you might succeed.

2. You're less likely to take negative risks. You respect yourself too much to put yourself in danger.

3. You're more likely to resist negative peer pressure.

4. You're less likely to go along with the crowd just to fit in.

5. You're strong. You can cope with the changes and challenges of life.

6. You're resilient. You can bounce back when life pounds you down with problems, disappointments, or failures.

7. You set goals for yourself and strive to reach them.

8. You feel free to explore your creativity and make the most of your talents, skills, and abilities.

9. You can let yourself be happy because you know you're worth it.

10. You have a positive attitude toward life.

"A strong, positive self-image is the best possible preparation for success in life."
Dr. Joyce Brothers

Sol Gordon's
7 Cardinal Mistakes of Self-Esteem

Sol Gordon is Professor Emeritus of Child and Family Studies at Syracuse University. He has written many books including The Teenage Survival Book *and* How Can You Tell If You're Really in Love? *Dr. Gordon has this to say about low self-esteem: "Everybody has* tzuris *(that's Yiddish for 'troubles'), but people who feel inferior seem to have more than their share. Eleanor Roosevelt once said, 'No one can make you feel inferior without your consent.' Why, in fact, so many people give their consent is an enduring mystery." Are you making some of these self-esteem mistakes?*

1. **Comparing yourself unfavorably to others.** There will always be people who appear to be handsomer, prettier, richer, luckier, and better-educated than you. What's the point of comparing? We are all created equal. We are all created to serve in a special way.

2. **Feeling you won't amount to much unless....** Choose your favorite ending to this sentence: a) someone falls for you, b) someone marries you, c) someone needs you, d) you earn a lot of money, e) your parents are satisfied with your achievements. In fact, you have to be someone to be attractive to someone else. You have to be self-accepting before you can please someone you care about. If you don't amount to anything before someone wants you, you won't amount to much afterwards, either.

3. **Thinking you must please everyone.** You must first please yourself... and thereafter, only people you care about. Those who try to please everyone end up pleasing no one.

4. **Setting unreasonable goals for yourself.** Lower your standards to improve your performance. You can always advance beyond today— tomorrow is always another day.

5. **Looking for THE meaning of life.** Life is not a meaning, it is an opportunity. You can only find the meaning of life at the end of it. Life is made up of meaningful experiences—mainly of short duration, but repeatable.

6. **Being bored.** If you are bored, then it is boring to be with you. If you are bored, don't announce it. It is especially unattractive to bemoan how you don't like yourself, or that you have "nothing to do." If you have nothing to do, don't do it in company.

7. **Deciding that your fate is determined by forces outside yourself.** Mainly, you are in control of your life.

My Personal Bill of Rights

You may feel that you have no rights at all—because you can't yet vote, you can't yet drive, and you can't yet live on your own. In fact, you have many basic rights simply because you're a human being. These are some of the rights you have. Do you exercise your rights?

1. I have the right to think for myself.
2. I have the right to learn and grow.
3. I have the right to decide what I believe.
4. I have the right to express my beliefs, opinions, and views.
5. I have the right to choose my life's direction.
6. I have the right to say no.
7. I have the right to say yes.
8. I have the right to have and express my feelings.
9. I have the right to be listened to and taken seriously.
10. I have the right to stand up to people who tease me, criticize me, or put me down.
11. I have the right to make mistakes and not do my best all the time.
12. I have the right to make my wants and needs known to others.
13. I have the right to be different.
14. I have the right to be treated with respect.
15. I have the right to respond when someone violates my rights.

"All human beings are born free and equal in dignity and rights."

From Article 1
of the Universal Declaration of Human Rights

Read the whole document online:
www.un.org/Overview/rights.html

5 Ways to Build Your Self-Confidence

1. **Learn to handle your feelings.** Like every other person, you'll have days when you feel angry, sad, hurt, frustrated, or stressed out. Don't let these feelings overwhelm you. Find ways to let your emotions out—physical activity, talking to someone, writing in a journal. When you learn to cope with your feelings in positive ways, you'll feel stronger inside.

2. **Know that you're responsible for your behavior.** Other people may try to influence you with their words. They may pressure you to do things you don't want to do. They may put you down to make themselves feel better. Instead of lashing out at those people or letting them talk you into doing something you don't want to do, stop and take a deep breath. Realize that you always have a choice—and that choice is to do what's right for you. Even though it's hard to stand up to pressure or harsh words, you can do it. You'll feel more secure and confident if you do.

3. **Become a decision-maker.** You're probably used to having decisions made by your parents, teachers, or other authority figures. But you're also getting the chance to make more decisions for yourself: which classes to take, which activities to get involved in, who to hang out with, how to spend your time, and so on. Making decisions takes confidence and builds confidence. Give yourself the opportunity to make more decisions in your life. It helps to ask for advice from friends and adults you trust. You may also want to write down the pros and cons of each decision, and look at your options carefully. If you end up making a choice that you later regret, don't beat yourself up. This is all part of being human. Let yourself learn from your mistakes.

4. **Focus on your life, not on other people's lives.** It's easy to look around and compare yourself to people you think are "better" than you. You may see cliques or popular people who seem to have more confidence and power than you do. You may convince yourself that these people are "perfect" and that their lives are so much happier and more interesting than yours. Don't let yourself fall into the trap of comparing yourself to others. Instead, focus on your life and your goals. What can you do to improve your life? Make a list of actions you can take. If you really want to make your life better, start on your list today.

5. **Be your own cheering section.** Remember that how you talk to yourself plays a big part in how you see yourself. Instead of focusing on what's going wrong in your life, tell yourself what you're doing

right. Instead of thinking, "I really screwed that up," you might think, "That didn't go the way I wanted it to, but next time, I'll know the right thing to do."

Top 10 Reasons Why You Look Hot

Don't like the way you look? Look again. Want more insights into issues affecting teens? Visit www.youthNOISE.com.

10. You may think it's the eyes or the walk, but what really attracts you to that cutie in math class is the confidence.

9. There are 3 billion women who don't look like supermodels and only 8 who do. The numbers are even more dismal for guys.

8. The average woman weighs 144 pounds and wears between a size 12–14. The average man is about 5' 9" and weighs 172 pounds.

7. It's much easier and way more fun to live life if you aren't totally obsessed with what you look like every minute of every day.

6. If you're going to get hung up on fat and calorie intake, then you'll miss out on life's greatest treats (can you say ice cream and cookies?!?).

5. People will only notice what you think are gross features if you complain about them and point them out.

4. Dimples and freckles are considered defects or flaws. Says who?? One person's "flaw" is another person's beauty trait.

3. You'll feel like a lot better person (and have way more self-confidence) if you focus more on having an attractive personality than an attractive physique.

2. If you feel good about yourself, others will feel a lot more comfortable and relaxed with who you are inside and out.

1. Think about it: Would you want to hang out with someone who hated himself?

"Believing in yourself and liking yourself
is all a part of good looks."
Shirley Lord

The 6 Pillars of Character

In 1992, a group of educators, youth leaders, and ethicists met in Aspen, Colorado and defined six values that are central to the lives of all ethical people, regardless of their differences. The Six Pillars of Character^{SM} have since been endorsed by many cities, counties, school districts, and chambers of commerce; the U.S. Senate and House of Representatives; the YMCA; and more. Do you live according to the Six Pillars of Character? To learn more about them, visit www.charactercounts.org.

1. **Trustworthiness.** Be honest • Don't deceive, cheat, or steal • Be reliable—do what you say you'll do • Have the courage to do the right thing • Build a good reputation • Be loyal—stand by your family, friends, and country.

2. **Respect.** Treat others with respect; follow the Golden Rule • Be tolerant of differences • Use good manners, not bad language • Be considerate of the feelings of others • Don't threaten, hit, or hurt anyone • Deal peacefully with anger, insults, and disagreements.

3. **Responsibility.** Do what you are supposed to do • Persevere; keep on trying! • Always do your best • Use self-control • Be self-disciplined • Think before you act—consider the consequences • Be accountable for your choices.

4. **Fairness.** Play by the rules • Take turns and share • Be open-minded; listen to others • Don't take advantage of others • Don't blame others carelessly.

5. **Caring.** Be kind • Be compassionate and show you care • Express gratitude • Forgive others • Help people in need.

6. **Citizenship.** Do your share to make your school and community better • Cooperate • Stay informed; vote • Be a good neighbor • Obey laws and rules • Respect authority • Protect the environment.

12 Reasons to Tell the Truth

Uh-oh. You've been caught doing something you shouldn't do. Or maybe you haven't been caught (yet), but you're afraid you will be soon. Should you tell the truth or not? The answer is YES, and here are 12 reasons why.

1. "You'll never get mixed up if you simply tell the truth. Then you don't have to remember what you have said, and you never forget what you have said."—Sam Rayburn

2. Telling the truth means that someone else won't get blamed for what you did.

3. "The truth is always the strongest argument."—Sophocles

4. Telling the truth gives you a chance to explain what really happened. Maybe it's not as bad as you think or as bad as other people think.

5. Telling the truth usually gets you into less trouble than lying.

6. "Telling someone the truth is a loving act."—Mal Pancoast (Think about it.)

7. Telling the truth is less stressful than lying. You don't have to worry about someone else eventually learning about your lie(s).

8. Telling the truth helps the people you care about trust and respect you more. Lying destroys trust and respect.

9. "People deserve... the truth. They deserve honesty."—Bruce Springsteen

10. Telling the truth helps you feel calm inside. Lying makes a knot in your stomach.

11. Lying is a trap. The truth can set you free and let you move on with your life.

12. "You never find yourself until you face the truth."—Pearl Bailey

> "A half truth is a whole lie."
> *Yiddish Proverb*

9 Reasons to Go to Church, Temple, Mosque, or Meetings

Maybe you're battling your parents over religion. Maybe you think that organized religion is a crock or a crutch, or you've got better things to do with your time. If so, this list is for you.

1. **Religious communities reduce risky behaviors.** Teens who are involved in a church, synagogue, parish, mosque, or other faith community are half as likely as those who aren't to use alcohol or other drugs, have sex too soon, or attempt suicide.

2. **Religious communities teach values.** This leads to responsible decision-making and positive choices. Teens who say no to risky behaviors often do so because of their values. *Tip:* Many schools and other organizations shy away from teaching values. Your religious community may be the only place you go (outside your family) where people talk openly about values. You need adults in your life who aren't afraid to say "This is right" or "That's wrong"—even if you don't always agree with them.

3. **Religious communities are intergenerational.** You'll meet, worship with, and get to know people of all ages—adult leaders, younger teens, children, grandparents. *Tip:* Society is increasingly age-segmented. Your religious community may be one of the few places you go where you have regular contact with principled, caring adults.

4. **Religious communities provide caring and support.** You'll form relationships with religious education teachers, youth group leaders, peers, friends, relatives, and mentors who care about you and are there for you in good times and bad.

5. **Religious communities have high expectations for their young people.** They motivate teens to grow and mature, succeed and achieve.

6. **Religious communities provide opportunities to be contributing members of a group.** You'll participate in meaningful activities and perform useful roles. Along the way, you'll learn and practice problem solving, decision-making, and goal setting.

7. **Religious communities encourage service to others.** All major faith traditions include an emphasis on service, and many congregations make service an integral part of their youth program.

8. **Religious communities nurture social competencies and leader-ship.** Most give teens opportunities to lead, plan programs, become peer ministers, and care for younger children.

9. **Religious communities offer stability.** Over the course of your life-time, many things will change. You'll graduate from schools, leave home to live on your own, move into and out of neighborhoods, and probably switch careers more than once. But no matter where you go, you can always find a community of people who share your faith and values. Most large religious organizations have congregations around the world. Your religious community can be a source of support, encouragement, and affirmation throughout your life.

5 Steps to Taming Your Temper

Do you feel angry a lot of the time? What if you had a special thermometer that could read your anger level all day long? How high would the level go? How often would it reach the hot zones? Too much anger is bad for your health. It's bad for your relationships. It's bad for your life. Here's how you can keep your anger from getting the best of you.

1. **Know your "anger buttons."** What always (or almost always) makes you mad? Getting teased? Being told to do something you don't want to do? Being told you can't do something you want to do? Getting criticized? Seeing someone else being treated unfairly? Not getting what you want? Being ignored? What else? Figure out what your anger buttons are. Then, if someone pushes one, you can stop, take a deep breath, and pull yourself together. Just because you've gotten mad in the past doesn't mean you have to react that way now.

2. **Know your anger "warning signs."** Your body usually tells you when you're getting mad. You may feel hotter. You may get shaky. You may feel as if your thoughts are spinning out of control. Your head or stomach may start to hurt. You may feel jumpy, helpless, or ready to burst. You may want to yell or cry. You may squeeze your hands into fists. The next time you're mad, notice how you feel. Those are your warning signs—your personal "heads up" that you may be about to explode.

3. **Think about what your anger may be masking.** Anger often hides another, deeper feeling. Your anger may be covering up fear, frustration, sadness, shame, disappointment, jealousy, or guilt—feelings that are hard to face or talk about. It's easier to get mad than to admit to yourself that you're jealous of someone or ashamed of something you did. The next time you get angry, stop and think about what's really going on. Ask yourself: "What happened that made me get angry? Besides feeling mad, how did I feel when it happened?" Answering these questions can help you understand your feelings better and decide if you need to talk to someone about what's going on. Plus, you'll be thinking instead of letting your anger build.

4. **Cage your rage.** Anger is a strong emotion, but you're stronger. You can choose how to handle yourself. You can choose to walk away from whoever or whatever is making you mad. You might say, "I need a few moments to pull myself together." Or, if you can't remove yourself from the situation, take several deep breaths. Breathe until your body and mind feel calmer and more relaxed. Now you can think more clearly.

5. **Decide what to do.** Once you've pulled yourself together, figure out what to do instead of lashing out. Doing something is important because it means you're taking action. Here are four positive things you can do:

- *Stick up for yourself.* Suppose you're angry because someone insulted you. Tell the person how you feel. You might say: "I don't like what you said. I want more respect." Or suppose you've been treated unfairly. You might say, "This isn't fair. Let me tell you what really happened."

- *Talk it out.* Find a friend or a trusted adult who will listen and give you advice, if you want advice. If you need to tell someone that she or he has done something that angered you, do it calmly. You might say, "I feel upset about the way you treated me. I'd like to talk about this."

- *Express your anger in a healthy way.* Write about your feelings in a journal or diary. Write a song or a poem. Draw or paint your feelings. Express them in clay, or build them with a hammer and nails. Play an instrument, sing, or dance. It may sound dumb, but it really works to let your feelings out in creative ways.

- *Help start an anger-management group.* Talk to your teacher, school counselor, youth group leader, or someone at your place of worship about starting a group for teens who want to learn to handle anger in positive ways.

> "Anger is a momentary madness,
> so control your passion or it will control you."
> Horace

5 Ways to Handle Embarrassment

Have you ever wished you could vanish from the planet because of something you said or did? Everyone has embarrassing moments. Here's what to do the next time you think you've made a fool of yourself.

1. **Admit that you're feeling embarrassed.** Don't get defensive or try to hide your feelings. You might even laugh and say, "Whoa! Am I ever embarrassed!" The feelings will pass more quickly if you don't try to cover them up or pretend they don't exist.

2. **Forgive yourself.** You made a mistake. It happens. Stop beating yourself up. If you've hurt or embarrassed someone else, apologize. Sometimes this is the hardest part, but it's important to say you're sorry, because it will make both you and the other person feel better.

3. **Know that the whole world didn't notice.** So you said or did something embarrassing. It may feel as if *everyone* is staring at you. This probably isn't true. Most people are much too concerned about their own mistakes to focus on yours.

4. **Move on.** Put the embarrassing moment where it belongs: *in the past.* Push yourself if you have to, but get on with your life. If someone kids you about what happened, say, "Oh, yeah! That was pretty embarrassing." Laugh and show that you can handle the teasing. Other people will soon forget about the embarrassing moment—and so will you.

5. **Think before you act or speak.** Remembering this will save you from some embarrassing moments. There's no guarantee that it will prevent *all* embarrassments, but it can help reduce them. And when you slip up, repeat steps 1–4 to recover more quickly.

5 Ways to Handle Insecurities

Have you ever felt as if you're really two people in one? A cool, outgoing you—and a shy, awkward, not-so-cool you? Are you confident on the outside, unsure of yourself on the inside? Do you worry that you wouldn't be accepted if people knew the real *you? Try these tips for handling self-doubts and insecurities.*

1. **Make a list of your strengths.** You might include things like, "People know they can count on me," or "I'm a good listener." Or you could list any special skills you have, like telling jokes, drawing, singing, playing soccer, or being a good student.

2. **Make a list of your weaknesses.** What traits are preventing you from being happy or self-assured? Forget about looks for a moment. Focus on personality traits that need work, or skills you might improve on. *Examples:* "I put off things until the last minute." "I don't always tell the truth about how I feel."

3. **Keep both lists the same size.** If you think of five weaknesses, come up with five strengths. If you have a hard time identifying your strengths, ask a parent or friend for suggestions.

4. **Review your strengths.** How do you feel about them? Does the list include things you don't usually give yourself credit for? If so, give yourself credit now. And think about how you can use these strengths

more than you already do. Write down your ideas so you can turn them into goals.

5. **Review your weaknesses.** Identify the weaknesses you can live with for now, and think about the ones you want to work on. Don't tackle everything at once. Instead, choose one weakness and develop a plan of action. *Example:* If you want to stop putting things off until the last minute, think of ways to get more organized about deadlines. Maybe you can break a long-term project into several smaller steps. This way, you'll be more likely to make steady progress toward your main goal. When you successfully complete one long-term assignment, you'll feel more motivated to start the next one without procrastinating. Before long, "I'm organized" might be one of your strengths.

IO Tips for Solving Almost Any Problem

Everyone has problems. How do you solve yours? Try these tips for making life easier.

1. **Don't assume that all problems are negative.** Try to view some as opportunities to use your brain and take positive action.

2. **Separate problems into categories.** Which are related to goals in your life? Which are a result of being disorganized or not planning ahead?

3. **Break down problems into as many elements as possible.** Then break down these elements into steps. Then take each step one at a time.

4. **Learn to distinguish real problems from fantasy problems**—ones you've made up in your head. Maybe you're just imagining that a problem exists. Unnecessary worrying is a waste of brain power.

5. **Work backwards.** Don't focus only on the solution. The best one may not be obvious at the beginning. Instead, focus on the problem-solving process.

6. **When faced with an especially sticky problem, outline it on paper first.** List the things you *want to do* about it. Then list the things you *can do* about it. Do the two lists match up?

7. **Gather information.** If any of your friends have dealt with similar problems, find out what they did. Ask adults you trust—your parents, teachers, school counselor, religious leader, mentor.

8. **Develop backup plans.** If things don't turn out the way you want them to, what will you do then?

9. **Be flexible in the way you approach problem solving.** Most of us develop problem-solving styles that turn into habits. We approach problems in the same old way, time after time. Maybe you need a change.

10. **Don't be afraid to talk to yourself.** Some of the most successful problem solvers think out loud.

> "What one has to do usually can be done."
> *Eleanor Roosevelt*

6 Reasons to Keep a Journal

The word "journal" comes from the French jour, *meaning "day." It's related to the word* journee, *or journey. Keeping a journal is an easy and rewarding way to record your life's journey. Even if you only write a few words, try to do it every day.*

1. Journaling can help you remember things that happen in your life. It's fun to look back at what you were doing and thinking last month, last year, or the year before. It's fascinating to see how you've changed and grown.

2. Journaling can help you understand yourself. In your journal, you'll probably write about things that matter to you. Looking back at what you've written can help you get to know yourself better.

3. Journaling can help you handle your feelings. Writing about your feelings makes them seem more manageable.

4. Journaling can help you like yourself better and appreciate the person you are. After you've been journaling for a while, look back at some of the things you've written. You might see that you're a creative person with a lot of talents, skills, and ideas.

5. Regular journaling can help in the healing of anxiety, depression, grief, and loss. If your life isn't going so well right now, this is a great time to start a journal.

6. Journaling is relaxing. It lowers your blood pressure and heart rate. Journaling about stressful events can put them into perspective and calm you down.

12 Reasons to Write

A journal, poems, short stories, plays, essays, your memoirs, a Weblog.... It doesn't matter what you write, as long as you write something. *Here's why.*

1. **Writing helps you discover who you are.** When you put pen to paper and pour out your thoughts, you begin to discover what you know about yourself and the world. You can explore what you love or hate, what hurts you, what you need, what you can give, and what you want out of life. This helps you better understand yourself and your place in the world.

2. **Writing can help you believe in yourself and raise your self-esteem.** The very act of making something out of nothing produces a feeling of pride and a sense of accomplishment. Knowing that you're able to fill up a journal with your thoughts, write a story, or put together a research paper helps you believe in your own abilities, talents, and perseverance. Your increased self-confidence can inspire you to take more risks in your writing and in other creative activities.

3. **When you write, you hear your own unique voice.** Poet William Stafford once said that a writer is not someone who has something to say as much as someone who has found a way to say it. Writing allows you to communicate in your own words and voice, without the filters and blocks you might use when talking to people you want to please, avoid, connect with, impress, or run from. Writing also gives you an opportunity to listen to your own distinctive voice, recognize it, and know it better.

4. **Writing shows what you can give the world.** As you write, you can explore your particular talents, interests, and passions. What are you good at? What do you feel compelled to throw energy into? What do you want to improve? Writing allows you to delve deeper into yourself and put into words what it is you want to be and do. It helps you find your calling.

5. **As you write, you seek answers to questions and find new questions to ask.** Because writing forces you to sit and think, it can be a way of finding answers to questions in your life. Writing is introspective by nature; it gives you the opportunity to carefully review choices and decisions about everything from what to study, to who to hang out with, to how to tell someone what's on your mind. In the process of writing about your issues and examining your questions, you may find answers that are right for you.

6. **Writing enhances your creativity.** Creating anything means asking questions, dwelling in doubt and confusion, and finally reaching a breakthrough. When you write, you immerse yourself in the creative process. The more practice you get, the more easily you can transfer these skills to other areas of your life (school, activities, a job) that require creative solutions.

7. **You can share yourself with others through writing.** Many people believe that the written word allows for more freedom of expression than the spoken word. Writing lets you reveal aspects of yourself that don't always come across in face-to-face communication, phone conversations, or class discussions. Your writing self, in contrast to your talking self, has more time to reflect on what you believe, what you want to say, and why you think or feel a certain way.

8. **Writing gives you a place to release anger, fear, sadness, and other painful feelings.** Feelings are intense. They can hurt you to the core. (According to writer Oscar Wilde, their main charm is that they don't last!) When you're feeling angry, scared, upset, or depressed, it helps to get these emotions on paper rather than bottle them up. Writing is a safe way to release your feelings, explore them, and begin to cope.

9. **You can help heal yourself through writing.** It's no secret that many writers derive at least some healing benefits from writing. Whether it's their career, passion, hobby, or all three, writing offers writers a way to examine their wounds and, if they want, share them with the world. You, too, can take what has hurt you and turn it into something that helps you. The very act of creating can be a way to heal.

10. **Writing can bring you joy and a way to express it.** It's fun to put into words what's important and meaningful to you, then read what you've written. But the process of writing can be fun, too. It's exciting to put words onto paper and fill up pages with your ideas and opinions, not knowing exactly what you're going to say or what will come next. When you allow yourself to relax and see what happens on the page, you experience the thrill of creative expression.

11. **Writing can make you feel more alive.** The words, the images, the delight or grief that surfaces, the discoveries, the answers or questions that come to you as you write—all of this helps you feel more alive. Writing, like any art, is a way to connect with yourself, other people, and the world. In doing so, you may feel more involved, engaged, and interested in life. You may even be compelled to embrace it wholeheartedly.

12. You can discover your dreams through writing. Through the quiet and solitary act of writing, you can discover your greatest dreams (not what other people think they should be, but what really calls to you). You can think about these dreams and what you can do to start making things happen. Then you can write your way there.

> "Becoming a writer is about becoming conscious."
> *Anne Lamott*

Robert Sternberg's 10 Tips to Enhance Creativity

Robert Sternberg is IBM Professor of Psychology and Education at Yale University and a well-known authority on intelligence, learning, and creativity.

1. **Be motivated from *inside*, not *outside*.** Work to please yourself, not parents, teachers, or friends. Find things that excite you. Seek personal satisfaction from a job well done.

2. **Take time to think before you act.** Don't get carried away by the first idea that comes to mind. Instead, keep thinking until you're satisfied. Chances are you'll come up with a better idea.

3. **Practice stick-to-it-iveness.** Persistence pays, even when you're feeling frustrated, bored, or afraid you won't succeed. On the other hand, too much persistence can block progress, so know when to quit.

4. **Find out what you're best at, then use those abilities.** Now is a wonderful time to discover and develop your true abilities. Experiment, explore, take risks, and challenge yourself. You may find talents you didn't know you had.

5. **Finish what you start.** Follow through. Failure to complete tasks and projects can cramp your creativity. But if your current strategy isn't working, change it. If you have many unfinished tasks or projects, choose one and get it done. This success may motivate you to tackle another task... and another.

6. **Don't procrastinate.** Procrastination smothers creativity. The things you know you *should* do can weigh on your mind, crowding out creative thinking. If you're a procrastinator, do something about it today. Don't procrastinate in dealing with your procrastination.

7. **Don't let personal problems drag you down.** Everyone has personal problems from time to time. Life is full of joys and sorrow. The best thing to do is accept this fact and take it in stride. You may find that work helps take your mind off your problems.

8. **Strike a balance in your life.** Avoid taking on more—or less—than you can handle. If you try to do too much, you'll spread yourself too thin. But if you do too little, you'll miss out on opportunities and accomplish less than you could. Find the mix that's right for you.

9. **Know when to be creative—and when not to be creative.** Different kinds of thinking are appropriate for different kinds of situations. The key is learning how to make the right judgment call. For example, don't waste your creativity when answering problems on objective, multiple-choice tests. Save it for research projects.

10. **Make your environment a creative environment.** Are your friends creative? Do your parents and teachers support your creative efforts? Is your room at home an inspiring place to be? Decide which parts of your environment are under your control, then change them if they need changing. Creative people often see things differently from the way others do.

25 Quotes on Creativity

What does it take to be creative? You might find your answer or inspiration in these words from creative people—artists, writers, scientists, scholars, teachers, inventors, entrepreneurs, musicians, motivational speakers, cartoonists, and more.

1. "If you'd like to be more creative, just look at the same thing as everyone else and 'think something different.'"—Roger von Oech

2. "Leap and the net will appear."—Julia Cameron

3. "It's simple. You just take something and do something to it, and then do something else to it. Keep doing this, and pretty soon you've got something."—Jasper Johns

4. "Good ideas usually evolve out of pretty lame ones, and vice versa." —Gary Larson

5. "One of the advantages of being disorderly is that one is constantly making exciting discoveries."—A.A. Milne

6. "Do not fear mistakes. There are none."—Miles Davis

7. "Ideas are elusive, slippery things. Best to keep a pad of paper and a pencil at your bedside, so you can stab them during the night before they get away."—Earl Nightingale

8. "Making the simple complicated is commonplace; making the complicated simple, awesomely simple, that's creativity."—Charles Mingus

9. "Creativity comes from trust. Trust your instincts. And never hope more than you work."—Rita Mae Brown

10. "I look for what needs to be done.... After all, that's how the universe designs itself."—R. Buckminster Fuller

11. "Don't think! Thinking is the enemy of creativity."—Ray Bradbury

12. "Imagination is the beginning of creation. You imagine what you desire, you will what you imagine, and at last you create what you will."—George Bernard Shaw

13. "Be alone—that is the secret of invention: be alone, that is when ideas are born."—Nikola Tesla

14. "When all is said and done, monotony may after all be the best condition for creation."—Margaret Sackville-West

15. "All you need to do is to remember a tune that no one else has thought of."—Robert Schumann

16. "Creativity can be described as letting go of certainties."—Gail Sheehy

17. "Hitch your unconscious mind to your writing arm."—Dorothea Brande

18. "For me, the creative process, first of all, requires a good nine hours of sleep a night."—William N. Lipscomb Jr.

19. "Creativity is allowing yourself to make mistakes. Art is knowing which ones to keep."—Scott Adams

20. "If you are unhappy with anything...whatever is bringing you down, get rid of it. Because you'll find that when you're free, your true creativity, your true self comes out."—Tina Turner

21. "Any activity becomes creative when the doer cares about doing it right, or better."—John Updike

22. "The ability to play is essential to being a creative artist." —Dewitt Jones

23. "When in doubt, make a fool of yourself. There is a microscopically thin line between being brilliantly creative and acting like the most gigantic idiot on earth."—Cynthia Heimel

24. "Creativity is inventing, experimenting, growing, taking risks, breaking rules, making mistakes, and having fun."—Mary Lou Cook

25. "Follow your bliss."—Joseph Campbell

6 Good Things to Do for Yourself

Sometimes we get so busy that we forget to take care of ourselves. Then we wonder—why am I blue? Why don't I have any energy? What's wrong with me? Here are six things you can do for yourself, by yourself, that will always make you feel better.

1. **Choose something to do just for fun. Then do it whenever you can.** Forget the old saying, "Anything worth doing is worth doing well." Don't try to be perfect. Don't aim to be an expert at everything. Keep some things just for fun.

2. **Give yourself a treat every day.** This can be almost anything, as long as it's just for you. Listen to music. Take a bubble bath. Watch a movie you enjoy. Read. Sit in a park and listen to the breeze in the trees.

3. **Forgive yourself for something you did in the past.** We've all done things we wish we hadn't done. We've all hurt someone else's feelings. But we don't have to feel sad, guilty, or ashamed for the rest of our lives. Pick something from your past. Remember it one last time. Think about everything that happened. Then close your eyes and say, "I'm sorry, and I forgive myself." Let it go.

4. **Do at least one thing every day that's good for your body.** Take a walk, ride your bike, go for a run, or put on your skates. Physical activity boosts self-esteem, promotes a positive body image, and helps you get healthy and fit.

5. **Do at least one thing every day that's good for your brain.** Solve a puzzle or do a brainteaser. Read a book. Memorize part of a song, poem, or play. Listen to a concert on the radio. Visit a museum (real or virtual). Learn something new.

6. **Find adults you can trust and talk to.** Caring adults can help you solve your problems, face your fears, and reach your goals. Let your feelings guide you to the right people. Pick three or more you feel safe with. Pick those who care enough to listen and try to understand how you feel. This is one of the best things you can ever do for yourself.

8 Things That Make You One of a Kind

People often talk about teens as if they're all alike. In fact, there's no one else in the world exactly like you. Think of eight things that make you one of a kind. These might be likes, dislikes, beliefs, talents, qualities, or anything else you can think of. Be proud of the ways in which you're uniquely you.

1. _____

   _____

2. _____

   _____

3. _____

   _____

4. _____

   _____

5. _____

   _____

6. _____

   _____

7. _____

   _____

8. _____

   _____

"Let's dare to be ourselves, for we do that better than anyone else can."
Shirley Briggs

12 Things to Look Forward to from the GW Forecast

Based at George Washington University in Washington, D.C., the GW Forecast brings experts together online to forecast coming breakthroughs in science, technology, medicine, and more. Here's what they see for your future. To learn more, visit www.gwforecast.gwu.edu.

2008 Most people use PDAs (personal digital assistants).

2010 Translation software replaces foreign language teachers.

2013 Half of all household waste is recycled.

2014 Healthcare is computerized.

2015 Only 10 percent of all jobs are in manufacturing.

2018 Half of all goods are sold online.

2021 Automated highways take us where we want to go.

2025 Children are genetically designed.

2027 A permanent base is established on the moon.

2028 Humans land on Mars.

2043 Humans travel to a nearby star.

2044 Most people live to be 100.

Based on what you think will happen, or what you want to happen, write your own prediction for the future:

The Last Words of 16 Famous People

What have famous people said as they were dying or about to die? If your own "last words" were going down in history, what would you want them to be?

1. **"Now comes the mystery."** Henry Ward Beecher (1813–1887), abolitionist and clergyman

2. **"What's this?"** Leonard Bernstein (1918–1990), composer, pianist, and conductor

3. **"I don't feel good."** Luther Burbank (1849–1926), American horticulturist

4. **"Never felt better."** Douglas Fairbanks Sr. (1893–1939), American actor

5. **"What is the question?"** Gertrude Stein (1874–1946), American writer famous for her experimental prose

5. **"I don't know."** Peter Abelard (1079–1142), philosopher and teacher

6. **"Leave the shower curtain on the inside of the tub."** Conrad Hilton (1887–1979), founder of the Hilton hotels chain

7. **"Are you happy? I'm happy."** Ethel Barrymore (1879–1959), American actress

8. **"It has all been most interesting."** Lady Mary Wortley Montagu (1689–1763), English writer and world traveler

9. **"I am not the least afraid to die."** Charles Darwin (1809–1882), English naturalist, author of *On the Origin of Species*

10. **"Dying is easy. Comedy is difficult."** Edmund Gwenn (1875–1959), English actor who played Santa Claus in the classic movie *Miracle on 34th Street*

11. **"Why not? Why not? Why not? Why not? Yeah."** Timothy Leary (1920–1996), Harvard psychologist who urged American youth in the 1960s to "turn on, tune in, and drop out"

12. **"Tomorrow, I shall no longer be here."** Nostradamus (1503–1566), prophet; many people today believe that his verses predict the future

13. **"I'm going over the valley."** George Herman "Babe" Ruth (1895–1948), legendary baseball player

14. **"Everybody has got to die, but I have always believed an exception would be made in my case. Now what?"** William Saroyan (1908–1981), Pulitzer Prize-winning writer of plays, short stories, and novels

15. **"Go away. I'm all right."** Herbert George "H.G." Wells (1866–1946), English writer and social theorist, author of *The Time Machine* and *The War of the Worlds*

16. **"Please put out the light."** Theodore Roosevelt (1858–1919), 26th president of the United States

The 8 Clown Commandments

Lots of teens are clowning around. They're putting on costumes and makeup, learning tricks, developing characters, and entertaining at children's parties, nursing homes, and other places where people like to laugh. Check your local library for books on how to be a clown. Look around your community for clown classes and workshops. And don't forget to follow the Clown Commandments. To learn more about clowns and clowning, visit the Clowns of America International Web site: www.coai.org.

1. I will keep my acts, performance, and behavior in good taste while I am in costume and makeup. I will remember that a good clown entertains others by making fun of himself or herself and not at the expense or embarrassment of others.

2. I will learn to apply my makeup in a professional manner. I will provide my own costume.

3. I will carry out my appearance and assignment for the entertainment of others and not for personal gain or personal publicity.

4. I will always try to remain anonymous while in makeup and costume as a clown, though there may be circumstances when it is not reasonably possible to do so. I will remove my makeup and change into my street clothes as soon as possible following my appearance.

5. I will conduct myself as a gentleman/lady at all times.

6. I will not become involved in or tolerate sexual harassment or discrimination on the basis of race, color, religion, sex, national origin, age, disability, or any protected status.

7. I will do my very best to maintain the best clown standards of makeup, costuming, properties, and comedy.

8. I will appear in as many clown shows as I possibly can.

9 Tips for Changing Your Hair Color

1. Get your parents' permission *before* you take the plunge. True, it's *your* hair, but they'll have to look at it, too.

2. Give some thought to how you'll feel if you walk into the school cafeteria and everyone stares. Maybe you'll want to start with something close to your original color—or maybe not.

3. Decide how long you want your new color to last. This will determine if you use:

   • a *temporary rinse,* which lasts only until you wash your hair.

   • a *semi-permanent dye,* which stays on through a number of washings. You can only use a semi-permanent dye to make your hair darker, not lighter.

   • a *permanent dye,* which won't wash out. As new hairs grow in, they'll be your original color. Think roots.

4. If you want your new color to be vibrant and unnatural, you'll have to bleach your hair before you color it. Bleaching makes hair more porous. Porous hair absorbs more color. Bleaching also damages your hair and may cause scalp burns if it's too strong or you leave it in too long. Plus bleaching is permanent. It lasts until your hair grows out. You can bleach your hair on your own or with a friend's help, but make sure to read and follow all of the instructions. *Best bet:* If you can afford it, have a professional bleach your hair.

5. When you look at the picture on the front of a haircolor package, don't expect your hair to turn out exactly that color. The picture shows the color you're *adding to* the color already on your head— unless you bleach out all the color first. In other words, if your hair is a medium-brown and you use a medium-red dye, your final color won't be the medium-red shown on the box. It will be auburn—a combination of your brown and the dye's red.

6. If your hair is really dry or damaged, wait to color it. Use a strong conditioner for a few months first. Try some hot-oil treatments.

7. Don't perm or relax your hair on the same day you color it. That's too much stress for your hair.

8. If you end up with fried hair or a color that's totally wrong for you, get a stylist's help. Don't be embarrassed; they've seen it all before.

9. After you color your hair, wear a hat whenever you're in the sun. Ultraviolet rays can fade your color. Wear a swim cap in the pool, because chlorine reacts with the chemicals in your hair—and it's true that it can turn blond hair green. And treat your new hair extra-well with shampoos and conditioners specially created for colored hair.

How to Convince Your Parents to Let You Go to a Party

Parents are understandably suspicious of kids' and teens' parties. They're not there in person to see what goes on, and they've heard horrible stories (some of them true). If you're invited to a friend's party and you want to go, here's what to do.

1. **Give your parents as many details as you possibly can.** Tell them exactly where the party will be, who's hosting it, who else will be there (to the best of your knowledge), and what kind of party it will be. Just a social gathering? A dance? A pool party?

2. **Tell them that absolutely no alcohol or drugs will be available.** Again, this is to the best of your knowledge. You know and they know that you can't control what other people bring or do. But you can promise—and mean it—that even if someone does show up with illegal substances, you won't indulge.

3. **Tell them that the party will be chaperoned by your friend's parents.** Of course, this will have to be true, because the next thing you'll do is...

4. **Invite them to call the parents to confirm the details.** Give them the phone number and the parents' names. Encourage them to call. Tell them you really *want* them to call.

5. **Tell them how you plan to get to and from the party.** If they offer to drive you, accept. If someone else will be driving, promise that you won't ride with any driver who is under the influence of alcohol or other drugs.

6. **Plan to bring your cell phone or pager with you, if you have one, and leave it on.** That way, you can contact them if you need them—or they can contact you if they want to.

7. **Discuss what you'll do if the party gets out of hand.** If you feel uncomfortable or unsafe, or if you see evidence of alcohol or drug use, you'll leave the party immediately. You'll ask the person who

drove you to take you home. Or you'll call your parents if you need a ride. Or, if your parents won't be around, you'll call another adult they trust (something you'll have to arrange ahead of time). You'll also bring taxi money in case that's your only alternative.

8. **Discuss what you'll do if the party moves to another location.** This sometimes happens. Promise that you'll call your parents and let them know if it does. If this isn't acceptable to them, you'll come home.

9. **Agree on a curfew.** Promise to be home on time. Promise that if for some reason you're delayed—your ride left, or your ride has been drinking, or you have so much fun that you totally lose track of time—you'll call and explain.

10. **Agree that when you get home, you'll greet your parents and tell them a little about the party.** You won't just run to your room. You'll even give them a hug and a kiss if that's how you normally greet each other. This gives parents the chance to get close enough to tell if you've been drinking, smoking, or whatever.

11. **Agree ahead of time on the consequences of breaking any of these agreements.** This shows your parents that you're serious about keeping your word.

How to Convince Your Parents to Let You Have a Party

You've been invited to plenty of parties, and it's your turn to have one. It's right, it's polite, and it's only fair. Here's what you can do to bring even reluctant parents around to your way of thinking.

1. **Talk with your parents about what kind of party you'd like to have.** When do you want to have it? What time will it start, and what time will it end? How many people do you want to invite? (*Tip:* Parents generally prefer smaller parties.) What activities do you want to offer? (Videos, DVDs, dancing, volleyball in the yard?) What food and beverages do you want to serve? Don't just announce your plans. Invite their input and ideas.

2. **Tell them you want them to be there to chaperone.** This is important to them, and to the parents of the friends you invite. No parent in his or her right mind lets kids or teens go to unchaperoned parties. Say that if they want to invite other parents to help chaperone, that's fine with you.

3. **Decide where the party will be.** Only in the family room? Only in the back yard? In the party room of your apartment complex? What parts of the house will be off-limits? Which bathroom is okay for guests to use?

4. **Agree on who will pay for the food, beverages, decorations, etc.** If you can afford it, offer to pay. If you can't, see if they'll split the costs with you. What can you do for them in return? Extra chores? Baby-sit a younger sibling for free?

5. **Agree on a guest list.** Give them the names of the people you want to invite. Give them their home phone numbers, in case they want to call the other parents and tell them they'll be chaperoning.

6. **Agree on basic ground rules for how guests will behave.** You can't control other people's behavior—your parents understand that. But you can communicate your expectations to your guests.

7. **Agree on how crashers will be handled.** Uninvited guests should not be allowed in. Any exceptions? Maybe an invited friend who calls and asks if it's okay to bring someone else. Clear it with your parents first. What if an invited friend shows up with an extra guest? Promise to let your parents know if this happens.

8. **Agree that absolutely no alcohol or other drugs will be allowed.** Anyone who brings them will be asked to leave. Anyone who shows up under the influence will be asked to leave. If that person drove to your house, you'll make sure that he or she has another way home—a sober driver, the person's parents, or a taxi.

9. **Agree that guests may not leave the party and then return.** Let your guests know this rule. This reassures your parents that kids can't sneak off to use or get alcohol or other drugs.

10. **Agree that guests who get out of hand will be asked to leave.** If they don't listen to you, you'll tell your parents. Let your parents know that if this happens, you want them to be the "heavies." If the guests still refuse to leave, you'll call the police.

11. **Tell your parents that they don't have to disappear during the party.** It's okay with you if they greet your guests and stop in from time to time to see what's going on. Chances are, they won't, but they'll feel better knowing they can.

Michael Levine's 9 Tips
for Getting in Touch with Famous
People—and Getting an Answer

Michael Levine heads an entertainment public relations firm based in Los Angeles (www.levinepr.com). He is the author of The Address Book *and* The Kid's Address Book, *the first places you should turn if you need the current address of a famous person. Check your library or bookstore for the latest editions.*

1. **To reach a celebrity, you need a complete, correct address.** Start your search in the library, in reference books like *Who's Who in America, Current Biography,* and so forth. They often list celebrities' work addresses; you can write to them there.

2. **If you can't find a celebrity's address, try another approach.** Cartoonists can be reached through their newspaper syndicates; pop stars through their record companies; movie actors in care of the Screen Actors Guild. If people have been written about in a magazine article, send a letter to the magazine; if they appeared on a TV talk show, write to the producer of the program. Publications and TV shows won't give out famous people's addresses, but they will often forward mail.

To improve your chances of getting a personal response:

3. **Send photos of yourself.** These supply a human face to go with your letter, making it more personal, powerful, and hard to resist.

4. **Include a self-addressed, stamped envelope.** Celebrities have an unusually high volume of mail. Whatever makes it easier for them to respond helps tip the odds in your favor. Include your name and address on each page of a letter and on photos or anything else you enclose.

5. **Keep it short.** Notables are very busy people. Long letters tend to be put aside for future consideration...which never comes. If you're asking for an autographed photo, don't write four pages of prose.

6. **Make your letter easy to read.** Write it on a computer or type it if you can. Stay away from pencil and crayon.

7. **Be sure packages are easy to open.** Don't wrap gifts with yards of string and tape.

8. **Never send food.** If you mail brownies for a celebrity's birthday, they'll get thrown away for obvious reasons of security and spoilage.

9. **Set yourself apart from the flood of similar letters, especially if you ask for an autograph.** Don't mail a form letter; make your request specific. If you admire someone, say why. Flatter. Demonstrate your own creativity; if you write poetry, for instance, send a poem. Make your request original.

8 Tips for Remembering Your Dreams

Some people claim that they seldom or never dream. In fact, they do *dream—they just forget everything about their dreams as soon as they wake up. You can actually train yourself to remember your dreams. Try these tips.*

1. Start a Dream Journal. This can be anything you like to write in—a bound blank journal, a spiral-bound notebook, a pad of paper. Keep your Dream Journal and a pencil or pen next to your bed.

2. Every morning, *as soon as you wake up,* write down everything you can remember about your dream, or a few key words describing it. Dreams can disappear from your memory in less than five minutes, so don't wait to do this until you've gotten dressed or had breakfast. *Tip:* Date each page you write on. If you're like many people who begin Dream Journals, you may continue recording some or most of your dreams for the rest of your life. And you may go back and reread old Dream Journals from time to time. Dating your dreams can help to remind you of what was happening in your life when you had a particular dream.

3. Keep a glass of water next to your bed. Every night, *as soon as you start feeling sleepy,* drink the water and say to yourself, "Tonight I WILL remember my dreams." Repeat this phrase while you're falling asleep. Be sure to say "will remember" instead of "try to remember." This is called *autosuggestion.*

4. Use imaging to "set the stage" for your dreams. As you are falling asleep, picture yourself in a certain place and time. Make up a movie with yourself as the star.

5. Keep a record of important or unusual events that happen in your waking life. Try to draw connections between those events and the events that occur in your dreams. This will strengthen the links between your conscious mind and your unconscious mind.

If you're not ready to keep a Dream Journal but you still want to remember your dreams, try these tips:

6. Keep a tape recorder by your bed. "Talk" your dreams into it *as soon as you wake up.*

7. Tell your dreams to another person *as soon as you wake up*. *Note:* This is the *least* reliable way to keep a record of your dreams, because you can't count on someone else to remember them for you.

8. Keep a pad of blank paper by your bed and draw one or two images from your dreams *as soon as you wake up*. Use markers or crayons if you like to draw in color. Since your dream will fade quickly, you'll need to sketch quickly. You may want to write brief notes around or after your sketches.

> "We are the music makers.
> We are the dreamers of dreams."
> *Arthur O'Shaugnessy*

11 Common Dream Symbols and What They Mean

1. **Characters in a dream** may symbolize parts of you which resemble those characters.

2. **Bad dream characters** may indicate problems, fears, or concerns.

3. **A house** may symbolize your beliefs or attitudes.

4. **Water** may symbolize how you feel. For example, if you see water in a dream, is it stormy or calm? Frozen or free-flowing?

5. **Dead characters** may symbolize parts of you which are becoming less important in your daily life.

6. **Cars** may symbolize "getting around" in life. They can reflect either your personality or your physical body.

7. **Roads, paths, and highways** may represent choices or decisions. Pay attention to the types of roads you see in your dreams, and compare them. Is one paved? Is another overgrown with weeds? Where does each road seem to lead?

8. **Stones** (including gemstones, monuments, and memorials) may symbolize eternity. In dreams, a stone may symbolize your inner self—the part of you that lasts forever.

9. **A circle** may symbolize the whole self, because it is complete and perfect.

10. **A mirror** can show you another side of yourself.

11. **Crossing a bridge** may symbolize a change in attitude.

9 Colors and How They Make You Feel

Are you thinking of painting your room? Color can affect your mood. Some colors are soothing; others are energizing or even disturbing. Red clothes have been shown to raise blood pressure. Here's a short course on color theory.

1. **Blue** calms and cools. People are more productive in blue rooms. College students tested in a blue room were more likely to say they were happy and calm than students tested in red, yellow, or neutral rooms. Blue suppresses the appetite, maybe because it's associated with moldy food.

2. **Red** excites and warms. It stimulates the appetite, which is why it's so often found in restaurants. In one study, students gambling under red lights took greater risks than students under blue lights. Red can also feel oppressive and confining.

3. **Pink** soothes and tranquilizes. After a prison holding cell was painted pink, prisoners became less aggressive and hostile. Sports teams once painted locker rooms used by visiting teams pink in the belief that this made them more passive.

4. **Green** may increase stress, induce fatigue, and encourage passivity. Then again, many people find green to be soothing and refreshing. It's often used in hospitals.

5. **Brown and beige** appear to have a calming influence. In a room, they create feelings of security and intimacy.

6. **Yellow** has been associated with everything from diminished boredom to increased irritability. Some people find yellows cheering and energizing. Bright yellow can cause anxiety.

7. **White** communicates innocence, purity, and spirituality. A white environment can be calming and restorative or, if too harsh, cold and irritating.

8. **Purple** comforts and creates a mysterious mood.

9. **Black** is stylish and timeless. It can also be very, very dark and oppressive.

Decorating tip: Cool colors (blues, greens, violets) make a room seem larger than it is. Warm colors (reds, oranges, yellows) make a room seem smaller than it is.

18 Tips for Analyzing Your Handwriting

Graphology—the study of handwriting—can give you insights into your personality. Businesses hire graphologists to study the handwriting of people they are thinking about hiring. Police departments hire them to look at notes left by criminals. Write your signature on a piece of paper, then read these descriptions. Which ones match your signature? What does your handwriting say about you? (P.S. Some people think that graphology is reliable. Others think it's nonsense.)

1. **If your writing is large,** you think big. You like to be noticed.

2. **If your writing is small,** you're detail-oriented. You don't like to be in the public eye.

3. **If your writing slants to the right,** you like to show your feelings. You're sociable, active, and forward-moving.

4. **If your writing slants to the left,** you keep your emotions to yourself. You're unwilling to go out and "face the world."

5. **If your writing slants up,** you're optimistic.

6. **If your writing slants down,** you're tired or sad about something.

7. **If your writing is upright,** you're neutral and unemotional about many issues. You're self-reliant, calm, and in control of yourself.

8. **If your writing slants in many different directions,** you're unpredictable. You haven't yet decided where you want to go in life. (Many teenagers have this kind of writing.)

9. **If your writing is narrow,** you tend to be economical and hold "narrow" views of things.

10. **If your writing is broad,** you're somewhat uncontrollable. You like room to move and think freely.

11. **If your writing is dark** (from heavy pressure), you're determined and action-oriented. You feel "under pressure" to get things done.

12. **If your writing is light** (from light pressure), you dislike violence, loud noises, and bright light. You're sensitive, tender, and perceptive.

13. **If your letters are disconnected,** you concentrate on details instead of the "big picture." You have original ideas.

14. **If your letters are connected,** you like logic and order. You're good at understanding relationships and the way things "connect" to one another.

15. **If your writing has large spaces between words,** you need space. Sometimes you seem stand-offish. You're clear-headed and have an uncluttered mind.

16. **If your writing has narrow spaces between words,** you're a very sociable person who enjoys "getting together" with a lot of people.

17. **If you have unusual ways of crossing your t's and dotting your i's,** you're a creative person.

18. **If you leave openings in letters that are usually closed**—like a's, b's, d's, o's, and p's—you're open-minded.

8 Big Truths

These Big Truths are observations most people eventually learn from experience. Knowing them now will give you a head start on life.

Truth #1

If you lend a book, chances are you'll never get it back.

Truth #2

You'll save yourself a lot of trouble by following these two simple guidelines:

1. Don't say "no" when you mean "yes."
2. Don't say "yes" when you mean "no."

Truth #3

Most of the things you buy aren't nearly as attractive three months later, out of the store and out of the package. Keep this in mind and you'll pass up a lot of foolish purchases.

Truth #4

If you like yourself more after spending time with someone, he or she is a true friend. If you like yourself less, he or she is not a true friend.

Truth #5

The best predictor of future behavior is past behavior.

Truth #6

Nothing is as easy or as hard as it looks. Nothing is as good or as bad as it seems.

Truth #7

You can't get something for nothing. (Or: If something seems too good to be true, it probably is.)

Truth #8

You have to find your own truth.

25 Deep Thoughts About Life

For pondering, agreeing with, disagreeing with, or inspiring you to write your own Deep Thoughts.

1. "There is more to life than increasing its speed."—Mohandas Gandhi
2. "Besides the noble art of getting things done, there is the noble art of leaving things undone. The wisdom of life consists in the elimination of the nonessentials."—Lin Yutang
3. "Life is a zoo in a jungle."—Peter De Vries
4. "Sometimes the best way to deal with everyday life is to lay down on your mat and take a nap."—Joyce Bartels
5. "Life is made up of little things. True greatness consists in being great in little things."—Charles Simmons
6. "There are only two tragedies in life: One is not getting what one wants, and the other is getting it."—Oscar Wilde
7. "Some poems don't rhyme, and some stories don't have a clear beginning, middle, and end. Life is about not knowing, having to change, taking the moment and making the best of it, without knowing what's going to happen next."—Gilda Radner
8. "A life spent making mistakes is not only more honorable but more useful than a life spent doing nothing."—George Bernard Shaw
9. "Life is a do-it-yourself project."—Napoleon Hill
10. "There are only two ways to live your life. One is as though nothing is a miracle. The other is as though everything is a miracle."—Albert Einstein

11. "In the book of life, the answers aren't in the back."—Charlie Brown (Charles M. Schulz)

12. "Live every day as if it were your last, because one of these days, it will be."—Jeremy Schwartz

13. "If I were asked to give what I consider the single most useful bit of advice for all humanity, it would be this: Expect trouble as an inevitable part of life, and when it comes, hold your head high. Look it squarely in the eye, and say, 'I will be bigger than you. You cannot defeat me.'"—Ann Landers

14. "Live a balanced life—learn some and think some and draw and paint and sing and dance and play and work every day some."
    —Robert Fulghum

15. "Believe that life is worth living, and your belief will help create the fact."—William James

16. "Don't go through life, grow through life."—Eric Butterworth

17. "Hope for the best, expect the worst. Life is a play. We're unrehearsed."
    —Mel Brooks

18. "Life is 10 percent what you make it and 90 percent how you take it."
    —Irving Berlin

19. "Life is a great big canvas. Throw all the paint on it you can."
    —Danny Kaye

20. "I believe that we are here on the planet Earth to live, grow up and do what we can to make this world a better place for all people to enjoy freedom."—Rosa Parks

21. "The great thing to learn about life is, first, not to do what you don't want to do, and, second, to do what you do want to do."
    —Margaret Anderson

22. "You will find as you look back upon your life that the moments when you have truly lived are the moments when you have done things in the spirit of love."—Henry Drummond

23. "Everybody's a mad scientist, and life is their lab."—David Cronenberg

24. "This life is yours: Take the power to choose what you want to do and do it well. Take the power to love what you want in life and love it honestly. Take the power to walk in the forest and be a part of nature. Take the power to control your own life. No one else can do it for you. Take the power to make your life happy."—Susan Polis Schutz

25. "Here is the test to find whether your mission on Earth is finished: If you're alive, it isn't."—Richard Bach

10 Life Lessons from Teens

What are the 10 most valuable lessons you've learned in life? When students in one Minnesota school were asked that question, these were their Top 10 answers. If you want, you can add your own life lessons to this list.

1. Be yourself.

2. Do unto others as you would have them do unto you.

3. Keep a sense of humor.

4. Keep an open mind.

5. Respect others.

6. Set goals for yourself and work to achieve them.

7. Stand up for what you believe.

8. Pick your friends wisely.

9. Life isn't fair.

10. Clean your plate, because people are starving all over the world.

My Own Life Lessons

_____

_____

_____

_____

_____

_____

_____

_____

_____

_____

Acknowledgments and Sources

Many of the lists in this book have been adapted, excerpted, condensed, or expanded from previously published materials. I am indebted to the following publishers, organizations, Web sites, and individuals, who generously granted permission to reprint. They're listed here in the order they appear in the chapters. Every effort has been made to attribute original ownership. If you believe that proper credit has not been given for a particular list, please contact Free Spirit Publishing Inc., 217 Fifth Avenue North, Suite 200, Minneapolis, MN 55401-1299, so any errors can be corrected in future editions of this book.

HEALTH AND WELLNESS

"12 Serious Reasons to Laugh." Exclusive to *Life Lists for Teens*.

"8 Ways to Bring More Laughter into Your Life." Exclusive to *Life Lists for Teens*.

"7 Basic Needs All People Share." Adapted from *Stick Up for Yourself! Every Kid's Guide to Personal Power and Positive Self-Esteem* by Gershen Kaufman, Ph.D., Lev Raphael, Ph.D., and Pamela Espeland (Free Spirit Publishing, 1999).

"Maria Rodale's 5 Things That Really Matter." From "The Art of Living in Balance" by Maria Rodale. *Organic Style,* September/October 2002. www.organicstyle.com.

"4 Ways to Avoid Burnout." Adapted from *Perfectionism: What's Bad About Being Too Good?* by Miriam Adderholdt, Ph.D., and Jan Goldberg (Free Spirit Publishing, 1999).

"8 Ways to Cope with Bad News." Adapted from *HIGHS! Over 150 Ways to Feel Really, REALLY Good... Without Alcohol or Other Drugs* by Alex J. Packer, Ph.D. (Free Spirit Publishing, 2000).

"7 Ways to Handle Worries." Exclusive to *Life Lists for Teens*.

"8 Tips for Coping with Tragedy or Disaster." Based on a brochure developed by Project Heartland—A Project of the Oklahoma Department of Mental Health and Substance Abuse Services.

"11 Warning Signs That You're Under Too Much Stress." Adapted from *Fighting Invisible Tigers: A Stress Management Guide for Teens* by Earl Hipp (Free Spirit Publishing, 1995).

"17 Ways to Manage Stress." Adapted from *Stress Can Really Get on Your Nerves!* by Trevor Romain and Elizabeth Verdick (Free Spirit Publishing, 2000).

"4 Steps to Quitting Caffeine." Adapted from *HIGHS! Over 150 Ways to Feel Really, REALLY Good... Without Alcohol or Other Drugs* by Alex J. Packer, Ph.D. (Free Spirit Publishing, 2000).

"4 Steps to Feeling Peaceful." Adapted from *Fighting Invisible Tigers: A Stress Management Guide for Teens* by Earl Hipp (Free Spirit Publishing, 1995).

"7 Steps to Total Relaxation." Adapted from *HIGHS! Over 150 Ways to Feel Really, REALLY Good... Without Alcohol or Other Drugs* by Alex J. Packer, Ph.D. (Free Spirit Publishing, 2000).

"5 Ways to Deal with Sadness." Adapted from *Can You Relate? Real-World Advice for Teens on Guys, Girls, Growing Up, and Getting Along* by Annie Fox, M.Ed. (Free Spirit Publishing, 2000).

"9 Symptoms of Major Depression." Adapted from "Symptoms of Major Depression." Suicide Awareness Voices of Education (SAVE). © Copyright 1995–2002 SAVE. www.save.org.

"7 Things to Do When You're Depressed." Adapted from *When Nothing Matters Anymore: A Survival Guide for Depressed Teens* by Bev Cobain, R.N., C. (Free Spirit Publishing, 1998).

"11 Types of Helpers and What They Do." Adapted from *When Nothing Matters Anymore: A Survival Guide for Depressed Teens* by Bev Cobain, R.N., C. (Free Spirit Publishing, 1998).

"47 Signs That You Might Be a Perfectionist." Adapted from *Freeing Our Families from Perfectionism* by Thomas S. Greenspon, Ph.D. (Free Spirit Publishing, 2002).

"11 Tips for Fighting Perfectionism." Adapted from *Talk with Teens About Self and Stress: 50 Guided Discussions for School and Counseling Groups* by Jean Sunde Peterson (Free Spirit Publishing, 1993).

"6 Benefits of Failure." Adapted from *Perfectionism: What's Bad About Being Too Good?* by Miriam Adderholdt, Ph.D., and Jan Goldberg (Free Spirit Publishing, 1999).

"5 Reasons Why Misteaks Are Great." Adapted from *The Gifted Kids' Survival Guide: A Teen Handbook* by Judy Galbraith, M.A., and Jim Delisle, Ph.D. (Free Spirit Publishing, 1996).

"7 Resiliencies All Teens Need." Adapted from *The Struggle to Be Strong: True Stories by Teens About Overcoming Tough Times,* edited by Al Desetta, M.A., of Youth Communication and Sybil Wolin, Ph.D., of Project Resilience (Free Spirit Publishing, 2000).

"4 Myths About Acne." Adapted from *Don't Sweat It! EveryBODY's Answers to Questions You Don't Want to Ask* by Marguerite Crump, M.A., M.Ed. (Free Spirit Publishing, 2002).

"10 Tips for Fighting Acne." Adapted from *Don't Sweat It! EveryBODY's Answers to Questions You Don't Want to Ask* by Marguerite Crump, M.A., M.Ed. (Free Spirit Publishing, 2002).

"4 Safe Ways to Learn about Sex." Exclusive to *Life Lists for Teens.*

"10 Reasons Not to Get a Tattoo or Body Piercing... ." Exclusive to *Life Lists for Teens.*

"... and 10 Things to Do If You Decide to Get One Anyway." Exclusive to *Life Lists for Teens.*

"10 Reasons to Eat Right." Adapted from *The Right Moves to Getting Fit and Feeling Great!* by Tina Schwager and Michele Schuerger (Free Spirit Publishing, 1998).

"15 Reasons Not to Diet." Adapted from *The Right Moves to Getting Fit and Feeling Great!* by Tina Schwager and Michele Schuerger (Free Spirit Publishing, 1998).

"29 Clues to a Diet Scam." Exclusive to *Life Lists for Teens.*

"10 Tips for Sticking to an Exercise Program." Adapted from *HIGHS! Over 150 Ways to Feel Really, REALLY Good... Without Alcohol or Other Drugs* by Alex J. Packer, Ph.D. (Free Spirit Publishing, 2000).

"24 Warning Signs of an Eating Disorder." Exclusive to *Life Lists for Teens.*

"14 Do's and Don'ts for Helping a Friend Who Might Have an Eating Disorder." Exclusive to *Life Lists for Teens.*

"15 Ways to Create a Body-Positive World." © 2001, Advocates for Youth. www.advocatesforyouth.org.

"16 Safe Ways to Stay Awake." Exclusive to *Life Lists for Teens.*

"The National Sleep Foundation's 7 Sleep-Smart Tips for Teens." National Sleep Foundation. Copyright © 2001 WebSciences International. All Rights Reserved. www.sleepfoundation.org.

"8 Ways to Never Start Smoking." Adapted from *Taking Charge of My Mind & Body: A Girls' Guide to Outsmarting Alcohol, Drug, Smoking, and Eating Problems* by Gladys Folkers, M.A., and Jeanne Engelmann (Free Spirit Publishing, 1997).

"14 Tips for Quitting Smoking." Source: How Can I Quit Smoking? www.TeensHealth.org. © The Nemours Foundation.

"The Benefits of Quitting Smoking: A Timeline from the American Lung Association." Reprinted with permission © 2002 American Lung Association. For more information on how you can support to fight lung disease, the third leading cause of death in the U.S., please contact The American Lung Association at 1-800-LUNG-USA (1-800-586-4872) or log on to the Web site at www.lungusa.org.

"7 Reasons Why People—Even Smart People—Try Drugs." From www.freevibe.com, a site created by the White House Office of National Drug Control Policy (ONDCP).

"101 Anti-Drugs." From www.freevibe.com, a site created by the White House Office of National Drug Control Policy (ONDCP).

"The Truth About Alcohol: 9 Tips for Teens from NCADI." Adapted from "Tips for Teens: The Truth About Alcohol," National Clearinghouse for Alcohol and Drug Information (NCADI). www.health.org.

"NCADI's 7 Warning Signs of a Drinking Problem." Adapted from "A Guide for Teens. Does your friend have an alcohol or other drug problem? What can you do to help?" National Clearinghouse for Alcohol and Drug Information (NCADI). www.health.org.

"How to Help a Friend: FCD's 10 Steps for Conducting an Informal Intervention." Adapted from *FCD Update,* Fall 2002, pp. 4–5. FCD Educational Services, Inc. (617) 964-9300. www.fcd.org.

"If You Live with Someone Who Drinks Too Much or Uses Drugs." Adapted from "It's Not Your Fault!" brochure. National Association for Children of Alcoholics. www.nacoa.org.

"17 Helpful Toll-Free Numbers." Exclusive to *Life Lists for Teens.*

GETTING ALONG

"12 Tips for Making and Keeping Friends." Adapted from *The Gifted Kids' Survival Guide: A Teen Handbook* by Judy Galbraith, M.A., and Jim Delisle, Ph.D. (Free Spirit Publishing, 1996).

"Rate Your Friends: 15 Qualities to Look For." Adapted from *What Teens Need to Succeed: Proven, Practical Ways to Shape Your Own Future* by Peter L. Benson, Ph.D., Judy Galbraith, M.A., and Pamela Espeland (Free Spirit Publishing, 1998).

"16 Things to Say When Someone Teases You." Exclusive to *Life Lists for Teens.*

"4 Steps for Handling Betrayal." Adapted from *Can You Relate? Real-World Advice for Teens on Guys, Girls, Growing Up, and Getting Along* by Annie Fox, M.Ed. (Free Spirit Publishing, 2000).

"8 Steps to Conflict Resolution." Adapted from *The Bully Free Classroom: Over 100 Tips and Strategies for Teachers K–8* by Allan L. Beane, Ph.D. (Free Spirit Publishing, 1999).

"11 Rules for Fighting Fair." Adapted from "Rules for Fair Fighting" by Elaine Lovegreen, M.A. Published the week of March 4, 2002, in The Counseling Corner from the American Counseling Association. Copyright © 2002, American Counseling Association, All Rights Reserved. www.counseling.org.

"16 Steps for Mediation from the Resolving Conflict Creatively Program." From *Resolving Conflict Creatively: A Teaching Guide for Grades Kindergarten Through Six* by the New York City Board of Education and Education for Social Responsibility, Metropolitan Area, 1996. www.esrnational.org.

"8 Ways to Be a Better Talker." Adapted from *Knowing Me, Knowing You: The I-Sight® Way to Understand Yourself and Others* by Pamela Espeland (Free Spirit Publishing, 2001).

"5 Ways to Be a Great Listener." Adapted from *Knowing Me, Knowing You: The I-Sight® Way to Understand Yourself and Others* by Pamela Espeland (Free Spirit Publishing, 2001).

"7 Ways to Be a Terrible Listener." Adapted from *Knowing Me, Knowing You: The I-Sight® Way to Understand Yourself and Others* by Pamela Espeland (Free Spirit Publishing, 2001).

"8 Things to Try If You're Shy." Adapted from *Stick Up for Yourself! Every Kid's Guide to Personal Power and Positive Self-Esteem* by Gershen Kaufman, Ph.D., Lev Raphael, Ph.D., and Pamela Espeland (Free Spirit Publishing, 1999).

"8 Tips for Appearing Assertive." Exclusive to *Life Lists for Teens*.

"4 Myths About Friendship and Dating." Adapted from *Boy v. Girl? How Gender Shapes Who We Are, What We Want, and How We Get Along* by George Abrahams, Ph.D., and Sheila Ahlbrand (Free Spirit Publishing, 2002).

"8 Tips for Asking Someone Out." Exclusive to *Life Lists for Teens*.

"3 Things to Say When Someone Asks You Out." Exclusive to *Life Lists for Teens*.

"9 Rules for Breaking Up with Someone." Exclusive to *Life Lists for Teens*.

"9 Ways to Tell When Someone Is Lying to You." Adapted from *The First Honest Book About Lies* by Jonni Kincher (Free Spirit Publishing, 1992).

"10 Tips for Talking to Parents." Adapted from *The Gifted Kids' Survival Guide: A Teen Handbook* by Judy Galbraith, M.A., and Jim Delisle, Ph.D. (Free Spirit Publishing, 1996).

"7 Good Times—and 7 Bad Times—to Ask Your Parents for Something You Want." Adapted from *Bringing Up Parents: The Teenager's Handbook* by Alex J. Packer, Ph.D. (Free Spirit Publishing, 1992).

"12 Ways to Show Your Parents What a Fine, Upstanding, Totally Responsible Person You Really Are." Adapted from *Bringing Up Parents: The Teenager's Handbook* by Alex J. Packer, Ph.D. (Free Spirit Publishing, 1992).

"5 Steps for Getting More Freedom." Adapted from *The Gifted Kids' Survival Guide: A Teen Handbook* by Judy Galbraith, M.A., and Jim Delisle, Ph.D. (Free Spirit Publishing, 1996).

"6 Ways to Stay Close to Your Family." Adapted from *Too Old for This, Too Young for That! Your Survival Guide for the Middle-School Years* by Harriet S. Mosatche, Ph.D., and Karen Unger, M.A. (Free Spirit Publishing, 2000).

"12 Steps to Successful Family Meetings." Adapted from *How Rude! The Teenager's Guide to Good Manners, Proper Behavior, and Not Grossing People Out* by Alex J. Packer, Ph.D. (Free Spirit Publishing, 1997).

"A Bill of Rights for Children of Divorce." Adapted from *Problem Child or Quirky Kid? A Commonsense Guide* by Rita Sommers-Flanagan, Ph.D., and John Sommers-Flanagan, Ph.D. (Free Spirit Publishing, 2002).

"Code of Etiquette for Children of Divorce." Adapted from *How Rude! The Teenager's Guide to Good Manners, Proper Behavior, and Not Grossing People Out* by Alex J. Packer, Ph.D. (Free Spirit Publishing, 1997).

"Alex J. Packer's 10 Great Reasons to Have Good Manners." Adapted from *How Rude! The Teenager's Guide to Good Manners, Proper Behavior, and Not Grossing People Out* by Alex J. Packer, Ph.D. (Free Spirit Publishing, 1997).

"10 Ways to Swear Off Swearing from the Cuss Control Academy." Devised by James V. O'Connor, author of *Cuss Control: The Complete Book on How to Curb Your Cursing*, Three Rivers Press, 2000.

"12 Ways to Be a Great Guest." Adapted from *How Rude! The Teenager's Guide to Good Manners, Proper Behavior, and Not Grossing People Out* by Alex J. Packer, Ph.D. (Free Spirit Publishing, 1997).

"8 Tips for Writing a Thank-You Note." Adapted from *How Rude! The Teenager's Guide to Good Manners, Proper Behavior, and Not Grossing People Out* by Alex J. Packer, Ph.D. (Free Spirit Publishing, 1997).

"9 Ways to Be a Host with the Most." Adapted from *How Rude! The Teenager's Guide to Good Manners, Proper Behavior, and Not Grossing People Out* by Alex J. Packer, Ph.D. (Free Spirit Publishing, 1997).

STAYING SAFE

"11 Toll-Free Crisis Hotlines." Exclusive to *Life Lists for Teens*.

"16 Adults You Can Talk To." Exclusive to *Life Lists for Teens*.

"Adults I Can Talk To." Exclusive to *Life Lists for Teens*.

"10 Myths About Bullies and Bullying." Adapted from *The Bully Free Classroom: Over 100 Tips and Strategies for Teachers K–8* by Allan L. Beane, Ph.D. (Free Spirit Publishing, 1999).

"10 Things to Do When Someone Bullies You." Adapted from *The Bully Free Classroom: Over 100 Tips and Strategies for Teachers K–8* by Allan L. Beane, Ph.D. (Free Spirit Publishing, 1999).

"12 Things NOT to Do When Someone Bullies You." Adapted from *The Bully Free Classroom: Over 100 Tips and Strategies for Teachers K–8* by Allan L. Beane, Ph.D. (Free Spirit Publishing, 1999).

"Are You a Bully? 12 Ways to Tell." Adapted from *Bullies Are a Pain in the Brain,* written and illustrated by Trevor Romain (Free Spirit Publishing, 1997).

"13 Ways to Make Your School Safe." Adapted from *Early Warning, Timely Response: A Guide to Safe Schools.* © 2000 Center for Effective Collaboration and Practice. cecp.air.org.

"9 Things You Can Do to Stop School Violence." Adapted from "10 Things You Can Do to Stop School Violence." © 2000 DOSOMETHING.ORG. All rights reserved.

"6 Big Differences Between Flirting and Sexual Harassment." Adapted from *Sexual Harassment and Teens: A Program for Positive Change* by Susan Strauss with Pamela Espeland (Free Spirit Publishing, 1992).

"7 Ways to Tell If You're Flirting or Harassing." Exclusive to *Life Lists for Teens.*

"9 Things You Can Do to Stop Sexual Harassment in School." Source: "Harassment-Free Hallways: How to Stop Sexual Harassment in Schools" online guide (August 20, 2002). American Association of University Women (AAUW) Educational Foundation. www.aauw.org.

"25 Ways to Resist Negative Peer Pressure." Adapted from *What Teens Need to Succeed: Proven, Practical Ways to Shape Your Own Future* by Peter L. Benson, Ph.D., Judy Galbraith, M.A., and Pamela Espeland (Free Spirit Publishing, 1998).

"10 Tips for Staying Safe in Relationships." Adapted from *Boy v. Girl? How Gender Shapes Who We Are, What We Want, and How We Get Along* by George Abrahams, Ph.D., and Sheila Ahlbrand (Free Spirit Publishing, 2002).

"20 Ways to Tell If a Relationship Is Unhealthy." Adapted from *Boy v. Girl? How Gender Shapes Who We Are, What We Want, and How We Get Along* by George Abrahams, Ph.D., and Sheila Ahlbrand (Free Spirit Publishing, 2002).

"Dating Bill of Rights" from *Warning! Dating May Be Hazardous to Your Health!* by Claudette McShane, copyright © 1988. Used with permission.

"10 Things Teens Want Other Teens to Know About Preventing Teen Pregnancy." Source: "Thinking About The Right-Now: What Teens Want Other Teens To Know About Preventing Teen Pregnancy" © 2002, The National Campaign To Prevent Teen Pregnancy. www.teenpregnancy.org.

"3 Rules for Life from the National Center for Missing and Exploited Children." Source: "Know the Rules" brochure, Copyright © 1998 NCMEC. National Center for Missing and Exploited Children. www.missingkids.com.

"10 Questions to Ask Yourself Before You Run Away." Source: "We Can Help." Copyright © 2001 National Runaway Switchboard. www.nrscrisisline.org.

"12 Suicide Warning Signs from the National Association of School Psychologists." Source: "Save a Friend: Tips for Teens to Prevent Suicide." © 2002, National Association of School Psychologists. Adapted from "A National Tragedy: Preventing Suicide in Troubled Children and Youth." www.nasponline.org.

"5 Ways to Help a Friend Who Might Be Suicidal from the National Association of School Psychologists." Source: "Save a Friend: Tips for Teens to Prevent Suicide." © 2002, National Association of School Psychologists. Adapted from "A National Tragedy: Preventing Suicide in Troubled Children and Youth." www.nasponline.org.

"Do's and Don'ts When a Friend Is a Crime Victim." Source: "Tips for Teens," © 2002 National Center for Victims of Crime. www.ncvc.org.

"10 Ways to Keep from Being Ripped Off." Adapted from *The First Honest Book About Lies* by Jonni Kincher (Free Spirit Publishing, 1992).

"11 Tips for Staying Safe at an ATM Machine." Exclusive to *Life Lists for Teens*.

"The Chicago Police Department's 12 Tips for Staying Safe on Public Transportation." Source: "Public Transportation Safety," © 1998 Chicago Police Department. All rights reserved. 01 JAN 98. www.ci.chi.il.us.

"12 Things to Do If Someone Is Stalking You." Exclusive to *Life Lists for Teens*.

"How to Know If You're Being Abused—and What to Do." Exclusive to *Life Lists for Teens*.

"8 Do's and Don'ts for Calling 911." Exclusive to *Life Lists for Teens*.

SCHOOL AND LEARNING

"7 Keys to School Success." Adapted from *The Gifted Kids' Survival Guide: A Teen Handbook* by Judy Galbraith, M.A., and Jim Delisle, Ph.D. (Free Spirit Publishing, 1996).

"5 Steps to School Success: The Checkpoint System." Adapted from *School Power: Study Skill Strategies for Succeeding in School* by Jeanne Shay Schumm, Ph.D. (Free Spirit Publishing, 2001).

"10 Ways to Be Smart." Adapted from *The Gifted Kids' Survival Guide: A Teen Handbook* by Judy Galbraith, M.A., and Jim Delisle, Ph.D. (Free Spirit Publishing, 1996).

"Randall McCutcheon's 5 Reasons to Sit in the Front Row at School." Adapted from *Get Off My Brain: A Survival Guide for Lazy Students* by Randall McCutcheon (Free Spirit Publishing, 1998).

"8 Do's and 5 Don'ts for Class Discussions." Adapted from *School Power: Study Skill Strategies for Succeeding in School* by Jeanne Shay Schumm, Ph.D. (Free Spirit Publishing, 2001).

"5 Reasons to Take Notes in Class." Adapted from *School Power: Study Skill Strategies for Succeeding in School* by Jeanne Shay Schumm, Ph.D. (Free Spirit Publishing, 2001).

"19 Note-Taking Tips." Adapted from *School Power: Study Skill Strategies for Succeeding in School* by Jeanne Shay Schumm, Ph.D. (Free Spirit Publishing, 2001).

"16 Benefits of Doing Your Homework." Exclusive to *Life Lists for Teens*.

"10 Web Sites for Homework Help." Exclusive to *Life Lists for Teens*.

"10 Tips for Talking to Teachers." Adapted from *When Gifted Kids Don't Have All the Answers: How to Meet Their Social and Emotional Needs* by Jim Delisle, Ph.D., and Judy Galbraith, M.A. (Free Spirit Publishing, 2002).

"The Student Bill of Rights." Source: "The Student Bill of Rights" in *Engines for Education* hyperbook. Copyright © 2002. Engines for Education. All rights reserved. www.engines4ed.org.

"8 Steps to Stress-Free Studying." Adapted from *The Best of Free Spirit: Five Years of Award-Winning News & Views on Growing Up* by The Free Spirit Editors (Free Spirit Publishing, 1995).

"6 Ways to Remember What You Study." Adapted from *School Power: Study Skill Strategies for Succeeding in School* by Jeanne Shay Schumm, Ph.D. (Free Spirit Publishing, 2001).

"10 Test Preparation Tips." Exclusive to *Life Lists for Teens*.

"12 Ways to Keep Cool During Tests." Exclusive to *Life Lists for Teens*.

"12 Test-Taking Tips." Adapted from *The Gifted Kids' Survival Guide: A Teen Handbook* by Judy Galbraith, M.A., and Jim Delisle, Ph.D. (Free Spirit Publishing, 1996).

"4 Things to Do When Someone Tries to Cheat Off You." Adapted from *How Rude! The Teenager's Guide to Good Manners, Proper Behavior, and Not Grossing People Out* by Alex J. Packer, Ph.D. (Free Spirit Publishing, 1997).

"10 Ways to Learn New Words." Adapted from *School Power: Study Skill Strategies for Succeeding in School* by Jeanne Shay Schumm, Ph.D. (Free Spirit Publishing, 2001).

"100 Words All High School Graduates (and Their Parents) Should Know from the Editors of the American Heritage® College Dictionary." Copyright © 2002 Houghton Mifflin Company. www.houghtonmifflinbooks.com.

"5 Ways to Be a Better Speller." Adapted from *School Power: Study Skill Strategies for Succeeding in School* by Jeanne Shay Schumm, Ph.D. (Free Spirit Publishing, 2001).

"10 Ways to Smash Writer's Block." Exclusive to *Life Lists for Teens*.

"9 Do's and Don'ts of Giving Credit: Tips for Avoiding Plagiarism from the Purdue University Online Writing Lab." Source: "Avoiding Plagiarism" Copyright © 1995–2002 by Online Writing Lab (OWL) at Purdue University. owl.english.purdue.edu.

"13 Ways to Lighten Up at School." Adapted from *The Best of Free Spirit: Five Years of Award-Winning News & Views on Growing Up* by The Free Spirit Editors (Free Spirit Publishing, 1995).

"20 Ways to Change the Social Scene at School." Adapted from *More Than a Label: Why What You Wear or Who You're With Doesn't Define Who You Are* by Aisha Muharrar (Free Spirit Publishing, 2002).

"10 Ways to Build School Spirit." Adapted from *What Teens Need to Succeed: Proven, Practical Ways to Shape Your Own Future* by Peter L. Benson, Ph.D., Judy Galbraith, M.A., and Pamela Espeland (Free Spirit Publishing, 1998).

"The American Library Association's 12 Tips for Forming a Reading Habit." Source: "For Teens Only: Tips for Developing a Reading Habit" Copyright © 2001 American Library Association. www.ala.org.

"6 Ways to Find the Right Book to Read." Adapted from *School Power: Study Skill Strategies for Succeeding in School* by Jeanne Shay Schumm, Ph.D. (Free Spirit Publishing, 2001).

"10 Books Some People Don't Want You to Read." Source: "The Most Frequently Challenged Books for 2001" Copyright © 2002 American Library Association. www.ala.org.

"How to Start a Book Group." Exclusive to *Life Lists for Teens*.

"27 Clues That You're a Remarkable Reader." Source: "For Teens Only: Are You a Remarkable Reader?" Copyright © 2001 American Library Association. www.ala.org.

"21 Ways to Learn Something New." From *The Teenagers' Guide to School Outside the Box* by Rebecca Greene (Free Spirit Publishing, 2001).

GOING ONLINE

"9 Things You Can Do If You Don't Have a Home Computer." Adapted from *School Power: Study Skill Strategies for Succeeding in School* by Jeanne Shay Schumm, Ph.D. (Free Spirit Publishing, 2001).

"11 Signs That You're Web-Aware." Media Awareness Network Canada, 2002; adapted with permission. www.media-awareness.ca.

"10 Commandments of Email Etiquette." Exclusive to *Life Lists for Teens*.

"7 Things You Should Know about Online Privacy from the American Bar Association." Reprinted by permission from *Facts About Privacy and Cyberspace*. Copyright © 2000 American Bar Association. All rights reserved.

"12 Ways to Can Spam." Exclusive to *Life Lists for Teens*.

"2 Things to Do When You Get an Email Chain Letter—and 6 Reasons Why." Exclusive to *Life Lists for Teens*.

"6 Clues to Decoding a URL." Media Awareness Network Canada, 2002; adapted with permission. www.media-awareness.ca.

"6 Ways to Tell if a Web Site is Trustworthy." Media Awareness Network Canada, 2002; adapted with permission. www.media-awareness.ca.

"3 Rules for Doing Internet Research." Exclusive to *Life Lists for Teens*.

"6 Web Sites That Won't Insult You." Exclusive to *Life Lists for Teens*.

"12 Ways to Prevent Eye Strain." Adapted from *HIGHS! Over 150 Ways to Feel Really, REALLY Good... Without Alcohol or Other Drugs* by Alex J. Packer, Ph.D. (Free Spirit Publishing, 2000).

PLANNING AHEAD

"5 Keys to Success in Life." Adapted from *Cool Women, Hot Jobs... and how you can go for it, too!* by Tina Schwager & Michele Schuerger (Free Spirit Publishing, 2002).

"12 Ways to Get Control of Your Time." Exclusive to *Life Lists for Teens*.

"10 Tips for Procrastinators." Adapted from *Perfectionism: What's Bad About Being Too Good?* by Miriam Adderholdt, Ph.D., and Jan Goldberg (Free Spirit Publishing, 1999).

"10 Goal-Setting Steps." Exclusive to *Life Lists for Teens*.

"25 Quotes on Goal-Setting." Exclusive to *Life Lists for Teens*.

"10 Reasons Why Goals Are Worth Having." Adapted from *What Do You Really Want? How to Set a Goal and Go For It! A Guide for Teens* by Beverly K. Bachel (Free Spirit Publishing, 2000).

"My Life List." Exclusive to *Life Lists for Teens*.

"7 People Who Wouldn't Listen." Exclusive to *Life Lists for Teens*.

"12 Keys to Your Future Career." Adapted from *Cool Women, Hot Jobs... and how you can go for it, too!* by Tina Schwager & Michele Schuerger (Free Spirit Publishing, 2002).

"How to Find a Mentor: Tips from the National Mentoring Partnership." Source: "Find a Mentor," Copyright © The National Mentoring Partnership. www.mentoring.org.

"8 Ways to Make the Most of Your Mentorship." From *The Teenagers' Guide to School Outside the Box* by Rebecca Greene (Free Spirit Publishing, 2001).

"Follow Your Muse: 4 Steps to Success." Adapted from *HIGHS! Over 150 Ways to Feel Really, REALLY Good... Without Alcohol or Other Drugs* by Alex J. Packer, Ph.D. (Free Spirit Publishing, 2000).

SAVING THE WORLD

"10 Myths About Teens—and How to Set the Record Straight." Source: "Ageism. What's up with that?" © 2000 DOSOMETHING.ORG. All rights reserved.

"10 Ways to Handle Hate Words and Slurs." Adapted from *More Than a Label: Why What You Wear or Who You're With Doesn't Define Who You Are* by Aisha Muharrar (Free Spirit Publishing, 2002).

"5 Tips for Talking Nice." Adapted from "Tips for Positive Speaking." SHiNE (Seeking Harmony in Neighborhoods Everyday). www.shine.com.

"8 Ways to Combat Hate from the Anti-Defamation League." Source: "101 Ways to Combat Prejudice: Close the Book on Hate Campaign Pledge." © 2001 Anti-Defamation League. www.adl.org.

"12 Ways to Become More Tolerant from the Southern Poverty Law Center." Excerpted with permission from Teaching Tolerance © 2000, Southern Poverty Law Center, Montgomery, AL. www.tolerance.org; www.splcenter.org.

"3 Reasons to Become More Tolerant." Adapted from *Respecting Our Differences: A Guide to Getting Along in a Changing World* by Lynn Duvall (Free Spirit Publishing, 1994).

"13 Things You Can Do to Promote Diversity." © 2000 DOSOMETHING.ORG. All rights reserved.

"11 Ways to Remember 9/11." Source: "Stand with Courage... One Nation, One Spirit: A Personal 9/11 Remembrance." © Copyright 2002, White House Commission on Remembrance. All rights reserved. remember.gov.

"A Kind Act I Can Do." Exclusive to *Life Lists for Teens.*

"5 Ways to Fight Ad Creep." Exclusive to *Life Lists for Teens.*

"35 Possible Places to Volunteer." Adapted from *Cool Women, Hot Jobs... and how you can go for it, too!* by Tina Schwager & Michele Schuerger (Free Spirit Publishing, 2002).

"18 Great Reasons to Serve Others ." Source: *Volunteering and Giving Among American Teenagers 12 to 17 Years of Age* (Washington, DC: Independent Sector, 1996). indepentsector.org.

"5 National Days of Service." Exclusive to *Life Lists for Teens.*

"10 National Programs That Promote Youth Service." Exclusive to *Life Lists for Teens.*

"8 Steps to Volunteering as a Family." Adapted from *Children as Volunteers* by Susan J. Ellis, et al., © 1991, Energize, Inc. www.energizeinc.com.

"7 Ways to Connect with Others Who Care." Exclusive to *Life Lists for Teens.*

"8 Steps to a Service Project from the Points of Light Foundation." Source: "Start a Service Project" © 2002 Youth Outreach, The Points of Light Foundation. All rights reserved. www.pointsoflight.org.

"8 Do's and Don'ts of Successful Volunteering from the Prudential Spirit of Community Awards." Source: "Dos and Dont's of Successful Volunteering" from *Catch the Spirit! A Student's Guide to Community Service,* published by The Prudential in cooperation with the U.S. Department of Education, copyright 1996. Used with permission. www.prudential.com.

"11 Ways to Make Service Last from Youth Service America." Source: "Global Youth Service Day Tool Kit." Youth Service America. www.ysa.org.

FOCUS ON YOU

"10 Reasons Why You Need Self-Esteem." Adapted from *Stick Up for Yourself! Every Kid's Guide to Personal Power and Positive Self-Esteem* by Gershen Kaufman, Ph.D., Lev Raphael, Ph.D., and Pamela Espeland (Free Spirit Publishing, 1999).

"Sol Gordon's 7 Cardinal Mistakes of Self-Esteem." Adapted from *The Best of Free Spirit: Five Years of Award-Winning News & Views on Growing Up* by The Free Spirit Editors (Free Spirit Publishing, 1995).

"My Personal Bill of Rights." Exclusive to *Life Lists for Teens.*

"5 Ways to Build Your Self-Confidence." Adapted from *More Than a Label: Why What You Wear or Who You're With Doesn't Define Who You Are* by Aisha Muharrar (Free Spirit Publishing, 2002).

"Top 10 Reasons Why You Look Hot." Source: "Top 10 Reasons Why You Look Hot" by Deb Boxill and Heather Keets Wright. © 2000 Save the Children Federation, Inc. All rights reserved. www.youthNOISE.com.

"The 6 Pillars of Character." © Josephson Institute of Ethics — Reprinted with Permission. CHARACTER COUNTS! And the Six Pillars of Character are service marks of the CHARACTER COUNTS! Coalition, a project of the Josephson Institute of Ethics. www.charactercounts.org.

"12 Reasons to Tell the Truth." Exclusive to *Life Lists for Teens.*

"9 Reasons to Go to Church, Temple, Mosque, or Meetings." Adapted from *What Teens Need to Succeed: Proven, Practical Ways to Shape Your Own Future* by Peter L. Benson, Ph.D., Judy Galbraith, M.A., and Pamela Espeland (Free Spirit Publishing, 1998).

"5 Steps to Taming Your Temper." Adapted from *How to Take the Grrrr Out of Anger* by Elizabeth Verdick and Marjorie Lisovskis (Free Spirit Publishing, 2002).

"5 Ways to Handle Embarrassment." Adapted from *Can You Relate? Real-World Advice for Teens on Guys, Girls, Growing Up, and Getting Along* by Annie Fox, M.Ed. (Free Spirit Publishing, 2000).

"5 Ways to Handle Insecurities." Adapted from *Can You Relate? Real-World Advice for Teens on Guys, Girls, Growing Up, and Getting Along* by Annie Fox, M.Ed. (Free Spirit Publishing, 2000).

"10 Tips for Solving Almost Any Problem." *It's All in Your Head: A Guide to Understanding Your Brain and Boosting Your Brain Power* by Susan L. Barrett (Free Spirit Publishing, 1992).

"6 Reasons to Keep a Journal." Exclusive to *Life Lists for Teens.*

"12 Reasons to Write." Adapted from *Write Where You Are: How to Use Writing to Make Sense of Your Life: A Guide for Teens* by Caryn Mirriam-Goldberg, Ph.D. (Free Spirit Publishing, 1999).

"Robert Sternberg's 10 Tips to Enhance Creativity." From "Think Smart! 12 Ways to Avoid Brain Drain Poster" (Free Spirit Publishing, 1999).

"25 Quotes on Creativity." Adapted from *The Best of Free Spirit: Five Years of Award-Winning News & Views on Growing Up* by The Free Spirit Editors (Free Spirit Publishing, 1995).

"6 Good Things to Do for Yourself." Adapted from *Stick Up for Yourself! Every Kid's Guide to Personal Power and Positive Self-Esteem* by Gershen Kaufman, Ph.D., Lev Raphael, Ph.D., and Pamela Espeland (Free Spirit Publishing, 1999).

"8 Things That Make You One of a Kind." Exclusive to *Life Lists for Teens.*

JUST FOR FUN

"12 Things to Look Forward to from the GW Forecast." Exclusive to *Life Lists for Teens.*

"The Last Words of 16 Famous People." Exclusive to *Life Lists for Teens.*

"The 8 Clown Commandments." Source: "Code of Ethics: The Eight Clown Commandments." Clowns of America International. www.coai.org.

"9 Tips for Changing Your Hair Color." Exclusive to *Life Lists for Teens.*

"How to Convince Your Parents to Let You Go to a Party." Exclusive to *Life Lists for Teens.*

"How to Convince Your Parents to Let You Have a Party." Exclusive to *Life Lists for Teens.*

"Michael Levine's 9 Tips for Getting in Touch with Famous People—and Getting an Answer." Source: *Tricks of the Trade,* edited by Jerry Dunn (Boston: Houghton Mifflin Company, 1991). Used with permission of Michael Levine.

"8 Tips for Remembering Your Dreams." Adapted from *Dreams Can Help: A Journal Guide to Understanding Your Dreams and Making Them Work for You* by Jonni Kincher (Free Spirit Publishing, 1988).

"11 Common Dream Symbols and What They Mean." Adapted from *Dreams Can Help: A Journal Guide to Understanding Your Dreams and Making Them Work for You* by Jonni Kincher (Free Spirit Publishing, 1988).

"9 Colors and How They Make You Feel." Adapted from *HIGHS! Over 150 Ways to Feel Really, REALLY Good... Without Alcohol or Other Drugs* by Alex J. Packer, Ph.D. (Free Spirit Publishing, 2000).

"18 Tips for Analyzing Your Handwriting." Adapted from *Psychology for Kids: 40 Fun Tests That Help You Learn About Yourself* by Jonni Kincher (Free Spirit Publishing, 1995).

"8 Big Truths." Adapted from *The First Honest Book About Lies* by Jonni Kincher (Free Spirit Publishing, 1992).

"25 Deep Thoughts About Life." Exclusive to *Life Lists for Teens.*

"10 Life Lessons from Teens." Adapted from *The Best of Free Spirit: Five Years of Award-Winning News & Views on Growing Up* by The Free Spirit Editors (Free Spirit Publishing, 1995).

Index

About the Author

Pamela Espeland has written and coauthored many books for teens, children, and adults including *What Teens Need to Succeed, What Kids Need to Succeed, Stick Up for Yourself!, Succeed Every Day, Making the Most of Today, Making Every Day Count, Bringing Out the Best,* and *Knowing Me, Knowing You.* She lives in Minneapolis, Minnesota, with her husband, John Whiting, their cat, Happy, and two miniature dachshunds, Lily and Chloe.

Visit us on the Web!
www.freespirit.com

Stop by anytime to find our Parents' Choice Approved catalog with fast, easy, secure 24-hour online ordering; "Ask Our Authors," where visitors ask questions—and authors give answers—on topics important to children, teens, parents, teachers, and others who care about kids; links to other Web sites we know and recommend; fun stuff for everyone, including quick tips and strategies from our books; and much more! Plus our site is completely searchable so you can find what you need in a hurry. Stop in and let us know what you think!

Just point and click!

If you liked **LIFE LISTS FOR TEENS**, you'll also like
WHAT TEENS NEED TO SUCCEED and **MORE THAN A LABEL.**

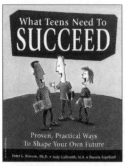

WHAT TEENS NEED TO SUCCEED
Proven, Practical Ways to Shape Your Own Future

Teens have the power to shape their futures, change their lives for the better, and make a difference in the world. This book shows them how!

1-57542-027-9, $14.95

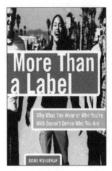

MORE THAN A LABEL
Why What You Wear or Who You're With Doesn't Define Who You Are

Freak. Prep. Goth. Loser. Teens share the truth behind the label: what hurts, what helps, and what anyone can do to make a difference.

1-57542-110-0, $13.95

Want to know more about **MAKING POSITIVE CHOICES, COPING WITH CHALLENGES, KEEPING IT TOGETHER,** and **MAKING A DIFFERENCE?**

Proven, practical ways for teens to succeed in all areas of life— starting today!

BUSINESS REPLY MAIL

FIRST-CLASS MAIL   PERMIT NO. 26589   MINNEAPOLIS MN

POSTAGE WILL BE PAID BY ADDRESSEE

free spirit PUBLiSHiNG®
Department 785
217 Fifth Avenue North, Suite 200
Minneapolis, MN 55401-9776

Free Spirit Publishing
Your SELF-HELP FOR TEENS®
source for over 20 years.

BUSINESS REPLY MAIL

FIRST-CLASS MAIL   PERMIT NO. 26589   MINNEAPOLIS MN

POSTAGE WILL BE PAID BY ADDRESSEE

free spirit PUBLiSHiNG®
Department 785
217 Fifth Avenue North, Suite 200
Minneapolis, MN 55401-9776